Pure Sport

Pure Sport: Practical Sport Psychology explains in everyday language the whys and wherefores of contemporary sport psychology – pinpointing what works and what doesn't when it comes to performance enhancement.

As the title suggests, *Pure Sport* goes back to basics by highlighting practical concerns for those who are involved with competitive sport at every level – from junior club to international elite. Drawing on their considerable experience as both academic researchers and applied sport psychologists, the authors present a powerful array of techniques for channelling and harnessing mental skills with the goal of improving sporting performance. The interventions that they describe have all been tried and tested in competitive settings, but here, for the first time, the psychological techniques underlying them are brought together in a single volume that uniquely blends sound theory with good practice.

Liberally sprinkled with practical examples, evocative photographs and clear diagrams, *Pure Sport* is essential reading for anyone with an active involvement or interest in sport. It will help coaches, teams and sports people alike to develop their mental edge and so realise their true potential in sport and through sport.

John Kremer is a Reader in Applied Psychology at Queen's University, Belfast, where he has lectured since 1980. A graduate of Loughborough University, he has been actively involved in sport and exercise psychology since the mid-1980s as a practitioner, researcher and teacher. He continues to work with a wide range of individuals and teams at both club and international level.

Aidan P. Moran is a Professor of Cognitive Psychology and Director of the Psychology Research Laboratory in University College, Dublin. He has gained an international reputation for his research on concentration, mental imagery and expertise in athletes. He is a psychology consultant to many of Ireland's leading athletes and teams, and is a former Official Psychologist to the Irish Olympic squad.

Pure Sport

Practical Sport Psychology

■ John Kremer and Aidan P. Moran

Routledge
Taylor & Francis Group

LONDON AND NEW YORK

First published 2008
by Routledge
27 Church Road, Hove, East Sussex BN3 2FA

Simultaneously published in the USA and
Canada
by Routledge
270 Madison Avenue, New York NY 10016

Reprinted 2008 and 2009 (twice)

*Routledge is an imprint of the Taylor &
Francis Group, an Informa business*

Copyright © 2008 Psychology Press

Typeset in Sabon by RefineCatch Limited,
Bungay, Suffolk
Printed and bound in Great Britain by
TJ International Ltd, Padstow, Cornwall
Cover design by Anú Design

This publication has been produced with
paper manufactured to strict environmental
standards and with pulp derived from
sustainable forests.

*British Library Cataloguing in Publication
Data*
A catalogue record for this book is available
from the British Library

*Library of Congress Cataloging-in-
Publication Data*
Kremer, John, 1956–
  Pure sport : practical sport psychology /
John Kremer and Aidan P. Moran.
    p. cm.
  Includes bibliographical references and
index.
  ISBN-13: 978-0-415-39557-1
  ISBN-13: 978-0-415-39558-8
1. Sports–Psychological aspects. I. Moran,
Aidan P. II. Title.
  GV706.4.K744 2008
  796′.01–dc22
              2007031862

ISBN: 978-0-415-39557-1 (hbk)
ISBN: 978-0-415-39558-8 (pbk)

Dedication

To our families – thank you.

Contents

List of illustrations and tables

Figures

Photographs

Chapter 1

Chapter 2

Foreword

> 'Think about it!'
> 'You're only as good as your last game.'
> 'Keep your eye on the ball.'
> 'No pain no gain.'
> 'Concentrate!'
> 'There's no "I" in team.'
> 'When the going gets tough, the tough get going.'
> 'Winning isn't everything – it's the only thing.'

As this collection of clichés reveals, sport psychology had already made its presence felt long before sport psychologists ever came on the scene. In fact, from the first time the human race ever chose to compete through the medium of sport, it is probable that the mental side to preparation and performance has played a significant if often haphazard and unregulated role. Sometimes this has been a positive influence, sometimes not – we can all recall those occasions when a few ill-chosen words, or personal negative thoughts, have taken their toll on performance, leaving us to ponder on what could have been rather than what was.

Our intention in *Pure Sport* is simple. It is to help you to explore what can be, or in other words your sporting potential, whether as a competitor, manager or coach. At the same time, in writing this book, we had no intention of simply adding to the burgeoning industry of applied sport psychology. Since the 1960s there has been a proliferation of practitioners, some good, some bad, backed by a library of books for those seeking to find that elusive winning edge.

That literature often serves a slightly different purpose from our own because our intention is to help you take charge, and for you to manage your own sport psychology; to direct but not to be directed. To achieve this goal we draw heavily on our lengthy and accumulated experience as both academics and practising sport psychologists, helping you to sift the wheat from the chaff and ultimately to bring together a coherent package of advice.

Too often in the past, sport psychologists have been hauled in to provide the snake oil or panacea for individual or team problems. Sadly, too often a vital ingredient has been left out of the recipe – you. We aim not to hog the limelight nor to bewilder you with science but to equip you with knowledge, insight and skills so that you can manage your own sport psychology, even to the point of recognising those occasions when it may be necessary to call on outside advice. In effect we aim to talk ourselves out of a job, but we are confident that the package of psychological skills will equip you to sustain a sporting career whatever may come your way.

Charting a path for the uninitiated through sport psychology has been a daunting task, and one, we must admit, we have avoided for far too long! In the past it has been easier to preach to the converted or those already working in or about to enter the discipline of sport psychology. In this book we have left that audience aside and focused our attention on those who can often be made to feel like outsiders but who have every right to be centre stage. We have enjoyed the challenge and we hope you enjoy the journey.

Finally, we'd like to acknowledge gratefully the help we received from Ms Julitta Clancy (indexer) and also from the Publications Scheme of the National University of Ireland.

John and Aidan

Chapter   1

Starting

Introduction

How a swing doctor and a mind reader bolster the home defence.[1]

England need group therapy.[2]

SPORT PSYCHOLOGY IS NEVER far from the headlines. Whether reporting the preparation for golf's Ryder Cup, or the problems facing England's soccer manager, hardly a week seems to go by without some reference in the media to the role that sport psychology has played in individual or team performance.

It hasn't always been this way but, from humble beginnings, sport psychology has now developed into a high-profile, international enterprise, with very few elite sportspeople now likely to finish their careers without having crossed paths, or even swords, with a sport psychologist somewhere along the way.

Experiences with sport psychologists are likely to be many and varied, good and bad, with the absence of quality controls causing serious headaches for the professional organisations that are trying to bring some discipline to the world of applied sport psychology. For example, headlines such as 'Golf psychologist banned after scuffle'[3] raise serious doubts about the ethical standards of certain people who work in this field. Make no mistake, the range of goods on offer is vast and the sort of work that is brought together under the umbrella of sport psychology can feel overwhelming, but there is no need to panic just yet.

One piece of advice to keep firmly in mind when approaching this field is to proceed with caution. Don't be tempted to take on board all available advice uncritically, but filter selectively and be prepared to reject any material that appears hard to digest or unpalatable. In golf and many other sports, many a career has been damaged by the fruitless search for the elusive kernel of knowledge among the countless sport psychology books that clutter the shelves of most bookstores. In the same way that sports involving hi-tech equipment such as cycling can attract

Pelé (courtesy of Inpho Photography)

'technofreaks' (those who are constantly on the lookout for the latest piece of kit or equipment to lose an ounce or give them the edge), there is a real danger that a craving for ever more psychobabble can become another dangerous addiction that never quite leaves you.

And sometimes the advice you are given needs to be taken with a large pinch of salt! As a case in point, it is amusing to discover from Pelé's autobiography that he was almost excluded from the Brazilian team that won the 1958 World Cup in Sweden on the basis of the rather odd advice given to the manager, Vicente Feola, by the team psychologist, Dr Joao Carvalhaes. Briefly, this advice suggested that Pelé was 'infantile' and lacked the necessary fighting spirit required for success. Fortunately, Feola had the wit to ignore this advice and proclaimed, 'If Pelé's knee is ready, he plays.'[4] A similar example of psychobabble comes from a story told by Magnus Hedman, the former Glasgow Celtic goalkeeper.[5] Apparently Hedman consulted a sport psychologist in the 1990s:

> The first thing he asked me was what I would do if I found an intruder trying to break into my apartment – I told him I would attack the guy and kick him down the stairs. So he says to me 'I want you to imagine the penalty area is your apartment and you have to kick out like that to protect your goal.' I knew then he had never thought about referees and me getting sent off in every game I played for violent conduct. So, I decided I would handle my own problems after that.

Leaving psychobabble aside, our purpose in writing this book is simple. It is to pull away some of the mystery that can surround the topic and in the process make sport psychology more accessible to those who may not have a background in psychology but who do have an interest in the mental side of sport.

We are aware that we are entering a very crowded marketplace but, practising what we preach, we regard this as a challenge, not a threat. In delivering this material, we do not intend to overview the field in detail or to defend some of the practices that may have been dubiously peddled under the guise of sport psychology. Instead what we would like to do is pick out a well-signposted route map, to help you sort the good from the bad and the plain ugly and ultimately to equip you with the knowledge and the skills to use sport psychology to your advantage.

Who are we?

What can we bring to the party that others have not already provided? For one thing, over the years we have gathered together quite a few T-shirts. To be more precise, between the two of us, we have been fortunate enough to have accumulated

TABLE 1.1   Sports we have worked with

Aerobics	Golf	Outdoor bowls	Table tennis
Archery	Gymnastics	Paralympics	Tae kwon do
Athletics	Handball	Rowing	Tennis
Badminton	Hockey	Rugby League	Trampolining
Basketball	Horse racing	Rugby Union	Triathlon
Boxing	Hurling	Sailing	Volleyball
Camogie	Ice hockey	Shooting	Waterskiing
Canoe/kayak	Indoor bowls	Showjumping	Weightlifting
Cricket	Judo	Skiing	
Cycling	Karate	Snooker	
Dancing	Motorcycling	Soccer	
Darts	Motocross	Squash	
Fencing	Mountaineering	Surfing	
Gaelic football	Netball	Swimming	

well over 30 years of applied experience working in competitive sports both team and individual, amateur and professional (Table 1.1).

Along the way we have had the privilege of working with national and international athletes (including several world champions) and teams from a wide range of sports. Yes, we have made mistakes, and inevitably we have had our ups as well as our downs, but more than anything, working either together or separately, we have endeavoured to continue to learn about how theory can best be translated into sensible and workable practice.

Good theory, good practice

To our clients, the underlying theory will not always have been upfront, but rest assured, it will have informed our practice. We can make that statement with a degree of confidence because, in contrast to many applied sport psychologists, we have continued to pursue our applied work alongside our academic careers, lecturing and researching within university psychology departments.

We feel passionately that the interplay between these two careers, spanning the pure and the applied, has been invaluable in developing a critical awareness of the subject area and providing the ability to translate that knowledge into workable practice. For example, consider the age-old idea that there can be only one winner in sport – and that winning always takes place at someone else's expense. Well, if you subscribe to that theory, you may end up losing interest in your sport just because you suffer a few defeats in your competition against others. As it happens, many top-class athletes such as Tiger Woods have a rather different view of success.

Specifically, they define it not in terms of being better than others but by performing better than they themselves did before.

An underlying theme of this book is that, in the words of a famous psychologist called Kurt Lewin, there is nothing so practical as a good theory.[6] We agree wholeheartedly, but at the same time there is nothing so useful for theory as the acid test of practice. Many of our previous publications focused on underlying academic and theoretical issues. Now is the time for us to redress the balance by writing specifically for non-specialists, and we hope to do so in a language that will not confuse and bewilder but may throw light on how you continue to ignore the mental side of your sport at your peril.

In so many sports the extraordinary advances in sport science over recent years have made it increasingly difficult to find that winning edge or X-factor to keep you one step ahead of the pack. Sport psychology is one frontier that remains to be fully explored, but it is not territory that should be frightening. With the right guides there are many established practices that can be adopted with confidence and that do not require a doctorate in psychology as a basis for exploration.

We aim to act as guides on this journey, hoping to inspire and to empower, but not to overpower with technical jargon or complicate what are often simple messages. We hope we succeed but ultimately we will leave that for you to judge.

Why *Pure Sport*?

At first glance this may seem a rather strange title for this book, but after long discussions we decided that these two words best capture our combined approach to applied sport psychology. That is, we do not set out to raise false expectations about the mysterious power of the mind. Instead our approach is purely to allow you to engage with sport itself, pure sport – unadulterated by hype or hysteria. At the end of the day, consistently playing your chosen sports to the best of your ability is what matters most. To achieve this goal, along the way it is vital that you have identified, harnessed and trained your mental skills to ensure that your physical capacity is what limits you, and not any excess psychological baggage.

When the proverbial boots have been hung on the nail for the very last time, a sportsperson should want to be able to reflect on a sporting career confident that the psychological did not stand in the way but acted in concert with the physical, the technical and the tactical in helping realise sporting potential – whatever that may turn out to be. No one dimension should ever be afforded pre-eminence; instead it is the synergy operating between them all that can help to maximise potential.

To enjoy pure sport more than anything we would ask you to travel with an open mind and with the optimism that you have the capacity to learn, to develop and to change. Too often, budding careers in sport have been thwarted because of an ill-timed comment to the effect that the person does or does not 'have it'. Once you apply the label (e.g. 'he's a natural'), it sticks and it can add an unnecessary burden, suggesting that the person can sit back and rely on his or her talent alone. But we should never forget that, as Gary Player once remarked, 'You must work very hard to become a natural golfer!'[7]

In the Western world in particular, we have been shown to be far too quick to apply labels that can so easily impose arbitrary limits on potential. A study comparing the mathematical ability of Western and Asian children found that one simple factor helped explain why those from the East consistently outperformed those from the West. It wasn't teaching techniques or investment in resources – it was that schools did not give credence to the idea that you are either good or bad at sums or numbers. Teachers in the East assumed that everyone had the potential to be good, and so the journey of discovery could be undertaken with optimism.[8]

As with mathematics, in relation to many of the psychological skills described in the book, all we ask for is an acceptance that many of these skills and techniques can be learned and can be developed, just as physical skills can be sharpened over time and with effort. Granted there will be limits to the potential for development or change, but surely it is better to travel hopefully and explore what those limits may be rather than passively accept the hand of fate.

Toughening up

Sport psychologists deal with a wide range of personal issues through their work but some topics seem to crop up time and again, including how to develop mental toughness. The resilience to cope with pressure and rebound from failure, allied with the determination to persist in the face of adversity, is one example among many of a psychological characteristic that should not be left to chance but can be nurtured. After all, most of us can't claim to be born mentally tough – we become so by learning from our experiences – learning that focusing on what can be done *right now* (what we call 'positive action') is the key to overcoming any difficult problem, and we'll explore this idea in greater detail later in the book.

Resilience to deal with the peaks and troughs of a sporting career can be taught so long as the right psychological ingredients are brought together, including a dose of realism. For example, the technofreak mentioned earlier may be someone who has not learned to accept personal responsibility for failure, or who clings to unrealistic expectations of success. To defend their fragile ego, such people constantly turn to external explanations as a form of protection. Through a tailored intervention, this self-defeating approach can be replaced with a more balanced acceptance of appropriate ways of explaining what happens – which then will help the person deal with successes and failures in a way that strengthens character and hardens resolve for future challenges.

Ultimately, mental toughness, along with so many psychological characteristics relating to sporting success, does not have to be the preserve of the fortunate few but can become the right of us all. Throughout the book we will bring together what we regard as the essential ingredients for success, but at the start of this journey all that we require is optimism, open-mindedness and a positive willingness to learn.

Change management

In many respects sport psychology is about change management. An old joke springs to mind.

How many shrinks does it take to change a light bulb?
Just one – but the light bulb must really want to change.

This sentiment resonates powerfully in the world of applied sport psychology where so often the best-laid plans fail because of individuals' unwillingness genuinely to engage with what is happening around them. This may be because of suspicion or more deep-seated personal psychological problems. Sadly it is often true that many of those who are most resistant to sport psychology are those who have the most to gain, and their resistance itself sometimes speaks volumes. Arrogance can be a thin veil disguising a lack of confidence or low self-esteem, but without a genuine willingness to engage, the enterprise is doomed to failure before it even begins.

At the other extreme are those whose resistance to change is entirely justified because they have already proved that they have what it takes to succeed at the highest level. From our experience, their number is not great, but in these cases there is nothing to be gained from disturbing a winning formula. As the saying goes, if it isn't broken, don't fix it. That said, it is a brave person who says they have nothing left to learn – even if it really is the case that they have nothing left to learn!

The word 'change' in the context we are using it here should not be interpreted as implying a root and branch cognitive restructuring. Such radical surgery is unnecessary and could prove to be dangerous and counter-productive. More often it is about rediscovering ingredients that were already there but may have been lost over time as a career has developed.

One of the most significant casualties can be the lightness that goes with pure enjoyment of an activity that may have become a job of work as a sporting career advances. Interestingly, the legendary basketball coach John Wooden (see Chapter 9) claimed that a crucial characteristic of successful sports teams is that they have players who not only work hard but *love what they do*.[9] Later chapters

Vince Lombardi (courtesy of Inpho Photography/Getty Images)

will explore these issues in more depth, but for many athletes, the growing significance of competition and winning can present special problems.

Vince Lombardi exemplifies this issue. He was the highly successful coach of the American football team, the Green Bay Packers, in the 1960s, and one of his most memorable quotes was 'Winning isn't everything, it's the only thing.' Shortly before he died of cancer in 1970, it is rarely reported that he openly acknowledged the danger of adopting this 'must win' mentality. In his own words:

> I wish to hell I'd never said the damned thing. I meant the effort, I meant having a goal. I sure as hell didn't mean for people to crush human values and morality.[10]

In some respects this is a sad epitaph, but it is also an honest acknowledgement that a healthy sense of balance or perspective can sustain a successful sporting career just as successfully as the 'eyeballs out' approach adopted so often in the past.

Our approach

In putting this book together, we have elected deliberately not to follow just one theory or perspective. Instead we welcome the freedom to range across the discipline of psychology in search of approaches, techniques and ideas that can help us to provide the sporting edge for you. Over the last 80 years, sport psychologists have been working with countless teams and individuals and during that time have made full use of a wide range of psychological approaches. By now, if any single approach had proved itself to be the gold standard, there would be a strong consensus in terms of day-to-day practices. That does not appear to be true. Instead there are still almost as many ways of doing sport psychology as there are sport psychologists – and there is a wide variety of theoretical perspectives to choose from in this field.

Rather than preaching or trying to convert you to one of these particular theoretical perspectives, we have tried to pull together the sorts of interventions that have been shown to work. Returning to an earlier theme, this is what we mean by there being nothing as practical as a good theory. Some interventions are well grounded in literature and research principles; others tend to 'float' theoretically and may need to be tied down before it is safe to proceed. Some have borrowed principles from other domains, including work and health psychology, whereas others have grown within the world of sport. Whatever is the case, the acid test is captured by two simple questions. Does it work? And can it be justified in terms of relevant literature? We are confident that the approaches that we shall outline have been there and done just that – on both of these counts.

Sport psychology: what it isn't

Before proceeding to describe what sport psychology actually *is*, it may be useful to outline what it most definitely *isn't*. It would be fair to say that over the years sport psychology has not always enjoyed universal acclaim, as the following quotes illustrate:

> *Ronnie O'Sullivan (snooker)*
> 'I tried a sport psychologist once and I never really got anything out of it . . . if you're on, you're on; if you're off, you're off, and there's not a lot you can do about it.'[11]

> *Goran Ivanisevic (tennis)*
> 'You lie on a couch, they take your money, and you walk out more bananas than when you walked in!'[12]

> *Michelle Wie (golf)*
> 'I'm not really interested in sports psychology. It makes me feel like a crazy person.'[13]

Ronnie O'Sullivan, Goran Ivanisevic and Michelle Wie (courtesy of Inpho Photography)

Many elite sportspeople's encounters with sport psychology must have seriously prejudiced their view of what is on offer. For example, one rugby coach with whom one of us worked briefly had learned his trade in South Africa. Over lunch (at a secret venue!) he immediately recalled with horror the antics of a self-styled sport psychologist, a Mr Motivator, who was brought into the changing room just prior to kick off to psych up the team. Let's just say he has since viewed anyone labelled as a sport psychologist with a considerable degree of suspicion. And perhaps his scepticism is justified in many cases. For example, in 2004, a young man contacted Leicester City soccer club with unsolicited psychological advice for the team manager about improving the team's performance. Rather than presenting his qualifications or experience, he took the bizarre step of attempting to smash a plank of wood in front of the manager with his bare hands! Similarly, Gary Player was sceptical of the growing trend for using sport psychologists in professional golf:

> When you need to put a two iron on the back of the green to win the Open, how is a psychologist going to help you? If he hasn't got the experience what can he tell you? I'm not totally against psychologists but you have to do a certain amount yourself.[14]

Interestingly, this last point echoes a crucial theme in this book – the importance of self-empowerment. Indeed, stories of the antics of well-meaning but perhaps not-so-well-informed practitioners would definitely frighten the horses, and are legion in the trade. Such gimmicks may have an immediate impact and can be eye-catching but are not likely to sustain long-term development.

Other sport psychologists cast themselves not in the role of showman but as doctor or physician, bringing succour to the sick and needy of the sporting parish. This role is also difficult to sustain, as it works from the assumption that the client is ill and so needs a cure. Most sportspeople are not psychologically 'sick' in these terms but are seeking ways not to become 'better' but 'better than ever before' at what they already do well. The medical model (that is, the idea that behavioural 'symptoms' may reflect some kind of underlying 'illness' that needs to be treated)

Gary Player (courtesy of Inpho Photography)

does not apply to the majority of the work of a sport psychologist, and what is more, it would immediately set the wrong tone for the relationship.

A more appropriate model, and one which we subscribe to, casts the sport psychologist more as a sport *consultant* offering informed advice and support to his or her client to help realise potential, secure in the knowledge that the person will not dread the next trip to the surgery.

Of course, there are occasions when it becomes clear that a person's problems *are* clinical in nature. At this stage it is time to step aside and bring in those who are trained to deal with these matters. This situation does not arise all that often but it can happen – and when it does it is very useful to have appropriate networks to tap into. For example, excessive exercise, even characterised as exercise addiction, can suggest a range of psychological disorders linked to low self-esteem and body dissatisfaction. Those with clinical training may be better positioned to identify and treat such problems, especially when they extend to obsessive-compulsive symptoms.

Equally, when exercise is being used inappropriately to control weight or body shape, clinical problems may not be far away. Among female athletes and in particular those involved in what are known as 'aesthetic sports' (including ice skating, gymnastics and dance), a common problem is known as the female athlete triad (FAT) – amenorrhoea (failure to menstruate), osteoporosis (weakening of the bones) and eating disorders (anorexia and bulimia), the last often appearing when injury or retirement has prevented training.

Among young men a growing and not unrelated issue is known as 'muscle dysmorphia' or the pursuit of exaggerated masculine body shapes, often through gym work coupled with dietary supplements and drugs. In these cases, someone with training in clinical methods will be much better equipped than a sport psychologist to help the person deal with the problem.

Across the globe, it is unlikely that the demand for sport psychology has ever been higher. For example, mental skills advisers have been used by teams ranging from the golfers in the 2006 Ryder Cup to various soccer teams competing in the 2006 World Cup. As teams and individuals constantly strive to find the winning edge, it becomes increasingly likely that a sport psychologist will be around to help find that edge. However, these powerful market forces can be dangerous, especially when demand has the potential to outstrip the quality supply of trained professionals. In these circumstances caution must be exercised in both promoting and developing sport psychology, with appropriate regulation of those who describe themselves as sport psychologists and due regard to the subject's limitations and weaknesses alongside its strengths.

In practice, very often the work of a sport psychologist does not need to be sexy, glamorous or high profile. In fact these 'in-your-face' types of intervention can lose sight of basic principles, including the fact that it is what goes into the changing room (the players) that is far more important than an injection of vim from a so-called expert. The focus of attention must always be the sportsperson, and he or she should be encouraged to take responsibility at the heart of affairs, along the way developing a strong network of support that includes specialists from all types of disciplines.

Sport psychology: what it is

Sport psychology can be different things to different people and should be sufficiently flexible to cater for all. The term itself describes all those activities where psychological theory and methods are applied to understand and improve sporting performance.

To a coach or sportsperson it may refer to someone brought in to help the team or individual before the season or to prepare for an important game or tournament. To a sport scientist it may describe that branch of the discipline that focuses on the brain and central nervous system and their influence on sport performance. To a health psychologist it may be about physical activity and well-being in general.

Each definition is appropriate for its own target audience. Some focus on practical application; some highlight professional or academic concerns. At the very least the diversity of interpretations should help highlight the various sources of influence and the broad church which we now know as sport psychology. Of course, an important issue to consider here is whether or not one has to be a *psychologist* to be a sport psychologist. Our answer to that is yes, for without a professional knowledge of the disciplines, the potential to evaluate different approaches, their strengths, weaknesses and effects, will be restricted. Likewise, the potential for causing hurt or damage will increase without an understanding of underlying psychological principles.

Cutting to the chase, for most sportspeople sport psychology is about any mental activity that relates to performance and performance enhancement. The potential to use this material to aid performance is enormous. It has been estimated by some that it takes at least 10,000 hours of practice for anyone to be able to claim that they have become expert in their chosen sport.[15] Sadly, that effort is so often wasted not because of physical or technical limitations but because not even a fraction of that time has been spent working on mental preparation.

Reflections

For a moment, reflect on the number of top-class, elite sportspeople (such as Paul Gascoigne in soccer, John Daly in golf, or Alex Higgins in snooker) who never truly realised their potential; those who hit the heights on rare occasions and showed the world what they were capable of doing but then failed to light the flame again. Very often their weaknesses reflected psychological issues that could so easily have been addressed.

What is more, the higher the sporting ladder any person climbs, the more that difference between winning and losing can come down to the head, and not the body – who rose to the big occasion, who folded under pressure. Sport psychology can help athletes realise their physical potential but it cannot make a silk purse out of a sow's ear and should not pretend it can. Fortunately the number of sportspeople who can truly say that they have explored the limits of their physical capabilities remains small and so the future for sport psychology looks healthy.

Sport psychology, when used alongside other sciences, can help a sportsperson look forward to achieving consistent and repeatable good performances, and eventually look backwards over a career that is not littered with regrets and lost opportunities. Developing the mental edge should not be left to chance or crisis management when the wheels have finally come off, or as the last minute fix. Instead the most effective work often takes place away from competition and involves honing mental skills, sometimes from an early stage in a career, and putting in place procedures that will stand the test of any challenge, big or small. The remaining chapters will explore how this can be achieved.

A brief history of sport psychology

> We argue more about the navigation of ships than about the training of athletes, because it has been less well organised as a science.
>
> (Aristotle, *Nicomachean Ethics*, 4th century BC)

Don't imagine that sport psychology is just flavour of the month or a flash in the pan. So long as there has been sport, there has been talk of the mental side and there has been sport psychology. Centuries before the modern era of professional sport, athletes spent as long preparing mentally as physically for competition. For example, the tetrad or 4-day system became accepted practice for all Greek athletes, leading up to the celebration of their collective and individual well-being through the games. According to the tetrad system, day 1 was set aside for *physical preparation* while day 2 moved on to the psychological and in particular *concen-*

Ancient Greek athlete (courtesy of iStockphoto)

tration. Day 3 was characterised by *moderation* with day 4 reserved exclusively for *relaxation*.

In many ways this was a very early example of 'tapering', a pre-competition regimen that is now universal in many sports and in particular swimming. It is interesting that the main emphasis in tapering today is on physical preparation while the mental side is often left to chance. In fact some research suggests that the psychological effects of tapering should not be ignored lightly, and it may be sensible to consider psychological conditioning alongside the physical in the days leading up to major competition. For example, mood state may dip in the absence of exercise and deliberate steps should be taken to ensure this does not happen.

Beware the filthy lucre!

Despite the advanced science associated with the ancient Greek games, they still finally succumbed to one of the most thorny motivational issues that sport psychologists still grapple with – the complications of extrinsic motivation or, to be more precise, money. According to a noted historian, it was professionalism that killed the games by promoting the message, 'at all costs avoid losing' through winner takes all, a message taken to its extreme by one heavyweight boxer called Melancomas, who succeeded in dancing around his opponent for two days without landing a single punch.[16] When winner takes all, fear of failure becomes a burden that even the most hardy can find hard to shoulder.

Sport psychology in the twentieth century

Despite this long-standing preoccupation with the psychology of sport, it was only in the 1960s that people began to market themselves as sport psychologists. Before that time there were a number of significant pioneers who plied their trade in the world of sport.

One of the earliest was a teacher and keen cyclist called Norman Triplett, who completed his master's thesis at the University of Illinois on his chosen sport. Consistently, Triplett found that times in both training and unpaced races were slower than in competition. This led him to the conclusion that the presence of others in competition served to release additional energy stores ('dynamogism'), which went on to improve performance.[17]

This pioneering study paved the way for later research on the topic of social facilitation – that is, if we are expert, the presence of others enhances performance of well-learned tasks while the less experienced perform new tasks less well in company. What is more, and predating the extensive literature on stress and anxiety in sport, Norman Triplett acknowledged that individuals, whether professional cyclists or children, often respond very differently to competition. Some rise to the challenge and perform better ('the arousal of their competitive instincts and the idea of a faster movement') while others are overstimulated by the prospect and actually perform worse in the presence of others ('going to pieces').

Twenty years later, Dr Coleman Roberts Griffith came to establish the first sport psychology institute at the University of Illinois. His interests were wide-ranging but always with a primary focus on practical application. This orientation is reflected in the content of his two celebrated texts, *The Psychology of Coaching* (1926) and *Psychology and Athletics* (1928), especially the former, which outlines guiding principles for successful coaching. He put these principles into practice in his work as a consultant but with only limited success. His interventions with the Chicago Cubs baseball team and the University of Illinois football team were far from plain sailing. The Cubs' president, Philip P. Wrigley, hired Griffith to find the psychological profile of a champion baseball player, but, with hindsight, pre-dictably he failed, much to the annoyance of Wrigley and the considerable amuse-ment of the players themselves, who apparently found the whole exercise highly entertaining.[18]

Elsewhere the history of sport psychology was quite different. Behind the Iron Curtain, from 1945 onwards, it is reported that there was more open-mindedness to practical interventions and recognition of the advantages that could be gained if scepticism was put aside. For example, some of the pioneering work on relaxation skills in the USSR ran in parallel with the Soviet space programme, and similar techniques to train cosmonauts were then used to prepare Eastern bloc athletes for the 1976 Olympics.

Myths and realities

The sometimes bizarre relationship between sport and 'psychology' in Eastern European countries revealed itself during the course of the World Chess Championship in 1978. In an early round of the championship, when playing a fellow Soviet player, Boris Spassky, Viktor Korchnoi had become paranoid over Spassky's gaining access to his biorhythm chart. He went on to accuse Spassky of deliberately directing 'psi' waves against him during games, waves that he then employed a team of Swiss parapsychologists to intercept. In the grand finale, his opponent, Anatoly Karpov, was accompanied by the renowned Soviet parapsychologist Dr Vladimir Zukhar, who sat prominently in the front row of the stalls 'psyching out' Korchnoi. In desperation, Korchnoi retaliated by hiring two Americans to help him meditate and 'psych out' Zukhar. The story then moved from the sublime to the ridiculous, as the Americans were exposed as alleged criminals who were actually on bail for attempted murder! Their banishment from the hall was followed swiftly by Korchnoi's resignation in game 32.[20]

Although the 1960s marked the real launch of sport psychology in the West, it was not until 1988 that a sport psychologist actually accompanied the US Olympic team in an official capacity. However, from the 1960s onwards, in the USA and Western Europe, a growing number of people, some from academic backgrounds but not all, began to make a living from sport psychology. Many simply learned on the job while others used their educational experience (especially in sport science) to inform their work. Today there is a wide array of professional sport psychologists across the globe working with teams and individuals, amateur and professional. Many of the earlier misgivings have been cast aside, but some sports still cling to the attitude of 'I didn't get where I am today by using a shrink'. Thankfully their number dwindles by the day.

Quality control

As in any scientific endeavour, rigour, discipline and quality control should be central to the work of a sport psychologist. Unfortunately, over the years, people have tried to use the title or mystique of psychology to exploit the vulnerable or uninformed. To avoid falling prey to such characters it is important to check the credentials of anyone using the title 'sport psychologist'. For example, within the UK this title should be restricted to those who are officially chartered by either the British Psychological Society or the British Association of Sport and Exercise Sciences. Elsewhere it would be important to confirm the credentials with reference to the national societies governing either psychology or sport and exercise sciences. Fools rush in where angels fear to tread; a little research at the start of an intervention can avoid hurt later in the day.

Even within the discipline of psychology itself there are many variations on a theme when it comes to the types of support and advice that are on offer. Some practitioners may operate from particular psychological traditions that demand interventions with which you may be uncomfortable. For example, a psychoanalyst often interprets current issues with reference to unresolved conflicts that stem back to early childhood, including psychosexual conflicts. In contrast, a behaviourist focuses on the 'here and now' and may ignore underlying cognitive processes.

A very common approach adopted by many practising sport psychologists is known as cognitive-behavioural therapy (CBT). Without going into detail, this term covers a broad spectrum of techniques and strategies that can be employed to explore and strengthen the relationship between what we think, feel and do (the ABC of psychology – *a*ffect (feelings or emotions), *b*ehaviour (actions) and *c*ognition (thoughts)). The interventions are often practically based to deal with immediate issues, and have been shown to be effective in many applied settings.

To many athletes and coaches, professional sport psychologists may be viewed with a degree of suspicion because of previous negative experiences or stereotypical images. For example, practitioners may have failed to deliver the goods that they over-optimistically promised, or have packaged their services in such a way that clients had been turned off. Certainly, sport psychologists have often been regarded with suspicion by the media, at worst characterised as puppeteers who attempt to pull the athlete's strings with one goal in mind, performance enhancement, at whatever price and with little regard to the sensitivities or wishes of the individual or team concerned. This need not be the case. Many of the techniques reported in the following chapters are unlikely to shock or surprise and do not involve smoke or mirrors. Instead, when brought together into coherent packages and applied with a modicum of common sense, they will provide a solid foundation on which to build a successful sporting career.

Letting go

Before going ahead and working with a sport psychologist, it may be useful to make clear where the relationship will end. Along with overzealous coaches or pushy parents, sport psychologists may not always have fostered the long-term well-being of their clients for one reason above all others – they weren't prepared to let go. It is our strong belief that the state of maturity that should characterise a job well done is a healthy realisation that you are no longer needed, or at least not as much. Over time, as the player or coach develops, so the role of the sport psychologist naturally shrinks – looking something like the schema in Figure 1.1.

No sport psychologist should be in the business of controlling or encouraging dependency. This would fly in the face of what should be a primary goal – to empower and impart knowledge and so to encourage personal growth. This is also true of a great manager or coach, who should know when the time has arrived to

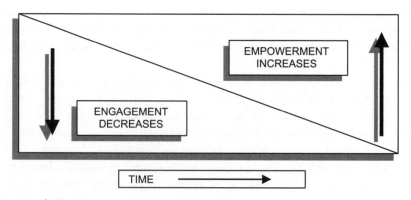

FIGURE 1.1 Letting go

occupy the back seat rather than the driver's seat (see Chapter 9). If we bear this in mind, it is interesting to note how often good coaches of 'under-age' teams are unable to make a smooth transition to coaching or managing senior squads. The styles and techniques that worked well with junior athletes will not necessarily inspire or motivate more mature individuals, and every sport is littered with examples of coach–athlete relationships that broke down because either one or both parties had not adjusted to changing times.

Returning to the role of sport psychologists, obviously there will always be occasions where they remain a useful sounding board but if the intervention has been successful, sportspersons should be increasingly self-sufficient, equipped with the skills and the knowledge to deal with whatever the world of sport may have in store across their career and at whatever level of participation.

Who can benefit?

One common misperception about sport psychology is that it is only for the elite, giving them that winning edge when all other angles have been covered. Nothing could be further from the truth. Making sure that the mental and physical work in harmony is a message for all ages and for all levels of ability with the goal of ensuring that whatever potential is there, it has been realised.

Remember Gary Player's earlier remark that it took him most of his playing career to become a natural. If the adoption of some core principles at an early stage of a career can reduce that long waiting time, there will be obvious benefits. There is no need to rely solely on experience to teach the hard lessons of sport. With careful mentoring these lessons can be imparted early in a career and so a solid and enduring foundation can be guaranteed.

In many respects the earlier the intervention the better, because with a sound foundation from which to build, the person can develop the physical and the mental in tandem. When these are out of synchrony, problems can lie in store at some stage in a career, as when the athlete's talent starts to bring unexpected reward.

The goal?

The goal of the sport psychologist is not as obvious as it may first have seemed. It is not to foster dependence, nor to blind with science, nor to build confidence to a level that is unrealistic and where disappointment is only a matter of time. Instead the goal of a positive intervention should be to mould a performance landscape characterised less by peaks and valleys and more by high, broad plains of routine and regular good performances.

To use the jargon, the lofty summits of 'peak performance' can be dangerous places to occupy. Those rare times when it all comes together naturally and effortlessly without conscious thought may occur occasionally during a sporting career, but they cannot be relied on week in and week out. Instead, a less dramatic but more realistic target to aim for could be above-average performance, or what is known as RGP (repeatable good performance).[19] This is attainable but only as long as you remain at the fulcrum of the enterprise. You, the athlete, must occupy centre-stage, drawing on whatever resources are necessary at whatever time and place is required, towards the goal of performance enhancement.

One common saying in sport is that you are only as good as your last game. That may be partly true from the point of view of a critical fan or coach, but from the player's perspective such an attitude would represent a psychological recipe for disaster. Lurching from game to game, waiting for the fickle finger of fate to play its unpredictable role in affairs, is not likely to encourage *confidence*, nor foster a belief in *control*, nor enhance long-term *commitment*, and increasingly it is taken that the balancing of these three Cs characterises a mentally strong athlete (see Chapter 2). When these three elements co-exist in a healthy state of harmonious interdependence, the sport psychologist can relax and walk away with a degree of satisfaction of a job well done.

Total preparation

We hope by now that you are oriented towards what sport psychology can achieve and how it can go about that task. This is not a separate enterprise but comes under the overarching philosophy of total preparation, where nothing is left to chance in the pursuit of maximising potential. The Greeks were probably the first to embrace this philosophy with enthusiasm, but now any committed sportsperson who seriously wants to succeed should regard this approach as obligatory, drawing on all the sport sciences in the pursuit of improvement.

As the margins between winning and losing become ever smaller, there is a growing need to ensure that all angles are covered. Sport psychology is not unique or special but sits comfortably alongside the other sport sciences, all combining to ensure that no avenue has been left unexplored. This journey does not have to be painful but can be an interesting voyage. We hope you enjoy the trip.

Chapter 2

Succeeding

Learn from yesterday, live for today, hope for tomorrow.

Albert Einstein

Introduction

A S THE SPORTS SCIENCES have become more and more sophisticated, the opportunities for finding a winning edge in terms of equipment, physical fitness, tactics or technique have reduced. In a strange way, the high incidence of drug cases in professional sport shows just how elusive that winning edge has become – and how desperate some athletes can be for success whatever the means and whatever the costs.

To see how sophisticated the drug-testing procedures have become, and in turn the extreme measures that sportspeople have taken to avoid detection, look at the website of the World Anti-Doping Agency[1] (WADA), including recent case law. For certain sports, the purity of the activity itself has now become so tarnished with suspicion that those sports are already starting to see the costs in terms of both participant numbers and public interest. It is a downward spiral that will be difficult to arrest.

Albert Einstein (courtesy of NASA)

To be clear at the outset, from a psychological perspective the response to the issue of using illicit drugs or any unlawful procedure, including cheating, must be unequivocal. Should an athlete choose that path, the door to a meaningful psychological intervention has closed firmly shut. In terms of the approach to sport that we advocate and outline in this book, it would be impossible to buy into our philosophy while cheating yourself and others. In the film *My Little Chickadee*, W. C. Fields famously remarked, 'Anything worth having is worth cheating for.' A great comedian but maybe not such a great sport psychologist.

A sporting life must be built on an honest mental foundation that can face the good times along with the bad times head on. At a more fundamental level, the question can be asked – why bother taking part at all when it will mean nothing when you look in the mirror? Yet again, this is a reminder that a mental approach to sport must come together in an integrated package. Leave out any ingredient and the recipe just won't work – and throw in other ingredients and the meal will be ruined.

Cheating, whether by drugs or any other means, may achieve short-term gain but will inflict long-term pain, both physically and psychologically. Rather than looking elsewhere the answer may lie within, only waiting to be discovered. While so many dimensions of sport science have now been exhausted, it is still true that the potential to unlock reserves of ability through the use of appropriate mental training is considerable, and so begins our search for success.

What makes 'the winning mind'?

The answer to this question has vexed sport psychologists over many years. In occupational psychology, throughout the twentieth century the quest was for the formula that defined a good business leader. In sport psychology, the challenge has been to find the winning mind or the champion's magic formula. It is probably no coincidence that one of the earliest documented sport psychology interventions was undertaken to try to identify the personal characteristics associated with success in sport. As mentioned in the previous chapter, Coleman Griffiths was employed by the president of the Chicago Cubs baseball team to identify the psychological profile of a champion player.[2] He tried hard but failed miserably, and he has not been alone. As with the search for leadership traits, the answer that researchers keep coming back to is that, 'It all depends', and depends in particular on a complex relationship between the person and the situation.

To any aspiring young sport psychologist who may think this is unfinished business, could we respectfully suggest that there may be more profitable ways of spending your time.

Your top five: what do they have in common?

In a sport of your choice, quickly jot down the names of five world-famous players. Now compare them in terms of temperament and personality. For example, are they all extrovert, introvert, intelligent, witty, stable, analytic, arrogant, charismatic, moody, or thoughtful? Are there any common traits or characteristics?

In reflecting for a moment on the psychological make-up of successful sportspeople, it does not take too long to realise that the search for a champion psychological profile is not only elusive but also illusory. In other words, there is *no* magic formula. Instead, what can be forged and shaped through a combination of nature (genetic predisposition) and nurture (development and experience) is a set of characteristics and mental strategies that will allow you to help realise your physical potential, and continue to realise that potential throughout your life. The rest of this chapter will elaborate on this idea.

Heading down the rocky road

A sporting career is best thought of as a journey. The road travelled can be rough, with potholes waiting for the unwary around every twist and turn. However, navigating down this path can be exhilarating and exciting, and the adventure itself should be as rewarding as the goal.

At the very start of this voyage, to assume that one's personality is static immediately presents us with a major obstacle to progress. From birth to grave, we grow and as we grow, we change, and nowhere is this more true than in sport and through sport. While there may be core aspects of our personality that endure, we continue to be moulded and shaped by our experiences, and especially our successes and failures.

Is it nature? Is it nurture?

From its birth as a scientific discipline, psychology has grappled with the nature/ nurture debate, and there is little point in retreading this well-worn ground here. To summarise, the jury is still out on the relative influences of genetic pre-disposition and experience in shaping our psychological make-up. Given the inconclusive evidence, it is safest to conclude that some combination of both nature and nurture defines who we are and what we are like. For our purposes, until concrete evidence emerges to suggest otherwise, let's be optimistic and assume that at least we have the potential to change. Otherwise our journey ends before it even begins.

Success is shaped by many things but in particular by the route you decide to follow down the rocky road, and how you deal with your experiences along the way. It is an old but true saying that we learn far more from our disasters than our triumphs, and our most profound and positive changes often occur as a result of how we deal with adversity. An old adage (and now a book by Maxine Schnall[3]) is, 'what doesn't kill you makes you stronger', or, as allegedly remarked by one of the most famous coaches of all time, Vince Lombardi, 'It's not whether you get knocked down, it's whether you get back up.'

Time and again, biographies of top sportspeople reveal that it was the knocks and the upsets that started to shape their later successes. For example, Jack Nicklaus failed to win a major before the death of his father. So, one important ingredient in the winning mind is dealing with adversity and using setbacks to learn, grow and come back stronger. Unfortunately, in the past, many sportspeople have relied on experience and time to help accumulate experience, but there are ways in which this learning process can be shortened.

In the beginning

Many young people set out on their sporting journey accidentally and for no other reason than they just happen to be good at a particular sport, or more usually, several sports that involve the execution of motor skills that rely on strength, dexterity and coordination. As time goes by, it is almost inevitable that their ability will be recognised – and what happens next can be just as predictable. Their talent will lead them into a competitive system that can start to take control. In the process, an activity that was once fun and inherently enjoyable may soon come to feel more like a job of work than a recreation. The burdens of expectation inevitably weigh more heavily as the stakes begin to rise and the level of competition increases, until eventually the lightness and vitality of youth become buried under the weight of a sporting career.

In many respects, what has happened here is that the naive innocence of youth has become infected not only by personal anxieties and ambitions but also by the collective expectations of those who continue to live in hope of what could be achieved. These are not always the Svengalis or puppeteers of sporting fiction or the 'pushy parents' so reviled by the sporting press. Such people exist but they are in the minority. More often these 'significant others' are sincere, well-meaning and highly motivated parents, teachers, coaches and relatives who want no more than the best for those they care for.

Sadly, through no fault of their own, these best intentions can end as a recipe for disaster, and one that many young athletes will have experienced. The high drop-out rates in adolescence from many sports, such as swimming, bear witness to the psychological damage that can be inflicted, and the careful nurturing that is required to sustain interest and enthusiasm through the many changes associated with the teenage years.

The reason why

Young sportspeople, and some not so young, eventually wrestle with a question that may not have even occurred to them in the past – why am I doing this? If the answer is not immediately to hand, or if the reasons are not sound, then problems will lie in store, and performance will suffer.

Two questions are critical in laying the mental foundation for success. Any hesitation in coming up with an answer to either of these questions needs to be explored further, to find out what may be interfering with these pure motives for participation:

Why am I doing this?
Who am I doing this for?

Why? Enjoyment and challenge. There is nothing complicated about playing sport for the intrinsic enjoyment of the activity, but other motives can come along to complicate matters considerably. It could be for others, for status, for money, for ego – all these motives come at a cost, for the activity itself becomes secondary to the primary need. This is not necessarily true of other motives such as competition, fitness or companionship where the sport itself remains paramount and the other motives are fortunate consequences of engaging in that activity – but enjoyment must still lie at the heart of the matter.

Who for? Again the answer is simple; it is primarily for yourself. If this ever fades from view or you feel that others seem to be benefiting more from what is happening than you, then there is a need to step back, reappraise and find a way of occupying centre-stage once more. This does not imply that a family row or worse must ensue, but often subtle but effective techniques can be used to redress the balance.

This is not being selfish because the goal will benefit everyone, but it is about rediscovering roots and remembering that when everything else is put aside, sport is fun and is inherently selfish, in the nicest possible way. The rewards that come along with a successful career in sport may be welcome, but they are no more than side effects and to give them more status than they deserve will not improve performance.

The middle

In the midphase of a career, other unexpected hurdles can present themselves. A difficult case can be the person who has already achieved – but maybe too much, too soon. Walking on the moon leaps to mind as an extreme example of the question of what else is there left to do? Both Neil Armstrong, the first moon walker, and Buzz Aldrin, the second, struggled psychologically coming back down to Earth (quite literally!) after the *Apollo 11* mission.

Sport is littered with examples of bright young stars who have burned brightly but briefly and ultimately failed to realise their undoubted promise. Dealing with such early success can be far more troublesome than dealing with failure because the scope for intervention is much more limited when there is no motivation to do anything while the successes keep coming.

Over the moon? (courtesy of NASA)

It takes great discipline to acknowledge the need for support in these circumstances and too often the chance is missed. Dealing with failure, by contrast, is much more straightforward so long as the individual is shown the way forward. It is at this juncture that good coaches, mentors and teachers really come into their own in shaping fledgling talent.

Less dramatically, it could be that earlier, sudden improvements in performance become less pronounced as a career progresses and as practice no longer reaps the same immediate rewards, or the practice itself becomes a chore. Once the buzz of discovering potential has dimmed and reality slowly creeps in, the person may have to come to terms with the physical limits of his or her potential. In team sports this can be less problematic, as the older player can continue on a journey to explore the team potential and maybe begins to assume other roles to help support the team or club. However, in individual sports the reality check can be especially hurtful. The next chapter in particular may be helpful in showing how these difficulties can be dealt with effectively.

Another obstacle that every sportsperson encounters at some stage is enforced rest through injury. When there has been a huge personal investment in a sporting life, the adjustment to either rest or retirement can be traumatic. A number of psychological models based on the grieving process have been developed to help understand this process.

In a far more positive vein, it is possible to see a period of enforced absence from sport as a time to develop other skills, including the mental. A time of injury can be used to return not in shape but in even better shape, and this is a theme to which we will return in Chapter 7. For example, when Roy Keane, the former captain of Manchester United, suffered a career-threatening cruciate knee ligament

Roy Keane (courtesy of Inpho Photography)

injury in 1998, he was forced to undertake an arduous programme of rehabilitation. During this physical recovery time, he benefited considerably by working on his upper-body strength in the gym, reducing his alcohol intake and establishing priorities for the remainder of his playing career. Remarkably, as he acknowledged in his autobiography, 'A bleak period in my professional life had changed me . . . time spent alone helped me figure myself out.'[4]

And the end?

At the far side of the sporting career may lurk a whole new set of mental pitfalls. As for retirement itself, the pain of sudden loss can be intense and, to be honest, cannot be sidestepped. This is especially true where people's sense of identity and whole lifestyle have been so firmly rooted in their sport. Instead, when the time is ripe there can be opportunities to see how that energy and expertise can be reinvested, but timing here is critical. Too soon and the rawness of loss may carry emotional baggage that interferes with rational decision-making. Too late and the sense of identity may have re-formed around alternative activities.

In many professional sports the end can be sudden and brutal, as age takes its toll. To the outsider the fall from grace can appear dramatic and with no safety net to break the descent. From the inside it is rare that signals have not been picked up that time is running out, and while denial may cloud judgement, usually there is a moment when a choice has to be made – do I jump or should I wait to be pushed? Research has considered the consequences for those who have not made the professional grade in several sports, including American football, basketball, baseball and soccer. Interestingly, usually being released from a contract is not as traumatic as may be imagined, and most players eventually find a level that is appropriate for the rest of their playing lives.

Coaches and managers must also deal with the end and, once more, timing is all. In a profiling session we carried out with coaches from many sports, one of the most important characteristics that was identified was 'knowing when to walk'. In many sports short-term goals dictate that a coach or manager must produce instant results, and when those results do not appear, room for manoeuvre can become cramped. 'Reading the runes' in these circumstances can ensure departure is planned and dignified rather than rushed and imposed.

Sport psychologists often find it difficult to work with more mature athletes, especially successful sportspersons who have been there so often that they feel there is nothing more to learn. Alternatively, there is the person who is struggling to come to terms with physiological changes associated with ageing and so vainly tries to recapture lost youth, often by pushing harder and harder but for diminishing returns. As one eminent coach once remarked, eventually there is only one solution for veteran athletes, the humane killer – but not always. Take Ed Whitlock, who became the only man on Earth known to have run a marathon in under 3 hours at the age of 70. Five years later, at 75, he was still much faster than 99 per cent of runners half his age. In 2006, at the Toronto Waterfront Marathon, Ed Whitlock ran 26.2 miles in 3:08 hours.

Travelling hopefully

At each stage of a sporting career different issues and challenges inevitably emerge and can derail the unwary. This is not an easy road to travel but with a few signposts and clear directions it can be a worthwhile and rewarding journey, with every step of the journey itself to be relished.

To look forward to this trip, one of the most important points to keep in mind is that you travel through a constantly changing landscape. For example, what worked or motivated you as a teenager will be quite different from what will inspire you as a veteran, and so the orientation at each stage of the journey must be dynamic and responsive, but throughout there will be one constant that should never change – a sense of who you are.

The person who begins this journey will not be quite the same as the one who ends it, but constantly striving to be someone else along the way will not help. Role models have their place but it should be a limited place. We can watch and learn, but beyond this the model can do more harm than good to self-esteem when we model rather than learn from. Modelling assumes uncritical acceptance; learning involves a more active process of filtering.

In a similar vein, certain teams and individuals have adopted the stance of 'doing what they did' to try to achieve success. That is, identifying a successful team or nation and then attempting to replicate that blueprint, as by importing 'foreign' coaches or styles of play. Rarely has this strategy yielded long-term results. Instead, a more likely outcome is a team with a confused identity, and a heightened sense of inferiority, as the role model remains elusively beyond their grasp. Cultures cannot be imported. The alternative is far more appealing and realistic – by all means, beg, borrow and steal but always remain true to yourself.

Having firmly attached this health warning, we may say that within sport there may be certain individuals with particular predispositions that may help at key stages in a career. For example, at present, there is a great deal of research interest in the characteristics that define mental toughness together with an assumption that all athletes need bucketsful. This may be true in many situations, as we have already noted, but, equally, mental toughness in one circumstance may be blind ignorance in another. Times change and the skills to deal with changing situations change, so no one person will ever possess all the answers, and no one can have the perfect psychological profile. Instead what each person brings is a unique set of qualities that define that individual, warts and all, and sadly a great many sporting careers have been blighted because people have lost sight of who they are and what makes them special.

Balancing the chip

So success involves always learning, respecting others but never standing in awe, and never trying to copy someone else. Recognise who you are, what makes you good, and, critically, what you need to work on to make you even better.

What else are we looking for? Well, there are certain characteristics linked to sporting achievement that can help to keep you moving down the road with a sense of purpose. For example, while champions may come in many different packages, it is often remarked anecdotally that there seems to be one common defining feature – they are never truly happy!

To be more accurate, whatever you achieve should never be quite enough. Some say that a truly well-balanced athlete carries a chip on both shoulders, and there may be a grain of truth in this statement. However, as with any characteristic, if carried too far this strength can become a weakness. For example, when reality never quite matches the heights of expectation, there is the potential for dis-enchantment, even sulking, and consequently losing motivation. Some of the most highly paid professional sportspeople have shown themselves to be guilty of this crime, not rising to the challenges posed by adversity but instead retreating into a small, grumpy world of self-recrimination, and in the process writing off a bad day at the office. In all these cases the key has to be balance – keeping the edge but keeping it in balance, and keeping the real world in view at all times.

When used positively, the chip can be a very powerful motivator at both an individual and team level. It is a trick that many great managers in sport have repeatedly used to their advantage, instilling a belief in their teams that what has been achieved is never quite enough – inspiring a hunger for success that can never be satisfied.

Healthy disrespect

As money continues to be poured into the pursuit of success in both amateur and professional sport, it is too easy to buy into the idea that resources will always win out, and that success can be bought. With this in mind, many teams and individuals participate in, or travel to, international tournaments, with no expect-ation of success because the form book tells them so. Rubbish! As long as that belief persists, the form book will prevail, but as long as there are those who are driven to tear up the form guide, sport will continue to prosper – along with the bookies.

31

The underdog label can be used in either a positive or a negative way, but it has great potential when carefully handled. As a negative, it can help maintain the status quo by keeping outsiders firmly in their place, and the label has hamstrung too many good players and teams over the years. If you let it, the label can provide a ready-made excuse for failure but only if you let it. From a positive motivational perspective, the underdog mentality, a healthy disrespect for authority, can work wonders so long as it is underpinned by a sufficient level of confidence. This does not have to extend to 'will win' – but instead, 'can win'.

Can win . . .

'Will win' is fragile, as nothing is that certain and entirely under our control. 'Can win' suggests we have the capability with the right motivation and circumstance, and is far easier to sustain in the long term. 'Can win' is sufficient to provide the drive to 'give it a rattle', and the great advantage of this strategy is that the burden of expectation is lifted from the shoulders of players, who are then allowed to go out and simply perform.

Many teams and individuals perform the first part of the underdog trick but often fail at the final hurdle when eventually succumbing to the status quo – otherwise known as the gallant loser. An example is a team that against all odds finds itself leading but then decides that the safest option is to defend that lead. In truth this becomes the riskiest option, as play becomes compressed into little more than a practice game of defence and attack. More rarely, a team will have the self-belief to know that what took them to that point can take them further, and that an honourable defeat is still a defeat and is unacceptable. When the going gets tough, the tough keep going.

Some situations allow the underdog tag to emerge naturally, but how can you hope to continue to persuade champions that they are still underdogs? This must be one of the greatest skills of sport management, but it is one that certain individuals have honed to perfection, constantly creating the impression that the world is 'agin us' and including match officials, administrators and the media. For example, Sir Alex Ferguson, one of the most successful managers in world football, likes to motivate his players by creating a 'them and us' mentality:

> Footballers are all different human beings. Some are self-motivators, they need to be left alone. . . . For some, you need causes, your country, them and us. . . . And those causes can be created by the manager.[5]

One common tactic used by those who espouse this philosophy is to gather together hostile press clippings and litter changing-room walls with the offending articles, or

Alex Ferguson (courtesy of Inpho Photography)

to foster a relationship with the media that is less than friendly. Any examples spring to mind?

... But dare to lose

Whether through such tactics or in other ways, what a good coach or manager is often trying to instil in players is a mentality that while the journey may be tough, the goal is within grasp ('can win'), but it won't happen by chance, and, critically, to be able to win you must acknowledge the prospect of losing. This is not negative but realistic and actually reflects the coming together of two psychological constructs that have long interested applied psychologists in many fields, including education and industry. Before going any further, try the short test in the box.

33

Winning and losing

Being honest with yourself, on a scale from 0 to 10, how would you rate your interest in winning (0 = no interest; 5 = moderate interest; 10 = crucial)?

Now, in terms of your fear of losing, on a scale from 0 to 10, how would you rate your fear of failing (0 = fear not important; 5 = moderately important; 10 = crucial)?

The literature suggests that need to achieve (NAch) and fear of failure (FF) combine to help determine our approach to competition.[6] Both are entirely independent psychological constructs. Contrary to popular belief, this means that it is possible to have a variety of scores, with very different profiles emerging, depending on the mix of this combination. Typically, scores are used to classify according to type, as shown in the box.

Winning, losing and typing

Type 1 – has a *low* interest in winning but a *high* fear of failing
These individuals often leave jobs unfinished or lose interest in activities. They avoid competition if possible but may choose to compete against someone they know they can beat, such as a younger brother or sister.

Type 2 – has a *low* interest in winning and a *low* fear of failing
These people feel indifferent to competition and would probably wonder why people make such a fuss about winning and losing. 'After all, it is only a game,' they may say.

Type 3 – has a *high* interest in winning but a *low* fear of failing
This type of people love competition, especially where the outcome is uncertain. They are full of energy for a particular goal and take calculated risks. They love to win but realise that losing is not the end of the world. They are very persistent and highly self-motivated.

Type 4 – has a *high* interest in winning and a *high* fear of failing
These individuals also enjoy competitive situations and take personal responsibility for outcomes, but failures cause self-doubt and lower their self-confidence. This worry over failing often reveals itself in poor sportsmanship, an unwillingness to take risks, decreased persistence, and sometimes a superficial air of arrogance. As a result of these factors, these individuals often fail to fulfil their potential.

Not surprisingly, type 3s often represent the best long-term investment for any sport and have the right ingredients to sustain a successful career.

Unfortunately the combination of circumstances that draws a young person into a sport, including the part played by significant others, can inadvertently produce not type 3s but types 1 or 4. These may then drift towards becoming type 2s and finally drop-outs from sport.

In terms of actual performance, those with a high FF often underperform not through lack of ability but through inhibition and an unwillingness to take risks. Poor performances then feed FF and so a downward spiral is created.

The bad news is that many young people do not derive the enjoyment they should from sport because of this combination; the good news is that it is not difficult to change the profile if there is a willingness to change. Unfortunately type 3s can also be characterised by arrogance and this complicates matters, as genuine engagement is not easy to sustain. These individuals often have developed remarkable defence mechanisms that make sure 'nothing sticks', including critical advice or even support. However, if there is willingness to change, the process relies on going back to basics by rebuilding the primary motives for taking part – for enjoyment and for yourself. This could include deliberately sidelining significant others and placing more and more personal responsibility on the shoulders of the athlete. With these foundations a more solid and secure basis for long-term growth can then be fostered.

Pause for thought: NAch and FF versus want to achieve (WAch) and hatred of failure (HF)

Looking well beyond the research literature to the reality of elite sport, the interplay between NAch and FF in determining performance and motivation is probably more complicated than may first appear. Somewhat naively, many sport psychologists still advocate an ideal psychological profile based on low fear of failure and high need to achieve. In reality, very often this is impossible to attain, particularly when the amount of investment in terms of time and effort has been so great that failure has real and tangible consequences. Indeed many top sportspeople would argue that avoiding FF is inadvisable, as it is 'fear' that continues to give them the edge.

In these circumstances alternative strategies may be needed to lose the inhibition attached to FF. If fear starts to cramp rather than help performance, it may be a case of working to turn fear of failure (a negative) into a more positive emotion – *hatred of failure* (HF). It is acceptable to hate the prospect of failure and all that goes with it, but to be afraid of that prospect is a different matter entirely. The former can inspire to greater efforts; the latter may conspire to constrain.

In a similar vein, even the expression 'need to achieve' (NAch) is worthy of a second glance. Need implies a natural force or drive that is outside our control.

A healthier term for you may be *want to achieve* (WAch) – 'wanting to' rather than 'needing to' may seem a trivial shift, but it is a significant move in terms of placing you in charge.

What lies beneath

Already we have identified a number of external factors that can have an adverse effect on performance and motivation, but what of internal or psychological mechanisms that can stand in the way of success? These are not pathological conditions that mark out those with clinical problems, but they are common mental processes that can interfere with the translation of positive motivation into repeatable good performance.

Very often these mechanisms serve to shield us from harm – for example, when we suffer failure or defeat. This short-term gain can prevent us from learning from our mistakes. To repeat an earlier point, without doubt the most effective learning potentially comes not from success but from failure, but we are not well programmed to take these messages on board.

Before going any further, try completing the short questionnaire in the box on the opposite page. If you compare your scores on each of the four questions for winning and losing, very often you will find that we are more inclined to take credit for success and find excuses for failure. So you should find relatively higher attribution scores for internal factors (1 and 4) under winning than losing, and vice versa for external factors when explaining why you lost.

What is more, whether the internal factor is stable (Q1 – ability) or unstable (Q4 – effort) and, equally, whether the external factors are temporary (Q2 – bad luck) or permanent (Q3 – opponents) will all have an influence on future motivation.

Use your head

If you are like many people, it could be that you are not taking sufficient credit for your successes and so feel that you have relatively little control over results. Clearly, whatever pattern emerges, in order to develop 'the winning mind' there are certain 'attribution styles' (ways of explaining events) that will be more effective than others. For example, in order for someone to draw on success it is often important to change the way you think about your performance – to work hard at acknowledging that a good performance was not due to luck or chance but reflected internal factors that are stable (skill) or unstable (effort), or that a poor performance should not be excused but can be drawn on to provide useful learning points that in turn can be translated into more effective practice.

Winning, losing and feeling

Winning

Think about the last time you won a sport competition, match, tournament or game and then indicate the extent to which you feel that each of the following was influential. (Rate each on a scale of 1 to 10 where 1 = not true and 10 = entirely true.)

1. To what extent do you feel your ability was a factor in the result?
2. To what extent do you feel the result was due to your good luck?
3. To what extent do you feel the result came down to your opponent's playing poorly?
4. To what extent do you feel the result was because you tried hard?

Losing

Now think about the last time you lost a competition, match, tournament or game and then indicate the extent to which you feel that each of the following was influential. (Rate each on a scale of 1 to 10 where 1 = not true and 10 = entirely true.)

1. To what extent do you feel your ability was a factor in the result?
2. To what extent do you feel the result was due to your bad luck?
3. To what extent do you feel the result came down to your opponent's playing well?
4. To what extent do you feel the result was because you did not try hard?

Another word makes its appearance at this point – *control*. The control that people believe they have over internal and external factors is vital. Almost all competitors believe that they can control effort; fewer intuitively believe that they can influence ability, but do remember, this must be an optimistic journey where change is possible. In fact we can learn to grow 'the winning mind' by putting the right formula in place when reflecting on our performance. High achievers will credit their successes to themselves and their ability, and will deal with failures in various ways, including finding positive ways that failure can be dealt with through increased effort and practice.

On the one hand, there may be occasions where there is a need to acknowledge mistakes in order to move forward from those mistakes. On the other hand, taken to its extreme, low achievers will blame themselves for mistakes and defeat, and will believe there is nothing they can do to change the situation. What is more, while high achievers explain success with reference to stable factors, low achievers talk about temporary factors beyond their control when explaining success – and so assume that the performance is not repeatable.

Each style then becomes self-fulfilling, generating a success circle for high achievers and a vicious circle for low achievers. That is, by attributing success to internal factors high achievers experience more personal pride in their success and so seek out achievement situations. They persist and try harder when the going gets tough, whereas low achievers do not attribute success internally and so become less motivated over time.

To use these styles effectively requires nothing more than common sense and a recognition that balance, yet again, holds the key to success, this time balancing the right style with the right occasion. At one extreme are those who have such well-developed 'external attribution styles' (that is, they always blame external factors for what happens to them) that they are 'Teflon coated' – nothing ever sticks. At the other extreme are those with such an exaggerated internal style (that is, they attribute the causes of significant events to themselves) that they take too much responsibility for things outside their control. The balanced approach lies midway between these extremes.

Any coach can extract key lessons from this work. The coach's task should be to instil the belief that success relates to effort and ability (internal causes), and that players are capable of again attaining the highest level of skill that they have shown in the past at any time in the future. Equally, strategies for dealing with failure must resist the temptation to excuse and instead find positive paths forward.

Before leaving this research, there is one further finding to note in passing, known by psychologists as the fundamental attribution error.[7] What this term refers to is the consistent finding that in comparison with those who play, those who watch overemphasise the role played by internal factors (skill and effort) in explaining results. The disastrous consequences for reconciling conflicting post-match analyses and opinions should be obvious!

Know yourself

We explain away successes and failures in ways that are not always productive, but being forewarned is being forearmed and reinforces a key component of 'the winning mind' – the capacity to be honest and self-reflective. The next chapter will explore the techniques involved in detail; for now, the principle is sufficient. A later chapter will also consider ways in which to manage stress so as to maximise performance (Chapter 4).

The complex relationship between stress, anxiety, physiological arousal and performance has intrigued sport psychologists for decades; for now, though, there is no need to become embroiled in these debates. Instead the key, yet again, is self-awareness – knowing what has worked in the past and having the skill and the discipline to recreate that state time and again in the future.

In essence, 'the winning mind' works hard to eliminate thoughts of luck or fate and instead takes control, reflecting on previous performances, and especially the 'head' that was carried into those games. This reflection is used to draft a formula for mental preparation that should never vary. Techniques such as biofeedback (e.g. pulse rate) and mental training (e.g. thought stopping, imagery) can then be used to hit the zone repeatedly, and to stay there. During play itself, other techniques can be brought in to achieve two primary aims – to keep the head in the present (not dwelling on past mistakes; not waiting for the final whistle), and to create an environment where thinking does not interfere with doing. It is here that the specialist skills of a sport psychologist can help to show which techniques work in which situation, and, again, what we have tried to do in the following chapters is outline these techniques.

Strangely, this means that 'the winning mind' needs to know when to think and when not to think. Too often all those countless hours of practice to make the difficult seem natural can be lost when thought interferes; this is otherwise known as *paralysis by analysis*. Losing confidence often refers to no more than the times when the spontaneous has become thoughtful, and stopping those thoughts is a vital skill, but not a difficult one to develop.

The foundation lies in sequencing and so preventing the contamination of one stage by another. Somewhat crudely, these stages can be referred to as follows:

Feck it
Do it
Think about it

1. 'Feck it' refers to that balanced state where the player performs knowing that all the hard work and preparation is behind and the primary task now is to play unfettered by doubts, worries or expectation – to give it a rattle.
2. 'Do it' involves making sure that the clock is not turned back during play itself; that is, the expert does not revert to the novice role by thinking about what should be happening spontaneously. This will only happen if analysis is not allowed to interfere with action, or at least if it does appear, it appears at the right time – for example, during breaks in play. A useful trick to remind yourself that analysis must begin and end is to draw a line on the back of your hand before you play, the line signifying that whatever has happened is past. Quite literally, this is drawing the line! Or if you are inclined to start taking it all too seriously, why not try a curved line (Figure 2.1), to remind you not to take yourself too seriously and that you are allowed to smile!
3. 'Think about it' is actually the most important phase, for without this the other two are impossible. Depending on the sport in question, there may be a

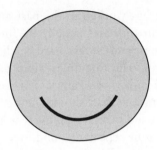

FIGURE 2.1 Draw the (curved) line

lot, little or no time for reflection during play itself. Whatever time there is should be used wisely, but the most important thinking time should take place almost as soon as play ends and before others have had an opportunity to judge or assess. Now is the time for a systematic and structured assessment of what went well, what went less well, and what must be worked on before the next time. This can then be used as a reference point for discussions with others on performance and will then frame subsequent practice (see Chapter 3).

Psychologists often describe their work in terms of three concerns – A, B and C. A or affect concerns emotion, B is behaviour, and C is cognition, and what this simple strategy actually achieves is a framework for coordinating and prioritising these three in order to produce optimal performance. That is, emotionally the individual must be right when entering competition, ready to meet the challenge, but not overwhelmed. During competition, behaviour should be pre-eminent, with cognition or emotion held firmly in check. Afterwards is the time for thought, to reflect and analyse and hence provide the basis for future action. In this way the winning mind harnesses A, B and C to produce effective performance.

Mental toughness: balancing 3 Cs (plus one)

As more pieces of the jigsaw fit into place, a clearer picture of 'the winning mind' should be starting to emerge. The image may not be alien to you because it is not about trying to make you something that you are not. Instead the core is you but you armed with a clear sense of purpose, an honest acknowledgement of what you are and what you can be, and also equipped with skills and techniques that can make sure that the sporting journey continues to excite you around every bend in the road. With the right guide, mental toughness will develop as the journey continues.

Balance remains critical throughout this journey, including the balancing of four constructs that can help tie together so many of the themes already introduced and that underpin mental toughness. Talk of the 3 Cs is not new in sport psychology but there have been many variations on the theme. The winning mind has the capacity to balance the 3 Cs. A successful athlete will continually monitor these three to ensure that when they act in concert they facilitate performance, and no single 'C' or attribute should ever be allowed to become too dominant.

Confidence, commitment, control

In the past it's perhaps true to say that too much emphasis was placed on confidence as the primary psychological attribute, when in fact it is joined with the other two as equal partners. Too much confidence can be as dangerous as too little, because too much may foster complacency, which in turn will lower commitment and control. Too little can have the opposite effect.

Likewise with commitment. Too much and there is a danger of losing control, and that will adversely impact on confidence. Too little and the performance will lack passion and hence may be too controlled. In this way, too much or too little of any one and the balance will be unhealthy. Keep them all in a harmony and you have a well-balanced athlete who will continue to feel good about what needs to be done and how to do it.

And challenge?

Challenge represents the fourth and overarching C. It encompasses the other Cs by defining the mental approach that must accompany you on each step of the journey. The steps on this journey should never be thought of as things to fear or to avoid; instead, they represent interesting tests of how far you have come and where else you may be going. At each stage of your sporting career there should remain that buzz of anticipation because the future is uncertain and the end of the journey is unknown. So the limits of your personal talents can be explored with a genuine sense of excitement and anticipation.

In this environment, change is the only constant as you continue to explore new challenges. And what of those who stand in your way, opponents? They are interesting obstacles to progress that must be dealt with, not according to reputation but according to the practical ways in which they prevent you from moving onwards and upwards.

Ever increasing circles

So when all is said and done, what is 'the winning mind'? Forget about a set of psychological ingredients that are magically plugged into your head to make you walk, talk and think like a champion. Instead of describing the winning mind as an object, think of it as the title for a journey of discovery, with you as the main character. As with any expedition, when you begin you will need help to prepare and equip yourself for what lies ahead. As time goes by, instead of taking on more and more baggage, and guides, your aim should be to lose these burdens and so travel lighter and lighter, enjoying the scenery along the way. The winning mind is open to these experiences, learning and growing as you go, with the skills at your disposal to deal with whatever may come your way.

Set against this foundation, the remaining chapters should help to equip you with the right skills and techniques, and as you continue to practise these skills, your role will expand as an ever increasing circle (Figure 2.2).

As your sporting career develops, you must continue to occupy centre ground, marshalling and adjusting the 3 Cs (control, commitment and confidence) as necessary, and enveloped in a mindset that sees every new experience, good or bad, as a fresh challenge. Meeting these challenges allows you to become secure and confident in who you are, what you are about, and what needs to be done constantly to find ways of improving. Over time the centre or circle will grow but at the right pace – not as a sign of arrogance or overconfidence but as an indication of growing independence and maturity. Grow the circle too slowly and you become cocooned in an unhealthy comfort blanket of overdependence; grow it too fast and you discard support before you should. Instead, think of shedding layers of bark – when you need them they protect; when it is time to grow, they no longer serve a purpose.

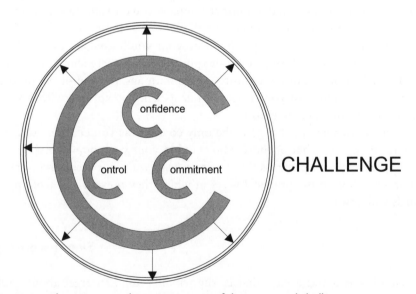

FIGURE 2.2 The 4 Cs: control, commitment, confidence . . . and challenge

Chapter 3

Reflecting

I think self-awareness is probably the most important
thing towards being a champion.[1]
Billie Jean King, winner of 39 women's
grand-slam tennis titles

Introduction

CHAPTERS 1 AND 2 AIMED to set out the principles that
will help guide you through the rest of this book. In
the longer term, these principles should shape a mental
approach to sport that will help you realise whatever your
sporting potential may be. Now is the time to start to translate theory into practice by providing the necessary tools
for effecting change, and we begin with the process of
reflecting or mirror gazing – defining who you are and what
you bring to your sport.

To help this process, one word in particular must be
uppermost in your thoughts at this time – honesty. Too
many sportspeople can lose their way because they delude
themselves or others – for example, by borrowing others'
identities – especially those who have already achieved
success.

While it may be useful to learn from others, you must

Billie Jean King (courtesy of Inpho Photography)

be at ease with who you are and understand what you are. Don't worry. We are not about to plunge into the murky depths of psychotherapy – that can be a journey from which it is not always easy to return unharmed. This self-assessment does not have to extend to all aspects of personality or temperament but only those that are directly related to sporting performance. As Chapter 2 makes clear, who you are remains at the core of the enterprise, but we are now concerned with fine-tuning those aspects of what *makes* you what you are to ensure that they help maximise your sporting potential.

In a more pragmatic vein, what we are suggesting is that you become familiar with the concept of mirror gazing or honest self-reflection. The story in the box on the opposite page illustrates what this means. This was a powerful lesson and one that the player never forgot. While we all assess our performances from time to time, it is rare that this evaluation will be thorough and systematic. Instead, quite naturally, we will be inclined to be selective, choosing only particular aspects of play that we consider most important or that we believe others will focus on. In this way we may lose a rounded or balanced picture of performance and come to highlight a small fraction of the total scene. This bias will then influence how we prepare, and so the cycle of delusion continues.

Mirror banging

Back in the changing room after playing one of his first games for his country, a rugby player is alleged to have let the rest of the team know exactly what he thought of their poor performances. Without realising it, he had broken an unspoken rule among the team at that time. Grabbing him by the throat, the captain shoved his face into a mirror and let him know in no uncertain terms that this was unacceptable behaviour. In fact, no player was allowed to discuss the game until physically he had looked into a mirror and asked himself the question – what did I do for the team? Only then had he earned the right to talk to his team-mates.

The alternative is to have immediately to hand tools that can be used to assess what has been done and what needs to be done, and these then provide the impetus for developing self-motivation skills known as profiling and goal setting. Profiling and goal setting together provide valuable techniques for helping an athlete become self-driven. In essence they enhance self-motivation, but before going any further it may be useful to clarify just what we mean by this word *motivation*.

What is motivation?

Ask anyone what motivation is and they are quite likely first of all to mention the things that motivate us, the motives that make us want to get out of bed in the morning and do something. In psychology, similar ideas long held sway and so, for example, Abraham Maslow famously described a hierarchical set of needs (Figure 3.1) that motivate or drive us to action.[2]

Moving from bottom to top of the hierarchy, the needs begin with the physiological, and then move to safety needs, belonging, esteem and, finally, self-actualisation needs. According to Maslow, we are only able to satisfy higher-order needs once those lower in the pecking order have been put to rest.

The model sounds entirely plausible until you test it against the real world and then you will find life is not quite so orderly. We each can and do prioritise different motives according to our personal life-choices at any time. So, for example, the artist may buy canvas at the expense of food, or the explorer may risk life and limb

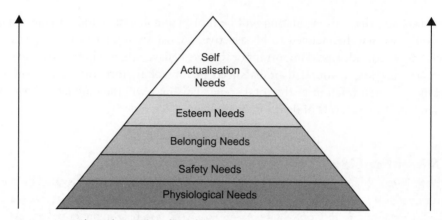

FIGURE 3.1 Maslow's hierarchy of needs

for no other motive than 'because it was there'. These may be exceptional examples but more generally we are far more flexible and sophisticated in our decision-making and the way we choose to prioritise motives than earlier prescriptive models of motivation would suggest.

Within sport psychology there have been literally hundreds of studies aimed at identifying the significance of different motives in determining participation and involvement in sports throughout our lives. With increasing evidence of obesity and related health problems among young people, most of this attention has fallen on the reasons why young people take part in sport. Intricate models of participation motivation have emerged to suggest that a whole host of personal and contextual variables interact to determine why we take part and continue to participate, with a critical distinction being made between extrinsic motives (doing it for rewards that are outside the individual – money, status, trophies, etc.) and motives that come from within or intrinsic motives (feeling good, self-realisation, enjoyment).

In general, this research suggests that intrinsic motives provide more powerful and sustaining sources of continued commitment than extrinsic motives, and that doing something for the sake of task accomplishment instead of ego enhancement is likewise more positive. In many ways, these findings have been used to underscore the philosophy that we have outlined in Chapter 2.

In recent years, the literature has taken forward the discussion of motivation from simple descriptions of motives and drives towards an understanding of the process of how these factors act to move us.[3] These models refer to a wide range of issues that can influence our commitment and our willingness to expend energy, but the core of these models is simple and it is worthwhile keeping in mind before we go on. In particular the model is useful for helping you understand and diagnose problems that may arise, including why it is that you or others don't seem to have the same enthusiasm as maybe you once had, and how this can be remedied.

These models describe motivation in terms not of content but process – the how and the why of what we do. The process of motivation is seen to hinge on the relationship between four factors:

effort   **how hard we are prepared to work**
performance **what we do, in training and competition**
outcome   **what we get out of what we do**
satisfaction **how we feel about the process.**

It is assumed that the four elements in Figure 3.2 relate in a systematic way that incorporates each of the ABC (affect, behaviour, cognition) aspects of psychology that we explained in Chapter 1.

To be motivated, you must recognise that an increase in the effort you are prepared to put in can be repaid in a positive change in performance – otherwise why bother at all? However, common sense dictates that an increase in effort does not automatically result in improved performance. Ability will play a part, as will the role that you are expected to play – your position in a team or the style of play you must adopt. You may be highly motivated but if you don't have the knowledge and skills, or you are being asked to do something which is inappropriate, then that effort will count for nothing.

Next you must not only believe that an increase in effort can change your performance but also that the change in performance, whether during training or in competition, will be reflected in outcomes that you genuinely value, including both intrinsic and extrinsic rewards. It is not absolute reward either but what you receive relative to those around you – am I getting as much, more or less than the next person for what I do? In other words, is it fair and so was it worth the effort? So, for example, I turn up for training without fail three times a week and work as hard as I can but never receive an acknowledgement whereas he swans in when he feels like it and yet always seems to attract the attention of the coach and is guaranteed his starting place. Why should I bother?

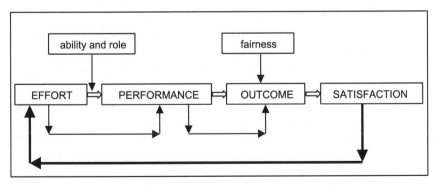

FIGURE 3.2 Modelling motivation

Only when you have expended effort, seen the performance and judged the outcomes (including success and failure) do you evaluate the whole process (was it worth it?), and this evaluation then determines your level of satisfaction, which in turn determines the effort you are prepared to invest in the future.

Profiling

Having understood motivation as no more than a process that energises us, we must now turn to the practice of motivating and ensuring long-term commitment. The technique of 'performance profiling' is now accepted practice across elite sport as a starting point in this process by way of systematically identifying strengths and weaknesses. For example, many national sports' institutes now routinely provide their elite performers with training diaries or logs to make sure that they are able to reference previous performances in moving onwards and upwards.

While profiling has attracted most attention in relation to top level sport, it can be useful in a wide range of contexts. What is more, it does not have to be restricted solely to post-performance analysis. At the start of a sporting career or season it is a very useful way of establishing what is there already and what is needed. At the end of a season it can be used to consider what has been achieved and what can be achieved. Also, the same techniques can be used by coaches as by athletes, where exactly the same principles apply.

A wide range of techniques have been used to profile, ranging from the highly structured to the less formal. Almost all will have scope to identify a list of attributes together with scores out of, say 10, to represent where you are and where you would like to be. Richard Butler, an eminent UK sport psychologist, pioneered the use of a particular device, the dartboard, as an easy visual tool for presenting profiles.[4] Each attribute is assigned a segment of the dartboard, and within each segment two colours usually represent the scores of 'where you are' and 'where you would like to be', typically out of 10. While useful, the number of segments on the board does restrict the attributes that can be shown, typically to between 16 and 20 (see Figure 3.3 on the opposite page).

As an alternative to the dartboard, a simple chart can be used. On the chart are listed all the attributes, skills, kinds of knowledge, techniques, etc., that are relevant to performance, and you are then asked to appraise honestly where you stand in relation to each.

To help you understand the process, we will use the example of a young golfer who is keen to win a place on the professional tour. He has already decided that he is willing to give this ambition whatever it takes over the next 12 months, and has the full support of his family and coach. The starting point of his journey has to involve an honest reflection on his current range of skills and attributes, ranging from the physical to the mental to the tactical.

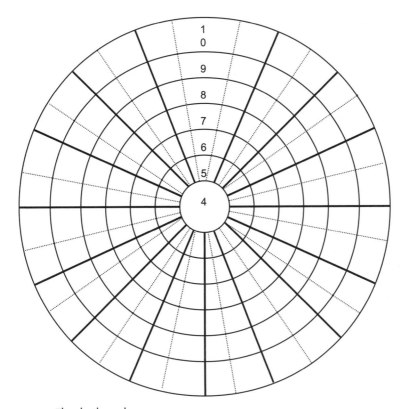

FIGURE 3.3 The dartboard

Quite deliberately, there is no need to put these into compartments, as this reinforces the impression that the approach emphasises total preparation, but the list could include what is shown in Table 3.1. You will note that the list does not include fundamental aspects of personality or self-identity but instead focuses attention on those skills and issues that are likely to be directly associated with golf.

The player could first of all complete the left-hand column and then the right, highlighting occasions where there is the greatest need for improvement. It is important to avoid the temptation of always putting '10' in the right-hand column. A '10' is often unattainable; instead, it is more sensible to give a realistic assessment of where it is possible to be by a certain time. After you have put down where you stand, it is useful to bring in as many people as possible to give an opinion as to whether the ratings are fair and realistic. The completed scale then provides a starting point for a goal-setting master plan to move from left to right – from where you are to where you want to be.

TABLE 3.1 Where am I and where am I going?

	Where I am	Where I want to be
Upper body strength	_____	_____
Leg strength	_____	_____
Bunker play	_____	_____
Putting	_____	_____
Chipping	_____	_____
Driving	_____	_____
Long iron	_____	_____
Short iron	_____	_____
Consistency	_____	_____
Control	_____	_____
Confidence	_____	_____
Commitment	_____	_____
Will to win	_____	_____
Imagery skills	_____	_____
Attentional styles	_____	_____
Lifestyle	_____	_____
Diet	_____	_____
Sleep patterns	_____	_____
Reading a course	_____	_____
Reading a green	_____	_____
Club selection	_____	_____
Shot selection	_____	_____
Relaxation skills	_____	_____
Time management	_____	_____
Fear of failure	_____	_____
Need to achieve	_____	_____
Thought-stopping techniques	_____	_____
Physical fitness	_____	_____
Flexibility	_____	_____
Knowledge	_____	_____
Listening skills	_____	_____
Social skills	_____	_____
Media/PR skills	_____	_____

Post-match profiling

The procedure described above will take time and is designed for longer-term planning. More immediately, after each competition it may be possible to come up with a shorter list that you can use to judge your performance, and before your next training session. Clearly there is scope in such a procedure to introduce attributes that the coach in particular would wish to highlight if that is an area that the team needs to work on. A typical example from rugby is shown in Table 3.2.

By adopting this systematic and personal approach to evaluation, you are avoiding all the pitfalls attached to focusing exclusively on immediate or high-profile issues. It forces a more rounded assessment, and can form a very useful basis of discussion between the player and the coach or manager. Often it is useful to have the player complete the form alone before sitting down with the coach and talking through scores and what can be done to bring about an improvement.

For coaches and performers alike, the techniques are not difficult to learn but more than anything they require the ability to offer an honest appraisal of strengths and weaknesses. A training log or diary could be used to support these profiles, providing an opportunity to comment on reasons why performance may have dipped or peaked at certain times.

TABLE 3.2 Match analysis

	Your performance (out of 10)									
Work rate	1	2	3	4	5	6	7	8	9	10
Distribution	1	2	3	4	5	6	7	8	9	10
Winning possession	1	2	3	4	5	6	7	8	9	10
Reading the game	1	2	3	4	5	6	7	8	9	10
Defence	1	2	3	4	5	6	7	8	9	10
Support	1	2	3	4	5	6	7	8	9	10
Consistency	1	2	3	4	5	6	7	8	9	10
Discipline	1	2	3	4	5	6	7	8	9	10
Team player	1	2	3	4	5	6	7	8	9	10
Communication	1	2	3	4	5	6	7	8	9	10

When you're hot, you're hot. . . . but

For some athletes, these techniques will be immediately welcome as they help reinforce their existing practices based on principles of personal control and agency – doing something about it. For those who are less analytic, there may be more resistance as the uncertainty attached to each performance continues to offer an unhealthy allure.

Que serra, serra

'Que serra, serra' (whatever will be, will be) is a sentiment that many sportspeople refuse to let go of without a fight – recall from Chapter 1 Ronnie O'Sullivan's philosophy, 'If you're on, you're on; if you're off, you're off.' It can be comforting to believe that the finger of fate can point in your direction at some happy and unexpected time, and as long as you keep hanging in there, things may change. National lotteries thrive on this sentiment – coupled with our poor understanding of statistical probability.

Unfortunately this mindset becomes a recipe for inconsistency, not improvement, because this reliance on luck or fate automatically reduces the scope for accepting personal control, and in the process, doing something about it. In relation to goal setting and self-motivation, this can create serious obstacles to progress.

Many sportspeople continue to cling to rituals and superstitions before performance in the belief that these will 'magically' reduce the risk of failure. Although pre-performance routines can improve concentration when used properly (see Chapter 5), they can, if used as superstitious crutches, actually increase the risk of failure because they take personal responsibility out of the equation and replace it with an external force or authority that is supposed to control destiny.

Make no mistake, dealing with these issues can be difficult; they often have to be handled extremely sensitively. Fortunately, reliance on these rituals will tend to reduce as the foundations of an effective intervention are laid down, but they can reappear during times of particular stress, seemingly as a way of coping with that anxiety. Again, perversely, reliance on superstition or fate will have precisely the opposite effect in the longer term by taking the person out of the driver's seat and turning them into a back-seat passenger. Anxiety and worry based on the uncertainty of outcome will flourish in this environment.

Before we continue, please do not imagine that our purpose is to fashion a sporting robot devoid of feelings and characteristics. Nothing could be further from the truth. The purpose is quite the opposite, to put the person first but in control and stripped of the baggage that may serve us well in other life domains but, in the context of improving performance in sport, will conspire to hold us back. Asking people to reflect on their performance is not an alien task. We all look back on what we have done well and badly but often we do this haphazardly and in a way that reinforces false impressions. Move it one step beyond, and instead of being a barrier to progress it becomes an aid.

Setting goals

Having established where you stand in terms of relevant skills, knowledge and attributes, and having identified where you need to be, the next step in the process must involve finding a way of travelling from here to there; from where you are to where you want to be.

For many years, goal setting has been embraced by business and management consultants, who use it as an essential part of motivational training programmes. More recently, sport has borrowed these ideas and applied them to help improve self-motivation in sport. Basic goal-setting procedures have become increasingly popular and accessible to coaches and athletes alike, and the principles have been frequently translated into popular language to encourage practical use. Goal setting can work and often does work, but it is not without its problems and these should not be glossed over. Instead what we intend to do is suggest how these principles may be applied before issuing a few heath warnings based on practical experience over several years.

The history of goal setting

Within sport, goal setting came to life in the 1970s. Probably still the most famous example of a systematic goal-setting procedure was that undertaken by the 1976 Olympic gold medallist, John Naber. The box below contains a statement in his own words.[5] Four years later John Naber won his gold medal in the 100 metres backstroke. Not only that, he won three others besides and a silver medal, and broke four world records in the process. Interestingly, Michael Phelps, the young American swimmer who has already won six Olympic gold medals and six world titles, is closing in on Mark Spitz's 1972 record and has set himself the goal of winning seven gold medals in the 2008 Olympic Games.

With a goal in mind

In 1972 Mark Spitz won seven gold medals, breaking seven world records. I was at home watching him on my living room floor. And I said to myself at that time, 'wouldn't it be nice to be able to win a gold medal, to be able to be a world champion in Olympic competition.' So right then I had this dream of being an Olympic champion. But right about then it became a goal. That 'dream to goal'

John Naber (courtesy of Inpho Photography/Getty Images)

transition is the biggest thing I learned prior to Olympic competition – how important it is to set a goal. My personal best time in the 100 back was 59.5. Roland Matthes, winning the same event for the second consecutive Olympics (1972), went 56.3. I extrapolated this, you know, three Olympic performances and I figured in 1976, 55.5 would have been the order of the day. That's what I figured I would have to do. So I'm four seconds off the shortest backstroke event on the Olympic program. It's the equivalent of dropping four seconds in the 440 yard dash. It's a substantial chunk. But because it's a goal, now I can decisively figure out how I can attack that. I have four years to do it in. I'm watching TV in 1972. I've got four years to train. So it's only one second a year. That's still a substantial jump. Swimmers train ten or eleven months a year, so it's about a tenth of a second a month, giving time off for missed workouts. And you figure we train six days a week so it's only about 1/300 of a second a day. We train from 6–8 in the morning and 4–6 in the evening so it's really only about 1/1200 of a second every hour. Do you know how short a 1/1200 of a second is? Look at my hand and blink when I snap my fingers, would you please? Okay, from the time when your eyelids started to close to the time they touched, 5/1200 of a second elapsed. For me to stand on the pool deck and say, 'During the next 60 minutes I'm going to improve that much,' that's a believable dream. I can believe in myself. I can't believe I'm going to drop four seconds by the next Olympics. But I can believe I can get that much faster. Couldn't you? Sure!! So all of a sudden I'm moving.

More generally, the use of goal setting as a motivational technique in sport can be traced directly back to Edwin Locke's goal-setting theory as developed initially in the world of business.[6] Underlying Locke's theory is the idea that behaviour is regulated by values and goals, with a goal defined as a conscious intention or, more simply, what the person is setting out to achieve. Goal-setting research has been carried out in a wide variety of situations, but regardless of the type of task or the individuals tested, the overwhelming majority of studies have shown that setting goals can lead to improved performance.

According to Locke, goals affect performance through four mechanisms. First, goal setting focuses attention; second, it mobilises effort in proportion to the

Michael Phelps (courtesy of Inpho Photography)

demands of the task; third, goals enhance persistence; and, finally, goals have an indirect effect in that they encourage people to develop strategies for achieving their goals.

Furthermore, Locke and his co-workers claim that a number of features relate to these performance effects. These features have taken on the status of accepted principles in the goal-setting literature, as outlined in the box.

Goal-setting principles

Difficulty: More difficult goals lead to a higher level of performance than easy goals.

Specificity: Specific goals are more effective than general subjective goals (such as 'do your best') or no goals.

Acceptance: To be effective, goals must be accepted by the performer, whether they are self-instigated or assigned by someone else.

Feedback: Goals will not be effective in the absence of feedback.

Planning goal setting

While not all of us have the extraordinary dedication of John Naber or other Olympian giants,[7] we can still draw on broadly similar principles to establish goals that will lead like stepping stones from where we are to where we want to be.

By profiling your performance or your skills/knowledge, you have already made considerable progress in delivering on goal setting. However, just because you can measure and assess does not mean that you are committed to action, so before going any further it is worthwhile pausing to answer the following questions:

• What would you like to achieve in your sport?
• How important is it to you?

There is no point in hurting yourself unnecessarily. If the goal is not important to you, there is no point in putting in place a regimen that is doomed to fail before it begins. This is not an admission of defeat but a realistic and sober assessment of what is important in your life and where your priorities lie. To downgrade sport to a recreational activity and then to invest an appropriate amount of time and energy in something that still matters but maybe not too much is fine, and there may still be scope for limited goal setting even in these circumstances.

However, if you have the level of commitment necessary to continue to improve, the next stage is to return to the results of your profiling and to identify, one at a time, each item on the list where there is room for improvement, and then to prioritise these in a sensible way that allows you to draw up a goal-setting master plan.

Reflect on where you are going and how you will get there (courtesy of iStockphoto)

And when is the best time to do this work? It is not during the heat of competition or following a run of poor form but during the close season, when you have had an opportunity to reflect on where you are going and how you are going to get there.

This master plan should include a timescale for each skill, attribute or area of knowledge, indicating where you are and where you want to be by a given date. The timescale, start date and end point for each should be tailored to that particular issue, always accommodating practical considerations and including the time and resources you have available. To keep this scheme in your thoughts, this plan could be presented on a large sheet that is pinned somewhere prominently to remind you of your schedule.

From a practical perspective, a Gantt chart offers a simple way of representing

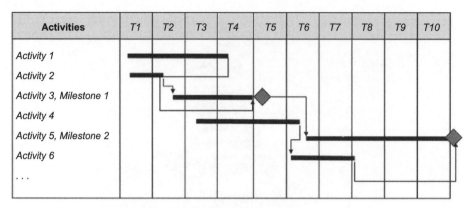

Activities	T1	T2	T3	T4	T5	T6	T7	T8	T9	T10
Activity 1										
Activity 2										
Activity 3, Milestone 1										
Activity 4										
Activity 5, Milestone 2										
Activity 6										
. . .										

FIGURE 3.4 Charting success

different timelines for different goal-setting activities, Many commercial software packages are now available to make the task of constructing a chart very easy. The charts allow you to see immediately the start and end points for each programme, and also significant checkpoints along the way. They also allow you to describe connections between the various activities. For example, you may wish to develop strength and flexibility before working on a particular skill or routine. An example of a typical Gantt chart is shown in Figure 3.4.

Doing goal setting

Having established a master plan, now is the time to look at each element of the plan in more detail, to work out a goal-setting routine for each element. To do this, for the sake of convenience, Locke's well-established principles are often presented to sportspeople by way of an acronym. Two of the most popular are SMART (specific, measurable, attainable, realistic and timely) and SCAMP. Of the two, we have found that SCAMP seems to capture the principles more completely, and sits easily alongside the philosophy we have outlined earlier. Whatever goals you set should be as outlined in the SCAMP box.

SCAMP!
S – Specific Don't set vague goals, such as get better. Specify exactly how much you want to improve and how you can measure it. Predict the extent of your improvement and you will work hard to achieve it.

C – Challenging/controllable Set performance goals at a level slightly ahead of your current ability, this means that goals are possible but also provide an interesting challenge. Also remember to keep your goals within personal control rather than depending on performance of others (e.g. performance not outcome).

A – Attainable Don't burden yourself with an impossible goal. All goals should relate to where you are now, and you should aim to improve yourself step by step. Don't be afraid to reassess goals if they prove to be unrealistic.

M – Measurable and multiple A sense of achievement is greatest and motivation enhanced most effectively when progress can actually be seen. Goals are best expressed in a form that can be measured objectively, such as seconds off time. Failing that, measure performance or characteristic on a subjective rating scale of 1 to 10; for example, rate ability to cope under pressure on a scale of 1 to 10. Also, multiple goals increase the probability of achievement.

P – Personal The goals you set must relate to you as an individual. Decide what you want to achieve; don't borrow other people's goals. This will enhance your commitment to these objectives.

To see what this can mean in practice, we will use the example of a tennis player who decides, among many other things and in consultation with her coach, that she wants to improve her first-serve accuracy. Exactly the same principles can be applied to any sport and any skill.

Worked example

An up-and-coming tennis player wishes to improve the accuracy of her first serve. At present she determines that when serving at maximum speed, she is able to hit the ball into an imaginary two-metre target circle in the receiving court three times out of ten on average. She then sets herself a realistic goal of being able to hit this target seven times out of ten by the start of the season in ten weeks' time. How does she achieve this? She works out a training programme that involves going to an empty court at her local club three times a week and on each occasion hitting 80 serves, 40 shots from each side of the court into four imaginary targets (ten per target) on each visit. She establishes weekly targets and records her performance on each occasion, including subjective rating, and charts her improvement over time. In the light of this continual feedback, she is able to check whether she is on line for achieving her goal and can adjust her practice over the weeks if necessary.

The rules of goal setting are simple. By answering each of the 10 questions in the box over the page, you should be able to develop a goal-setting programme for every skill or quality that you would like to improve. For each item on a profiling list it may be that one or several goal-setting procedures emerge. For example, under flexibility, there may be several stretching routines that you follow for different muscle groups. Nevertheless, the same principles would apply for each procedure.

You establish a baseline (such as how far beyond my big toe I can reach on a toe board). You then establish your goal by a given date (such as a further 10 cm) and then put in place milestones along the way where you measure and thereby establish and record progress made (for example, with ticks or stars on the Gantt chart).

The 10-step approach
1. Which aspect of performance do I wish to improve?
2. What associated skills/qualities/attributes must be developed?
3. What routines or practices will help me improve each of these?
4. How can I measure each?
5. What is my present level of attainment?
6. What level of performance would I like to achieve by a certain date?
7. What milestones do I want to put in place between the start and the end?
8. What level of performance do I want to reach by each milestone?
9. Who can help me monitor my progress?
10. Who can provide me with expert advice to quality-ensure the process?

Timetables can and should be modified to take into account changing circumstances including illness, injury or other commitments. Never forget that this procedure is designed to make you feel good about reaching targets; it is not about hurting yourself for failure. If the programme is too difficult or over-optimistic, always adjust, and never be afraid to seek advice from others.

Some skills or qualities are easy to measure; others are more difficult. Tests of strength or physical ability can often be measured without too much thought – for example, by the number of repetitions, the weight lifted or accuracy of performance. For certain lifestyle issues the means of measurement may be quite different. Sleep patterns may be no more than recording time to bed and time up, having first established an appropriate regimen. Diet may be expressed in calorific intake or type of food (and it should be immediately obvious that many diet clubs actually do no more than simple goal setting when trying to encourage weight loss).

Other skills or qualities may require more imagination, and this is especially true in relation to mental skills. However, with skills such as stress management (e.g. timing pulse rate), reaction time (e.g. timing performance on simple and complex reaction time tasks) or mental rehearsal (e.g. checking the match between the imagined and actual time it takes you to perform a certain task), it can be fun coming up with interesting ways of measuring performance. When all else fails, it may be a question of resorting to a subjective assessment of how you are feeling, or asking others to rate your performance against specified criteria.

This does not have to be a lonely process. Talk to other people and especially those with expert knowledge to make sure what you are doing is sensible, and try to involve them in the milestones to reassure yourself that your improvement is not fiction but fact. Ultimately, however, it is about you feeling good about your improvement rather than waiting for others to applaud.

Goal setting and the real world

So far all may appear rosy; here is what appears to be a relatively simple psycho-logical technique that will allow you to maximise your potential through structured planning and training. Unfortunately, this optimistic presentation can flatter to deceive, for goal setting is a prime situation in which popularity is based on per-ceived value but where application has become oblivious to significant theoretical and practical problems. This is not to abandon the approach but instead to suggest that it will only work and be effective in certain circumstances.

Some problems are linked to the way in which sport differs from the world of work where goal setting was originally developed. For example, there may be obvious differences in the reasons why individuals are actually involved in work or sport in the first place. Principally, the extrinsic rewards associated with work stand in contrast to the intrinsic motivators that are so crucial in maintaining an interest in many sports.

A further major distinction rests upon how goal setting is applied in sport and in work, and the relative emphasis which is placed on either *product* or *process*. Performance enhancement in business is normally directly related to an end product, increased productivity. However, in sport, it is often emphasised that goal setting should focus on process or performance, and not outcome. There is also debate as to whether setting distant, long-term goals can actually be demotivating, and so whether there is a need to introduce subgoals in order to sustain com-mitment. Our earlier discussion strongly suggests that while the long-term goals may light the fire it has to be constantly rekindled by short-term, realisable goals.

Clearly, the level of dedication shown by some top level sportspeople, includ-ing John Naber, would be beyond the reach of all but a very small minority, and to put in place such a highly structured programme would be unrealistic. This is where there is a need for a strong dose of realism to ensure that whatever regimen is put in place, it is tailored to the needs and characteristics of the individual. The flexibility of goal setting to accommodate individual differences is often ignored, and too many schemes have failed as a consequence. Instead, we must constantly adjust and readjust this motivational tool to meet changing times and changed people.

It is also worth noting that some critics of goal setting claim that it can interfere with competition unless handled with care. For example, in swimming it was noted that some swimmers could be seen to be over the moon even when finishing last in a heat or final because they had met their individual time target. It was as though the other swimmers had dissolved and the race had been reduced to nothing more than an individual time trial.

Swimmers (courtesy of Inpho Photography)

To counter this dangerous trend, North American swimming coaches have advocated a shift away from overreliance on specific performance goals and towards an accommodation of competitive goals; that is, to beat the person in the next lane. It should never be forgotten that many of the techniques we describe are a means to an end, and the end is tied to the intrinsic significance of competition itself. This is what makes sport enjoyable, and when the balance becomes tilted so dramatically that winning loses any emotional significance there are problems.

So you can now appreciate that what began as a simple story has evolved into a complex tale. Does this mean that goal setting should be abandoned? No, but it does remind us that it is not a panacea. Many highly motivated athletes may not need the rigours of a goal-setting programme to maintain their commitment, but in fact it may do no more than heighten their anxieties and raise unrealistic expectations. At the other end of the sporting spectrum there may be recreational athletes who would find the discipline of regimented goal setting to be a turn-off rather than a turn-on.

Ultimately, what we would suggest is that goal setting can be a powerful tool for sustaining self-motivation but should be applied with a modicum of common sense and should be tailored to the needs and circumstances of the individual. There are many variations on the theme and the trick is to find and use that variation which works well for you.

Chapter 4

Relaxing

It's one of the keys. Without emotional control, you cannot play . . . you cannot react. You have to know what you have to do. . . . You have to be cool.[1]

José Mourinho (former manager of Chelsea)

Introduction

WHETHER NOVICES OR WORLD champions, we are all inclined to feel butterflies in our stomachs when we cross the line and play competitive sport. First and foremost those nerves or butterflies reveal that it matters to you, and it *has* to matter; otherwise, why take part in the first place? This feeling is nothing to worry about though – it's entirely natural. In fact if you didn't experience that sensation, that would be even *more* worrying – because it may be a sign that you don't really care.

In common with most people, you probably don't relish the prospect of being tested, and in competitive sport the evaluation that you will experience is not only swiftly delivered but is often publicly observed. Each time we compete, we encounter the certainty of evaluation and the possibility of failure. Few of us enjoy failing but

José Mourinho, former manager of Chelsea (courtesy of Inpho Photography)

competitive sport, by its very nature, embraces uncertainty as to the eventual outcome (good or bad) regardless of our ability level.

Put these basic factors together and it becomes unavoidable that competition and nerves must go hand in hand, but the good news is that you don't have to let competitive occasions take over and get the better of you. With the right preparation and the right outlook, competing against others can continue to be a positive, exciting and rewarding experience, through the good times and the not so good. Let's face it, how else can you really find out how good you are at anything unless you are willing to test your limits?

At the outset, one point is very clear. José Mourinho was correct when he claimed that if you want to perform to the best of your ability in competitive sport you have to be cool in the heat of battle – head in the fridge, body in the oven. But how can you stay calm and controlled when there's a lot at stake? The purpose of the present chapter is to answer this question by investigating how to stay cool and to enjoy the challenge of sport.

We'll begin by explaining what being nervous means and we'll show why anxiety can be a help or a hindrance in sport depending on how you perceive it. After that, we'll examine some of the factors that make people feel nervous and how anxiety affects your performance, paying special attention to the well-known experience of 'choking' under pressure. In the final section of the chapter, we'll show you how to stay cool in pressure situations.

Head in the oven!

Before we begin, however, let's explore the difference between remaining cool and *losing your cool* in sport. Included in our analysis below is a fascinating contrast between the reactions of two world-class athletes to the cauldron of competition – Zinedine Zidane, the brilliant former French soccer international player, and Tiger Woods, the best golfer in the world.

Losing your cool . . . or staying cool?

For millions of fans, one of the saddest sights of the 2006 World Cup final was the dismissal of Zinedine Zidane (who had been voted player of the tournament

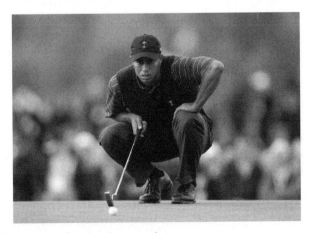

Zinedine Zidane and Tiger Woods (courtesy of Inpho Photography)

before this incident) for head-butting Italy's Marco Materazzi following an apparent verbal provocation. This violent loss of self-control under pressure occurred at a time when the teams were level. Significantly, it not only contributed to France's losing the match but also cast a shadow over the end of Zidane's career and his glittering achievements as a player. By contrast, consider the extraordinary attitude of Tiger Woods to the pressure of competition:

> The challenge is hitting good golf shots when you have to . . . to do it when the nerves are fluttering, the heart pounding, the palms sweating . . . that's the thrill.[2]

This quotation highlights two important ideas that may help you to stay cool under pressure. First, everyone gets nervous if they care about what they're doing. You may be surprised and consoled to discover that even Tiger Woods experiences the same type of anxiety symptoms (such as butterflies in the stomach, a pounding heart and sweaty palms) as the rest of us in competitive situations. Second, and more importantly, by using such words as 'challenge' and 'thrill', Tiger Woods shows us that he *labels* his nervous experiences differently from the way we usually do.

To clarify this point, whereas you probably look at a pressure situation as a threatening experience to be avoided at all costs, he has trained himself to regard it as an exciting opportunity to be welcomed and enjoyed. Put simply, he *thrives* on the experience of competitive pressure because he focuses on the challenge that it offers to his skills. It's simply a game. In the next section, we'll explore this idea of how our perception shapes our experience, but, for now, let's see what else we can learn from top level athletes' experiences of anxiety in sport.

To begin with, not all athletes manage to stay as cool as Tiger Woods does during sporting contests. For example, the England rugby star Jonny Wilkinson is renowned for his intense feelings of anxiety before matches:

> From the earliest times I can remember, I've been a very nervous individual – not nervous because of being scared, not physically scared, just frightened of letting myself down or letting other people down or just losing. It just causes that kind of anxiety.[3]

As before, this quotation yields several important insights into anxiety in sport. For example, it reveals that feelings of nervousness are usually triggered by psychological factors (such as worrying about not playing to your own high standards) rather than by fears of incurring physical injury. Also, Wilkinson's quotation shows us that world-class athletes are not afraid to admit that they feel nerves in certain situations. Indeed, there may be an advantage to this admission because, as another sporting champion, the golfer Nick Faldo, wisely observed: 'The player who recognises that he is nervous is streets ahead of the fellow who is in denial.'[4]

Another finding is that nervousness is not always a bad thing in sport – because it may force you to take appropriate action. The message here is that nerves can energise you by making your adrenalin flow. Consider this interesting observation by Sam Torrance, captain of the victorious European team in the 2002 Ryder Cup:

> If you're not nervous, then there is something wrong with you. Nerves create adrenaline and I told them to use that . . . to make you feel better, get pumped up, just get psyched up.[5]

A similar point was made by Mike Atherton, the former captain of England's cricket team, when he distinguished between

> two sorts of player: those who are quite placid people . . . who need an adrenaline flow to get them up for it, and so find nerves a real help. And then there are those who are naturally hyper for whom that additional flow may not be such a good thing.[6]

Other sports stars support this distinction between anxiety that helps your performance and anxiety that harms it. For example, according to Nick Faldo, there is a big difference between feelings of nervousness that are based on fear and those that stem from adrenalin. Whereas fear-based nerves are usually caused by a lack of confidence or a feeling of inadequate preparation, adrenalin-based nervousness stems from anticipatory excitement that can energise and thrill you.

Having explored elite athletes' views on staying cool under pressure, let's now explore what 'nervousness' means and what causes it in sport.

'Nerves'

In psychology, nerves or nervousness means anxiety or an unpleasant emotion with certain distinctive features. Among these characteristics are physical tension, a high degree of bodily arousal and persistent if vague feelings of apprehension and worry about some imminent event or situation.

Apparently, the term 'anxiety' is derived from the Latin word *angere*, meaning 'to choke'. This original meaning is interesting because the term 'choking' under pressure is well known in competitive sport. We'll return to this experience shortly. At this stage, however, let's summarise what is currently known about anxiety.

There are different types of anxiety

First, anxiety comes in different forms. Psychologists distinguish between nervousness that occurs as a temporary experience in certain specific situations (called 'state' anxiety) and nervousness that occurs as a stable personality characteristic in many different situations in everyday life ('trait' anxiety or a tendency to perceive almost any situation as potentially threatening). Typically, while state anxiety is short-lived and situation-specific, trait anxiety is longer-lasting and is a more deep-seated tendency to perceive almost every challenging situation as anxiety-provoking.

Another common distinction is made between 'cognitive' anxiety (worries, doubts and pessimistic predictions about the future) and bodily anxiety (the physical symptoms such as high arousal and a rapid heartbeat). Interestingly, these different types of anxiety appear to change in different ways during competition. Specifically, once a match starts, bodily anxiety tends to decrease but cognitive anxiety fluctuates, depending on how the event is going. For this reason, mistakes in sport are more likely to be caused by cognitive anxiety than by bodily anxiety (see Chapter 7 for a discussion of mistake-management techniques).

Anxiety is different from fear

Although anxiety resembles fear, there are important differences between these emotional states. For a start, anxiety usually lasts longer and is more vague or undifferentiated than fear. In fact, anxious people can't always explain exactly what they're afraid of, but they can feel a cloud hanging over them or a weight on their shoulders most of the time. Also, whereas you're usually anxious about the unknown, you tend to be 'afraid' of things that are known in the sense that they're either physically present (a steep ski slope) or are possible future events (being hurt in a tackle). Interestingly, Jonny Wilkinson understood this distinction between fear and anxiety very clearly when he revealed that:

> I am always nervous before a rugby match. I always have been.... The condition wasn't physical fear – my favourite part of rugby, then as now, was tackling. Instead, it was the thought of losing and letting myself down at something which meant so much to me.[7]

Usually, anxiety is triggered whenever you interpret a particular person, event or situation as posing a threat to you in some way. This perception of threat may be based on realistic or imaginary fears. For example, if you are a golfer standing on the first tee in the Captain's Prize, you will probably feel a little anxious even though realistically, your feelings in this case are completely disproportionate to the actual physical danger involved in this situation. On the other hand, if you are a novice skier facing your first steep slope with no instructor around, you have every reason to feel nervous because of the potential danger posed by this situation.

Anxiety is based on arousal

When you encounter a frightening situation (including the threat of physical harm), your body naturally activates a warning system that prepares you either to confront this source of danger or to run away from it. This so-called 'fight or flight' response to danger is a legacy from our primitive ancestors. It is triggered automatically whenever you *think* that you are in danger, regardless of the plausibility of the actual threat involved. It activates a host of bodily reactions such as a rapid heart-beat, increased blood pressure, the release of glucose into the bloodstream and a heightened state of 'arousal' or alertness – all of which help prepare you to respond to the anticipated emergency.

Interestingly, your arousal levels fluctuate significantly over time in response to the amount of stimulation you're receiving. Specifically, when you're bored, relaxed or asleep, your arousal level is low, but when you're afraid, angry or excited, your arousal levels rise rapidly. To be technical for a moment, in this latter state of high arousal, your brain's reticular activating system triggers the release of biochemical substances such as adrenalin and noradrenalin into the bloodstream so that your body will be energised and primed for action. So, how is arousal related to anxiety?

Well, on the basis that arousal is really just a state of alertness or stimulation, it is neither good nor bad in itself. The way in which you *label* it, however, is crucial. Put simply, psychologists believe that anxiety is simply an emotional label for a particular type of bodily experience – namely, an unpleasant state of high arousal. To explain, whereas some athletes regard rapid heartbeat, shortness of breath and butterflies in the stomach as welcome signs of being appropriately 'psyched up' or excited, others perceive exactly the same physical sensations as unpleasant indices of anxiety. Indeed, many athletes use the term 'flat' to describe their experience of feeling under-aroused, sluggish or lethargic before a match for which they would prefer to be more 'psyched up'. Given the fact that you can interpret or label a given level of arousal in different ways, is anxiety a help or a hindrance to your performance in sport?

Anxiety can either help or hinder – depending on how you interpret it

Earlier, we learned from Tiger Woods that a given set of bodily experiences can be labelled and interpreted in various ways. For example, shallow breathing and a rapid heartbeat can be seen as signs of either impending panic or mounting excitement.

69

This finding suggests that it is not the amount of arousal that affects your performance, but it is the way in which you interpret such arousal that matters (see 'Hitting the mark' box).

Hitting the mark

One of us was once consulted by an international sprinter who complained that pre-race anxiety was beginning to impair his performance in competitive athletics. Specifically, he said that his heart used to beat so fast before a race that he felt that rival athletes might even be able to hear it or see it as they prepared on the blocks. After some observation and analysis of his pre-race routine, we discovered a simple strategy to overcome this problem. We trained the sprinter to interpret his anxiety differently by convincing him to identify his pounding heart as the key in his body's 'ignition' – we trained him to believe that when it starts to beat fast, it simply means that he's now ready and primed for an explosive start.

Interestingly, a similar type of perceptual restructuring is practised by many top athletes. For example, research shows that successful gymnasts tend to perceive their pre-competitive arousal as a form of anticipatory excitement – a view that boosts their subsequent performance. Conversely, less successful athletes tend to interpret their arousal levels as unwelcome signs of impending failure. Based on such research, it is now widely accepted that bodily symptoms of anxiety can either help or hinder performance – depending on how you perceive them. To summarise, the way in which you label your arousal level plays a vital role in determining whether you feel challenged or overwhelmed by pressure situations.

In an effort to explore what anxiety means to you, try the exercise in the box below.

What does anxiety mean to you?

- What does the word *anxiety* mean to you? Do you think that it is helpful or harmful to your performance?
- On a scale of 0 ('not at all important') to 5 ('extremely important'), how important do you think that the ability to control anxiety is for successful performance in your sport?
- Do you prefer to be 'psyched up' or to be calm before a competitive event in your sport? Why? Please explain.
- What things make you anxious before a competition? How do these factors affect your performance? Explain.
- What things make you anxious during a competition? How do these factors affect your performance? Explain.

- What techniques do you use, if any, to cope with anxiety in your sport? Where did you learn these techniques?
- How would you like to react to things that make you anxious at present?

Anxiety affects you at different levels

In line with the ABC (affect, cognition and behaviour) approach that we explained in Chapter 1, anxiety affects you at three different levels – mental (or 'cognitive'), physical (or 'somatic') and behavioural. First, as we explained above, cognitive anxiety involves worrying or having negative expectations about some impending competitive situation. It usually leads to distractibility or 'task-irrelevant' thinking. By the way, research shows that among the things that athletes worry about most frequently are performing at a level below their expectations, being criticised by others, and experiencing physical injury.[8] The second level at which anxiety affects you is via bodily processes such as increased perspiration, a pounding heart, rapid, shallow breathing, clammy hands and butterflies in the stomach. The third component of anxiety is behavioural and includes tense facial expressions, agitation and general restlessness. Often, all three levels of the anxiety experience occur at the same time. For example, when Jonny Wilkinson was preparing to play in the 2003 rugby World Cup final, he admitted that on the morning of the game:

> The tension is eating into every pore. I try to sit down but it's impossible. My legs won't keep still. I pace the changing room. . . . I re-read my sheet of paper over and over again.[9]

We each have our own zone

The thousands of studies on the relationship between anxiety, stress and performance in sport reveal one thing above all others – we are all different. That is, while there may be general patterns, we each respond to stress in a unique way, and the person who is best placed to know how you respond is – yourself. From the techniques outlined in this chapter, it is quite possible to start to understand the level of stress or anxiety that works best for you, and then to develop pre-match routines that ensure you can hit that mark time and again. These should not come into play just before competition but can help lay down a blueprint for the longer term, so ensuring that the good times continue to roll.

Hitting the zone

Before moving on to consider ways in which you can manage your anxiety, it may be worthwhile spending a few moments reflecting on the level of anxiety that seems to work best for you.

Good times, bad times

The good time

First of all, think of an occasion when you felt that you played particularly well and close to your best. This may be recently or could be any time since you started to compete. Having thought of that time, now try to remember all the circumstances surrounding the event. This should include the whole build-up to the game – were you distracted or focused in the days and weeks beforehand; were there lots of other things on your mind; were you generally worried or chilled; were you angry or calm; did you sleep well beforehand; did you go to bed early, late or at the same time; on the day of competition did you laze around or busy yourself; were you deliberately thinking of the game or were other things dominating your thoughts; did you feel lethargic or energised; did you feel agitated or calm; did you arrive early or late; did you have too much time beforehand or not enough; what were the changing room and warm-up routines; how did you think about the opposition; was it an important game; were you underdog or top dog; were you home or away?

The bad time

Now think of an occasion when you felt that you performed particularly badly, and below your expectation and this was not because of injury or illness – you simply blobbed. Again try to remember all the circumstances leading up to and surrounding the event.

The good and the bad

Now think of other occasions when you performed either well or badly, and what led up to those performances. You can use this reflection to start to build a profile of the anxiety level that works best for you. One technique is to use this information to describe your stress level like a speedometer (where 0 = no stress and 100 = wired to the moon), and your goal is to put in place a regimen that will allow you to keep hitting the mark on the speedo, your zone, time and again, whatever the occasion.

This sort of reflection can inform a structured pre-competition routine that begins some time before competition and takes you through to the start of play. Built into this routine could be a number of biofeedback techniques that make sure you are not straying out of your zone. One of the easiest ways to monitor your emotional state is to take your pulse – on either your neck or wrist is easiest. When you become used to recognising what the rate of your resting pulse feels like, you can start to develop skills for moving your pulse rate to the desired level. This is not difficult; it simply involves playing with many of the imagery skills that we will describe in greater detail in Chapter 6.

Managing stress: taking control

To illustrate how easy it is to manage your stress level, try closing your eyes (after reading this!) while at the same time registering your resting pulse. Now bring to mind first of all those things that are causing you the most anxiety in your life at the moment. They can be inside or away from sport but try hard to immerse yourself in these worries. As you focus your thoughts on these sources of stress, you should detect your pulse rate rising. Now work hard to replace these anxious thoughts with the image of a place in the world that you find most relaxing – it could be somewhere quiet at home, in the countryside, or on holiday; anywhere that you are alone, and where you feel comfortable and at ease. Try bringing to mind the sights, sounds, smells and even feel of the place, and then have a single word that you can use as a cue for bringing this place to mind. As you work hard to focus on this quiet place, you should detect your pulse rate starting to fall, and with practice the change can be dramatic, and quick. If at first you don't succeed, keep practising and eventually you will have a powerful, self-driven stress-management tool always at your disposal.

Many top athletes intuitively would have developed similar techniques for making sure they perform to the best of their ability. Back in the 1970s, to the annoyance of many of his team-mates, one of the most talented rugby players of all time, the Welsh outside-half Barry John, would detach himself from the rest of the team during frantic pre-match build-ups by lying down quietly in the corner of the changing room. What was he doing? Hitting his zone.

What makes you feel anxious in sport?

As you would expect from such a complex psychological and physical response, nervousness in sport is caused by many factors. Here are the ones that have been identified as most important.

Barry John (courtesy of Inpho Photography)

Perceived importance of the game

Obviously, the more importance you attach to a sporting encounter, the more nervous you are inclined to become beforehand. Playing a friendly match is usually less stressful than playing a competitive match because there is little at stake besides your pride. But even a friendly match can make you feel anxious if you are aware that you are being watched by a coach or family member whom you are trying hard to impress. Clearly, the way in which you perceive the event is at least as significant as its competitive status.

Your expectations

Although it is difficult to tell which comes first, thinking and anxiety are strongly related. For example, if you set impossibly high standards for your performance, you will tend to become very anxious and possibly even give up whenever you encounter any major setbacks. For example, Ronnie O'Sullivan, the mercurial snooker player, made history in December 2006 when he took the unprecedented step of conceding a quarter-final match against Stephen Hendry when trailing 4–1 in a 'first to 9' frame match. Afterwards, he blamed his sudden exit on his apparent failure to satisfy his own high standards:

> Anyone who knows me knows I'm a perfectionist when it comes to my game and today I got so annoyed with myself that I lost my patience and walked away from a game that, with hindsight, I should have continued.[10]

Interestingly, there is evidence that athletes who display perfectionist inclinations tend to experience more anxiety than those who set their sights somewhat lower. This research shows us that a set of irrational beliefs lie at the heart of nervousness for most of us. If so, then we have to identify and challenge such beliefs as often as possible.

As a first step in this process, try the exercise in the box.

Are you being too hard on yourself?

What are your expectations of yourself when you compete in a match? To answer this question, ask yourself if any of the following thoughts seem familiar to you before or during a game.

- 'I must defeat my opponent easily in this match: If I don't, I might as well give up' (black-and-white thinking).
- 'If I miss this chance, I'm definitely going to struggle for the rest of the game' ('fortune-telling' or predicting the future).
- 'I/we always play badly when the weather is like this' (overgeneralisation).
- 'I know that X blamed me for a mistake even though s/he didn't say anything to me at the time' (mind-reading).

A common theme of the statements above is that they confuse facts with interpretations. In each case, you have put yourself under pressure by making a false assumption about your game or a possible result or by jumping to conclusions. Obviously, the solution here is to stop being so hard on yourself by learning to look at things differently. For example, clear your mind before you play and try to eliminate global words like 'should', 'must' and 'never' from your vocabulary.

Fear of failure

As Chapter 2 makes clear, every competitor suffers fear of failure from time to time, even those at the top of their sport. Ronaldo, the Brazilian soccer star, experienced a severe anxiety attack on the night before his team lost to France in the 1998 World Cup final. According to his team-mate, Roberto Carlos, this nervousness was triggered by a fear of failure: 'He was scared about what lay ahead. The pressure had got to him and he couldn't stop crying.'[11]

One way of overcoming this type of fear is to make a list of jobs that are under your control and then to visualise yourself performing these tasks smoothly. The idea here is that your mind can think of only one thing at a time so you're replacing a worry with an action plan. Sometimes, however, even world champions have to resist the urge to run away from a feared situation. Linford Christie, the 1992 Olympic champion sprinter, once remarked:

> I know I'll get shit-scared on the days I have to face the big races, terrified of failure. I always do. You want to turn and run back up that tunnel. But you know if you do, you will never come out again.[12]

These quotations show us that emergency action (such as forcing yourself to perform even when you don't want to) is often the best way of dealing with fear of failure.

Lack of confidence

If you have little confidence in your own abilities, you are likely to experience high levels of anxiety in competitive situations. Of course, the obvious solution to this problem lies in practising harder. This idea is expressed in advice attributed to the former golfer Sam Snead, for players who admit being afraid of certain shots: 'If you're scared of your 7-iron, go and practise it!'

Having explained the nature and causes of anxiety, let's explore now what we know about how nervousness can actually affect your performance.

How does anxiety affect performance?

Earlier, we suggested that the ability to regulate your level of arousal is a vital mental skill in competitive sport. Many athletes and coaches have developed techniques designed either to energise themselves when they feel flat or to lower their arousal levels when they feel too agitated before a match. For example, if you're a wrestler or a weightlifter, or are involved in other contact sports where high levels of physiological arousal are required for success, it may be important to develop psych-up strategies such as listening to inspirational music in the hours or minutes before a competitive event. Apparently, the song used most frequently by Premiership soccer players during the 2002–3 season was 'Lose yourself' by Eminem.[13] It was also used by the England rugby team on their way to play Australia in the 2003 World Cup final. Other sports may require much lower levels of arousal, and here the choice of music may be quite different.

Ideally, you should not choose music that is merely in keeping with your mood but instead, try to use it to manage your mood. If we are agitated, we are inclined to choose tunes with a fast, heavy beat, thus reinforcing our agitation. If this state is not helping you hit your zone, then it is important to select melodies that will. With this in mind, many athletes deliberately mix their own tapes for use prior to competition, deliberately choosing medleys that will help optimise their personal performance. These should not necessarily be tub-thumping or inspirational but should be deliberately chosen to create the right mood for your best performance.

Of course, music is not the only psych-up or psych-down strategy used in sport. In fact, some coaches believe that if players are taunted or made angry before they compete, their performance will be improved. One advocate of this rather bizarre theory was Laurent Seigne, a French rugby coach who is reported to have punched members of his team, Brive, before a match in order to raise their game![14] Arousal-regulation strategies are also used in precision sports such as golf, snooker and archery where performers need to calm down in order to play well. For example, the American archer Darrell Pace, twice an Olympic gold-medal winner, used a controlled breathing technique as a preparation strategy before competition.[15] A key component of this breathing technique was the attempt to synchronise the pattern of breathing in and out with his silent repetition of the word 'relax'. Of course, such strategies are not always effective. This leads us to one of the biggest problems of nervousness in sport – 'choking' under pressure.

Choking under pressure

Earlier in the chapter, we explained that the terms 'anxiety' and 'choking' are closely related. In sport, 'choking' under pressure happens when your performance is suddenly impaired by intense anxiety. Nervousness has prompted collapses in the performance of many athletes in individual sports such as golf. To illustrate, as a result of his anxiety, Greg Norman surrendered a six-shot lead in the final round of the 1996 US Masters' championship in Augusta, Georgia, and duly lost to Nick Faldo. On the last day of the event, he had a 78 and Faldo shot a 67. Other golfers who have admitted choking include Scott Hoch (who jokingly remarked, 'that's Hoch as in choke!'), who missed an 18-inch putt which would have earned him victory in the 1989 US Masters' event, and Stewart Cink, who missed a putt of a similar distance to win the 2001 US Open.

So widespread is the problem of choking that a language has accumulated across different sports – it is known by a variety of terms such as 'icing' (in basketball), 'dartitis' (in darts) and the 'yips' (in golf). Sports stars who have succumbed to this condition include golfers such as John Daly, Lee Trevino and Tom Watson and tennis players such as John McEnroe and Pat Rafter. Unfortunately, choking can affect athletes over a long period of time. For example, the Welsh golfer Ian Woosnam admitted that he had suffered from the 'yips' for a number of years.[16]

Fortunately for him, this problem disappeared when he made a technical adjustment to his stroke by switching to a 'broom handle' putter. Similarly, Eric Bristow, who won the world darts championship five times, choked so badly at

Ian Woosnam (courtesy of Inpho Photography)

times that he could not release the dart from his fingers. Like Woosnam, it took him several years to overcome this problem.

What is choking?

Technically, choking involves the sudden deterioration of normally expert skills under pressure. Perhaps the most fascinating aspect of this state of mind is not that it leads to poor performance but that it seems to stem from a motivational paradox. Specifically, the more effort that you put into your performance when you're extremely anxious, the worse it gets. In other words, choking under pressure occurs ironically because you're trying too hard to perform well.

The symptoms of choking in sport are broadly similar to those experienced when you're aroused physiologically. They include tense muscles, shaky limbs, rapid heart and pulse rates, shortness of breath, butterflies in the stomach, 'racing' thoughts and feelings of panic. In addition, choking may involve the sensation that you cannot seem to complete a stroke or movement that you can normally perform effortlessly. Indeed, golfers who suffer from the 'yips' often feel themselves getting tense over the ball and unable to complete a putting stroke. The former golfer and commentator Peter Alliss admitted that in one major tournament:

> I stood over the ball, lining up the putt and suddenly I was gripped by negative thoughts. I couldn't visualise the ball going in. I was frightened of failure and I could barely draw back the putter to make contact with the ball.[17]

Likewise, pitchers in baseball or bowlers in cricket who suffer from anxiety attacks suddenly feel as if they cannot release the ball. On one occasion Phil Edmonds, the former England cricket bowler, was so badly afflicted with anxiety that he ended up standing in the crease and lobbing the ball at the batter's end.

Choking reactions may also be characterised by a tiny muscular spasm that occurs just as the stroke is about to be executed. The Scottish darts player Jocky Wilson was legendary in his sport for the various tics and twitches that came to characterise his unique throwing action, especially in the latter stages of his career. By the way, one curious finding in the literature is that choking seems to occur more frequently in untimed individual sports (e.g. golf, tennis) than in timed team games (e.g. football, rugby). As yet, however, the precise reasons for this phenomenon remain unknown.

What causes choking?

Many psychologists regard choking as an anxiety-based, concentration difficulty rather than a personality problem. This distinction is important because it suggests that a tendency to choke in sport is not a character flaw but a cognitive problem

that arises whenever nervousness causes you to pay attention to the 'wrong' target –
anything that is outside your control or that is irrelevant to the task at hand
(see also Chapter 5). For example, if you feel anxious and begin to think too
much about yourself or the importance of the event in which you are competing,
you may find that your performance suffers. Technically, what's probably
happening is that you are trying to exert conscious control over skills that you
normally perform automatically. When such 'paralysis by analysis' occurs, your
skills can unravel before your eyes. Interestingly, this problem of having too
many thoughts at the same time may increase with age. For example, when Ian
Woosnam tried to correct his putting stroke after several years of the 'yips', he
revealed that

> putting shouldn't be hard . . . but that's where the mind comes in. So much is
> running through your mind – hold it this way, keep the blade square –
> whereas when you're young, you just get hold of it and hit it. When you get
> old too much goes through your mind.[18]

Having explored how choking can arise, we need to turn now to the issue of how to
control your anxiety and cope with pressure situations in sport.

Coping with pressure: the eight-point plan

Given the inevitability of performance anxiety in sport, we need to explore practical
strategies in an effort to reduce it. Before describing these techniques, however, let
us clarify two key points.

First, we must distinguish between *pressure situations* and *pressure reactions*
in sport. This distinction is extremely important because you need to understand
that you don't automatically have to experience 'pressure' (that is, an anxiety
response) in pressure situations. Second, you need to understand exactly what
effective anxiety control involves psychologically. In this regard, successful coping
involves any efforts that a person makes to master, reduce or otherwise tolerate
pressure. These efforts fall into two main categories. On the one hand, you could
confront the pressure situation directly. This strategy is known as 'problem-
focused' coping and involves such activities as gathering as much information as
possible in advance of the pressure to be faced or forming a plan of action to reduce
it. Alternatively, you could practise 'emotion-focused' coping, which involves
trying to change your interpretation of, and reaction to, the pressure situation in
question. Typically, 'problem-focused' coping techniques are advisable when you
are preparing for controllable sources of pressure (such as worrying about whether
you've trained hard enough or have packed all your gear for a game), whereas
emotion-focused strategies are usually more appropriate when the pressure

situation is largely uncontrollable (such as the possibility of facing a hostile reaction from fans of a team that you're due to play against soon).

Based on two key ideas – that pressure lies in the mind of the beholder and that different coping strategies are available to facilitate active coping – here is a summary of some of the most popular techniques used by athletes to deal with unwanted anxiety in sport.

Restructure the pressure situation in your mind

In general, you will experience pressure and associated anxiety symptoms whenever you believe that a current or impending situation threatens you in some way. For example, as a soccer player you may be apprehensive about making a mistake in an important match in front of your home supporters. Alternatively, as a swimmer, you may feel tense at the prospect of competing under the watchful eye of a feared coach. More generally, whenever there is a discrepancy between what you think you can do (that is, your assessment of our own abilities) and what you believe you are expected to do (that is, what you perceive as the demands of the situation), you put yourself under pressure. Psychologically, therefore, pressure is a subjective interpretation of certain objective circumstances (the 'pressure situation').

Another point to note is that although you cannot change a pressure situation, you *can* definitely change your reaction to it by a technique called 'restructuring'. Specifically, by restructuring a tough situation in your mind, you can learn to interpret it as a challenge to your abilities rather than as a threat to your well-being. To illustrate, consider what Jack Nicklaus, who is statistically the greatest golfer ever by virtue of winning 18 major tournaments, revealed in his distinction between feeling nervous and feeling excited:

> Sure, you're nervous, but that's the difference between being able to win and not being able to win. And that's the fun of it, to put yourself in the position of being nervous, being excited. I never look on it as pressure. I look on it as fun and excitement. That's why you're doing it.[19]

Interestingly, Clive Woodward, who coached England to World-Cup victory in rugby in 2003, used a restructuring technique called 'second-half thinking' with his players during the half-time break in key matches. The purpose of this strategy was to generate sufficient momentum to overcome the problem of 'slow starts' in the second half of games. It involved players changing shirts, pretending that the score was 0–0, and visualising the kick-off for the second half.[20] Another example of the use of restructuring in sport concerns Michael Phelps (see Chapter 3), the brilliant American swimmer who has won six Olympic titles and six world championships. He revealed:

Jack Nicklaus (courtesy of Inpho Photography)

You can look at pressure in two different ways. It's either going to hurt you or help you. I see it as something that helps me. If there's pressure on me or someone thinks I can't do something, it's going to make me work even harder.[21]

Unfortunately, this skill of perceiving pressure situations as challenges does not always develop quickly or spontaneously. At the same time, you can cultivate the skill through specialist advice and training. To explore this skill of cognitive restructuring for yourself, try the exercise in the box.

Turning pressure into challenge

The purpose of this exercise is to show you how to use a technique called cognitive restructuring to turn a feared pressure situation into a manageable challenge. To begin, think of a situation in your sport or daily life that usually makes you feel anxious. Now, describe this situation by finishing the following sentence:

'I hate the pressure of —— .'

Fill in the missing words with reference to the pressure situation you have experienced. For example, you might write, 'I hate the pressure of taking a short putt when a lot depends on it.'

Now, think of this pressure situation again. This time, however, I would like you to restructure it in your head so that you think about it differently.

'I love the challenge of —— .'

Please note that you are not allowed to simply repeat what you wrote before. You cannot say, 'I love the challenge of taking a short putt when a lot depends on it.' Instead, you have to pick something else to focus on in that pressure situation besides the fear of making mistakes. As we shall see in Chapter 5, the secret of maintaining your focus under pressure is to concentrate on something that is specific, relevant and under your own control. Usually, that means concentrating on some aspect of your preparation for the feared situation – you could write, 'I love the challenge of keeping my head steady every time I putt – no matter what the score is or who I'm playing against.' Notice how restructuring a situation can make you feel and think differently about it. You no longer see it as something to fear but as something that challenges your skills.

Having explained how to restructure pressure situations as challenges, our next step is to explore some practical techniques for reducing anxiety.

Learn to understand what your body is telling you

Despite their talent and experience, many top sportspeople have a poor understanding of what their body is telling them when they are anxious. In particular, they need to realise that anxiety is not necessarily a bad thing but merely a sign that they care. Without such awareness, we are all likely to misinterpret physical signs of readiness to act (such as a rapid heartbeat or a surge of adrenalin) as signals of impending disaster. So, the first step in coping with anxiety is to become tuned in to what it means. The lesson here is that you must learn to regard your bodily arousal as the platform for a good performance.

Use physical relaxation techniques

In the heat of competition, athletes tend to speed up their behaviour. This is not surprising in view of the 'fight or flight' reaction that we discussed earlier in the chapter. If you have experienced this problem, the obvious solution is to make a deliberate effort to slow down and relax whenever tension strikes. Of course, this advice must be tailored to the demands of the particular sport that you're playing. In fact, the feasibility of using physical relaxation techniques, such as progressive muscular relaxation, depends heavily on the amount of 'break time' offered by the sport in question. For example, in stop-start, untimed sports such as golf or tennis, there are moments where it may be possible to lower your shoulders, flap out the tension from your arms, and engage in deep-breathing exercises. Centring is a technique used in many sports, and can easily be adapted to meet the particular requirements of your own sport. For example, in rugby union, a hooker could easily introduce centring into the line-out pre-throw routine to ensure there is no tension in the upper body.

Centring

At any stage during play, it may be necessary to stop, take stock and take control. Centring enables you quickly and simply to counteract some of the changes associated with physical tension and associated loss of control. All it takes is a few seconds to 'calm yourself down' to a point where you regain the capacity to assess the situation accurately and then direct your concentration in appropriate ways.

1. Stand with your feet shoulder-width apart and knees slightly bent. Your weight should be evenly balanced between your two feet. The bend in your knees is important and should result in your being able to feel the tension in the muscles in the calves and thighs. The flexing counteracts a natural tendency to lock knees when you become tense.
2. Now, consciously relax your neck and shoulder muscles. Check this by making slight movements with your head and arms (see that they are loose and relaxed).
3. Your mouth should be open slightly to reduce tension in jaw muscles.
4. Breathe in from your diaphragm, down to your abdomen. Inhale slowly and, as you do, attend to two cues. First, notice that you extend your stomach as you breathe. Next, consciously maintain relaxation in your chest and shoulders. This helps you avoid allowing your chest to expand and shoulders to rise, thus increasing upper body tension. It also counters a tendency to tense your neck and shoulder muscles.
5. As you breathe out slowly, notice the feelings in your abdomen and your stomach muscles relaxing. Consciously let your knees bend slightly,

attending to increased feelings of heaviness as your body presses down towards the ground. The exhalation counteracts the natural lifting associated with breathing in, and the body does begin to feel more steady.

6.   As you have attended to the relaxing physical cues, you have simultaneously stopped attending to the things that were causing you to lose control. Now you should have recovered enough composure to deal in a constructive way with the situation you face.

To facilitate centring, some professional tennis players use a relaxation strategy whereby they visualise an imaginary area (usually located behind the baseline of a tennis court) that serves as a relaxation zone where they can switch off mentally during breaks in play (see also Chapter 6 for a discussion of mental imagery in sport). However, this procedure may be impossible to use in games where play is fast and mainly continuous (as in hockey or basketball). Also, another caution is necessary when teaching relaxation skills to athletes. In our experience, relaxation CDs do not work effectively with many sport performers because they are too passive for their needs. If you feel that you may benefit from relaxation skills, try converting the script in the box into a tape. It can be used as a general lifestyle tool, or helping to create the right environment for a good night's sleep. Closer to competition, the tape may help create the right emotional environment during a pre-competition routine, particularly for those who may be prone to overheating.

Self-directed relaxation

Lie down on a flat, firm surface.

Close your eyes and adjust your position so that you are stretched out making maximum contact with the ground. Raise and lower your head to stretch your neck, making sure your neck is not tilted backwards. Flatten your back and push away with your heels to stretch your legs. Take a deep breath and let it out slowly. Feel the weight of your body on the floor, take another deep breath, and let the floor support the full weight of your body.

Take a deep breath and slowly breathe out. Think of the word 'relax' and then pause. Breathe in deeply . . . breathe out slowly . . . breathe in deeply . . . breathe out slowly.

Now focus all your attention on your head. Feel any tension in your forehead. Just relax the tension in your forehead. Relax . . . (pause). Relax even deeper . . . and deeper . . . and deeper.

Feel any tension in your jaw. Just relax the tension in these muscles. Feel the tension flow away. Breathe in deeply . . . breathe out slowly.

Feel the relaxation in your facial muscles. Relax . . . then pause. Breathe in deeply . . . breathe out slowly (pause). Relax even deeper . . . and deeper . . . and deeper.

Now feel any tension in your arms, forearms, and hands. Just relax the muscles in your arms. Relax . . . (pause).

Feel any tension in your hands, fIngers or arms, and just relax the tension in these muscles. See the tension flow out of your body. Breathe in deeply . . . breathe out slowly.

Feel the relaxation in your arms and hands. Relax . . . (pause). Breathe in deeply . . . breathe out slowly (pause). Relax even deeper . . . and deeper . . . and deeper.

Now focus your attention on your neck and upper back. Feel any tension in the muscles of your neck and upper back. Just relax the tension in these muscles. Relax . . . (pause). See the tension flow out of your body. Breathe in deeply . . . breathe out slowly. Feel the relaxation in these muscles. Relax . . . (pause). Breathe in deeply . . . breathe out slowly (pause). Relax even deeper . . . and deeper . . . and deeper.

Remember to keep your facial muscles relaxed. Keep your arms and hand muscles relaxed. And keep your neck and upper back muscles relaxed. Keep all these muscles relaxed. Inhale deeply . . . exhale slowly. Feel the relaxation in all these muscles. Feel the relaxation even deeper . . . and deeper . . . and deeper.

Now feel any tension in your lower back and stomach muscles. Focus all your attention on these muscles and get them to relax. Relax these muscles fully. Feel the tension flow away. Breathe in deeply . . . breathe out slowly. Feel the relaxation in your lower back and stomach muscles. Relax . . . (pause). Breathe in deeply . . . breathe out slowly (pause). Relax even deeper . . . and deeper . . . and deeper.

Now feel any tension in your upper legs, both the front and back. Focus all your attention on these muscles and get them to relax. Relax these muscles fully. Feel the tension flow away. Breathe in deeply . . . breathe out slowly. Feel the relaxation in your upper legs. Relax . . . (pause). Breathe in deeply . . . breathe out slowly (pause). Relax even deeper . . . and deeper . . . and deeper.

Remember to keep your facial muscles relaxed. Keep your lower back and stomach muscles relaxed. And keep your upper leg muscles relaxed – keep all these muscles relaxed. Breathe in deeply . . . breathe out slowly. Feel the relaxation in all these muscles. Feel the relaxation even deeper . . . and deeper . . . and deeper.

Now feel any tension in your lower legs and your feet. Focus all your attention on these muscles and ask them to relax. Relax these muscles fully. Feel the tension flow away. Breathe in deeply . . . breathe out slowly. Feel the relaxation in your lower legs and feet. Relax . . . (pause). Breathe in deeply . . . breathe out slowly (pause). Relax even deeper.

With practice you can gradually combine the muscle groups together into larger units (e.g. head, neck and arms; torso; lower body) until the whole exercise takes only a few seconds. The golfer Sam Torrance used a similar procedure prior to almost every major tournament that he played in, although he wasn't lying on the floor but sitting on the toilet, and he knew he had reached the required state when the cigarette he was invariably holding fell to the floor!

Give yourself specific instructions

As we indicated earlier, anxiety is unhelpful because it makes us focus on what might go wrong (possible negative outcomes) rather than on what we have to do (the immediate challenge of the situation). Therefore, a useful way to counteract pressure in a competition is to ask yourself, 'What exactly do I have to do right now?' By focusing on what you have to do, you can learn to avoid the trap of confusing the facts of the situation (e.g. 'We're 1–0 down with ten minutes to go') with an anxious interpretation of those facts ('It's over, we're going to lose'). Hence a useful practical tip for coping with pressure is to give yourself specific commands (for example, you could say, 'go cross court' to yourself when preparing to receive a serve in tennis).

Use a pre-performance routine

A good way of slowing down and dealing with anxiety is to use 'pre-performance routines', or systematic sequences of preparatory thoughts and actions before important skills (e.g. golf putts, penalty kicks; see also Chapter 5). Routines are valuable because they take you from thinking about something to doing it (see 'Hitting the mark' box). By encouraging you to take one step at a time instead of worrying about what might happen in the future, they help you to focus on the present and rid yourself of thoughts of the past. Also, as routines teach you to focus only on what you can control, they cocoon you against the adverse effects of anxiety. They can also be valuable in providing the correct tempo, and some athletes take this further by setting these routines to a rhythm or music.

One Gaelic footballer who we worked with rediscovered his set piece kicking ability by developing a pre-performance routine that he had used when he was young but had abandoned as he moved up through the ranks. It involved setting the ball on the ground, looking at the target, looking at the ball, taking five steps backwards, three to the side, looking at the ball, looking at the posts – and then singing to himself, 'We built this city on rock and roll', as he ran up to kick the ball over the black spot!

Over time the script could be shortened but should always be there, in both training and competition. To make sure the correct tempo or timing is maintained, the words could even be set to a rhythm or song.

Hitting the mark

In a high-precision sport such as archery, it is vital that the flow or rhythm of each shot is constant but is controlled by a measured routine. Here is an example of one routine used in archery. The routine begins the moment the arrow is taken from the quiver. This also acts as the signal to stop the evaluation of the previous shot and focus all attention on the next.

1. **Check** – before loading the bow, a quick check that physically things feel right – this could include a breathing exercise. Only proceed when things feel right, and have the courage to begin again if they don't.
2. **Load** – the bow faces the ground while the arrow is loaded and the required tension is applied to the bowstring.
3. **Spot** – the bow is slowly raised until the arrow points to a predesignated spot on the adjacent wall.
4. **Stance** – a quick check that the whole body stance is good.
5. **Swing** – the archer rotates through 90 degrees until the arrow points to the target.
6. **Head** – checking that the correct head position is adopted.
7. **Gold** – attention focuses on the gold spot at the centre of the target.
8. **Squeeze** – the release mechanism is activated and the arrow flies.

Think constructively and encourage yourself

When you are anxious, your 'self-talk' (that is, what you say to yourself silently inside your head) tends to becomes hostile and sarcastic. Although such frustration is understandable, it is never helpful, as it usually makes the situation worse. So when you're talking to yourself, try to encourage yourself for your effort (positive reinforcement) or to instruct yourself on what to do next (guidance). For example, if you're an anxious table-tennis player, you might say to yourself, 'Come on, this point now. Attack the backhand.'

Get used to pressure situations by training in them

One of the best ways of developing mental toughness is to inoculate yourself against anxiety by practising under simulated pressure situations in training. For example, as part of their training for gold-medal success in the 1988 Olympics, the Australian women's hockey team practised under such adversity as gamesmanship (especially verbal taunting or 'sledging') and bad umpiring decisions.

Control your body language

If you are nervous, your shoulders will tighten, your breathing will increase, and your body movements will tend to become jerky. By making an effort to lower your shoulders, breathe more deeply, and slow down, you'll not only conquer your feelings of anxiety but you'll also send a more confident image to your opponents.

In summary, we have shown you that you can learn to cope with pressure situations by using a variety of psychological strategies. First, remember that pressure lies in the eye of the beholder, and so you must learn to restructure cognitively competitive events as opportunities to display your talents (the challenge response) rather than as potential sources of failure (the fear response). Second, you have to learn for yourself what level of stress works best for you and which combination of practical strategies can help bring you to your 'zone' before a competitive game. One way of doing this is to use simulation training and mental rehearsal to prepare yourself for the challenges that lie ahead. Third, you can benefit from using self-talk techniques to guide yourself through pressure situations. Finally, when anxiety strikes, you must be prepared to deepen your routines and to use physical relaxation procedures in accordance with the structure of your sport. In other words, remember the following advice – when the going gets tough, the tough *keep* going!

Chapter 5

Focusing

I was in my own little world, focusing on every shot.
I wasn't thinking of what score I was on or anything. . . . But today was probably as good as I have
ever played.
> Darren Clarke, Ryder Cup golfer, after he had
> shot a record-equalling round of 60 in the 1999
> European Open championship in Kildare, Ireland[1]

Introduction

'COME ON, CONCENTRATE!' Has a coach or fellow player
ever shouted this at you during a game? If so, you may
have noticed that this instruction rarely works well – for
a rather obvious reason. The problem is that although a
request to 'concentrate' may encourage you to try harder, it
fails to tell you *exactly* what to focus on in the situation in
question. The lesson from this everyday experience is clear.
Any instruction to concentrate is meaningless and ineffect-
ive unless it's linked to a specific job or action – preferably
one that is relevant, under your control, and one that you
can perform immediately. For example, if someone urges
you to 'hold the line' in soccer or to keep your 'head down'
in golf, you know exactly what job to concentrate on
straight away because your mind has a definite target.

Darren Clarke (courtesy of Inpho Photography)

Unfortunately, although this psychological principle is easy to understand, it is difficult to put into practice in competitive sport because so often your mind can be sidetracked by a host of situational factors – bad refereeing decisions, opponents' gamesmanship and even weather conditions on the big day. To make matters worse, you can even distract *yourself* by the way in which you think. Interestingly, this problem applies at all levels of sport. Imagine the jumble of thoughts that must have gone through the mind of golfer Paul McGinley as he faced a tricky six-foot putt to win the 2002 Ryder Cup for Europe against the USA at the Belfry. Should he concentrate on the ball, on the hole, on some technical aspect of his stroke action, or, simply, on not missing the putt because of its importance to his team? Fortunately for Europe, McGinley not only chose the right target to focus on – the line of his putt – but by holing out, he helped his team to victory.

Although winning rarely comes down to just one shot, it is definitely made more likely by good decision-making. And that's where McGinley showed wonderful mental strength. To explain, his choice of target was correct because it involved a specific, relevant action that was completely under his control. As he revealed afterwards:

> At no time did I even consider the mechanics of the stroke. Of course, I knew what the putt meant and what it was for, but I became absorbed in the line of the putt. I could see it exactly from beginning to end. My only job at that moment in time was to set the ball off on the line that I had chosen. That was the only thing I could control.[2]

Clearly, although sport is played with the body, it is *won* in the mind. But what exactly is this winning mental skill called 'focus' or 'concentration'? Why do we lose it so easily when we need it most? What kinds of distractions do we face in sport and what is the best way to deal with them? What are the building blocks of effective concentration? Perhaps most importantly, what practical techniques can you use to improve your concentration skills in sport? The purpose of this chapter is to answer these and other relevant questions. But before we begin, let's explore some important insights arising from what athletes tell us about their own concentration processes.

What winners do

We can learn a lot about effective concentration from athletes who produce winning performances in sport. In this regard, Paul McGinley's statement is fascinating for at least four reasons. First, it highlights the fact that in order to focus properly, you have to have a clear goal (in his case, to sink a putt) and be able to break that objective into action steps – one of which was to guide the ball down the line he had chosen. Second, it shows us that when you're under pressure, it is dangerous to think too much about the mechanics of your skills. Otherwise, you could experience the dreaded paralysis by analysis and your performance will suffer (see also our discussion of 'choking' in Chapter 4). This problem has been faced by Darren Clarke, another Ryder Cup golfer, who says, 'Whenever I'm thinking about technique, the ball disappears at all kinds of funny angles.'[3]

To avoid such difficulties, top sports performers have learned that technical analysis is best left to the practice ground. A third reason why McGinley's remarks are interesting is that they suggest that in order to perform to the best of your ability, you have to *clear* your mind of all distracting thoughts. This 'decluttering' principle of mental preparation is echoed by other winners in sport. For example, Michael Johnson (a three-times Olympic gold medallist in the 400 metres, and nine

Michael Johnson (courtesy of Inpho Photography)

times a world athletics gold medallist) deliberately cleared his mind before every race so that he ended up with only one thought:

> I have learned to cut out all the unnecessary thoughts . . . on the track. I simply concentrate. I concentrate on the tangible – on the track, on the race, on the blocks, on the things I have to do. The crowd fades away and the other athletes disappear and now it's just me and this one lane.[4]

Unfortunately, this skill of clearing your mind doesn't come naturally to most people – even world champions. That's why many of them turn to sport psychologists for help in this area. For example, Sonia O'Sullivan, a 5,000 metres Olympic silver medallist, paid tribute to the practical assistance that psychologists can provide in dealing with distractions:

> They're very useful, especially if you have a lot of stuff going on. If you're trying to do one thing but you're getting distracted by ten other things, they really help you to focus on what you're trying to do and just aim for that. And they help you to block out things . . . to just focus on one thing at a time.[5]

The final learning point from McGinley's statement is that when two opponents are evenly matched, victory is usually achieved by the one who is better able to focus on the task at hand while ignoring distractions.

Sonia O'Sullivan (courtesy of Inpho Photography)

This idea brings us to the main theme of this chapter. What separates winners from losers in sport is the ability to stay in the present and focus on what you can do right now rather than speculating about what might happen in the future. It is precisely this skill that helped Petr Cech, the Chelsea and Czech Republic goalkeeper, to set a record in the 2004–5 English Premiership soccer season by keeping 24 'clean sheets' (no goals) out of 38 matches in which he played:

> Everything is about concentration and that's what I've learnt this season. We have a great team and we're always on the attack so our opponents get maybe one or two chances in the game. Sometimes it can be one chance in 90 minutes and it's difficult to be concentrated for the right moment.[6]

Having learned some valuable lessons about effective focusing from winners in sport, let's explore what the term 'concentration' really means.

What is concentration or 'focus'?

In sport psychology, the term 'concentration' or 'focus' usually means paying attention to what is most important in any situation while ignoring distractions. But it has two other meanings. So, let's now clarify the three separate mental activities involved in concentration.

Selective attention

To begin with, concentration means focused or 'selective' attention – your ability to 'zoom in' on relevant information while ignoring potential distractions. To illustrate, if you are a goalkeeper in hockey waiting for a penalty corner from the opposing team, you must be able to focus selectively on the ball while ignoring the pushing and shoving among the players around you in the penalty area.

Conscious attention

Secondly, 'concentration' can mean conscious attention that involves making a deliberate decision to invest mental effort in something that is important to you. For example, at a team talk before an important match you will probably make a big effort to listen carefully to your coach's instructions. By contrast, you may find that your mind wanders when you're going out to a training session.

Unconscious attention

The third meaning of concentration is unconscious attention and concerns your ability to perform two or more skills at the same time. This type of mental time-sharing happens quite easily when one of the skills you are performing is highly practised. For example, if you play basketball regularly you should be able to dribble with the ball while simultaneously scanning the court for a team-mate who is in a good position to receive a pass.

Although all three aspects of concentration are important in sport, we're going to deal with the first and second of these processes in this chapter, because, to focus properly, you have to decide that you're going to pay attention in the first place (conscious concentration) and also be able to focus on some aspects of the situation while excluding others (selective attention). Let's now try to understand these processes a little more deeply.

The mental spotlight

Perhaps the best way to understand the skill of concentration is to imagine it as a mental spotlight that you shine at things of interest to you. In some ways, it is like the head-mounted torches that miners, divers and potholers wear in dark environments. Wherever they look, their target is illuminated. Similarly, you're in control of your own concentration beam. When you shine your mental spotlight at a target in the world around you (for example, as you look at your team-mates before the start of a match), you have an *external* focus of attention at that moment. But when you concentrate on your own feelings or bodily processes (as in listening to your heart pounding with excitement before kick-off), you have switched to an *internal* focus of attention. Typically, in team sports, an external focus of attention is required when you're reading a game, passing to a team-mate, or marking an opponent. By contrast, an internal focus is needed whenever you devise a game plan or rehearse a skill in your mind's eye before performing it (see also Chapter 6).

Another feature of your mental spotlight is that it has an adjustable beam. To explain, whereas a *broad* focus allows you to absorb lots of information rapidly, a *narrow* focus enables you to have only one thing on your mind. An example of a broad focus occurs when you quickly note your team-mates' positions just before you take a throw-in in soccer. On the other hand, a narrow focus occurs when you pick a specific spot to aim at before you take a penalty kick.

When we combine these ideas about the direction and width of your concentration beam, your focus at any given time falls into one of four different categories – broad external, broad internal, narrow external or narrow internal. Of course, whether the focus you've chosen is *appropriate* for the skill that you're performing is a very different question. As we learned from Paul McGinley and Darren Clarke, thinking technically about your skills while competing in sport is rarely helpful.

In the spotlight

Likewise, shining your spotlight on yourself is not a good idea, as it makes you self-conscious and worried about making mistakes. It is interesting that experienced marathon runners differ from novices in their capacity to switch between internal and external modes, knowing when to listen to their bodies (association) but also knowing when it is safe to turn off the monitor (dissociation). And focusing on what might happen in the future is also counter-productive as it encourages you to think too far ahead. We'll come back to these examples of focusing on the wrong target when we explore how you can lose your concentration in sport.

Where is your spotlight shining right now?

As we have just explained, your mind is always focused on a target – whether it's appropriate to the job that you're doing or not. Hopefully, you're concentrating on the words on this page right now, *but* if your mind is elsewhere, you won't even notice this sentance (or spelling mistake)! Anyway, having introduced the idea that there are different *types* of focus, let's outline what we know about them.

Four types of focus

A broad external focus

This type of focus involves the ability to read a game and quickly assess a situation for relevant information. For example, good midfield players must be able to quickly weigh up the best passing options available to them, having won a tackle. Peripheral awareness is the key here (especially in team sports) and involves the ability to integrate many different observations at a glance (experienced players can rapidly assess the position of team-mates and the formation of opposing players).

A narrow external focus

This type of focus is required whenever an athlete locks onto a specific target in the surrounding environment. For example, when rugby full-backs attempt a catch, they must focus solely on the dropping ball and ignore in-rushing opponents. Likewise, pistol shooters must focus on the bullseye before they press the trigger.

A broad internal focus

This focus is called upon when you're developing a tactical plan for a forthcoming match. This plan might require you to analyse your opponents' strengths and weaknesses.

A narrow internal focus

This type of focus is necessary when your mind has to concentrate on a single thought or idea such as your stride or breathing as you run a marathon. Interestingly, when you're nervous, you tend to adopt this type of focus – but the target is invariably unhelpful to the action (e.g. 'I'll never be able to keep up this pace' or 'I'm playing very badly at present').

At this stage, let's see if you can come up with some examples from your sport of the four different types of focus that we've just described.

Focusing

Every sport places concentration demands on its performers. Using the sport that you know best, try to identify the specific skills that go with each of the following types of focus:

- a broad external focus?
- a narrow external focus?
- a broad internal focus?
- a narrow internal focus?

Switching focus

As we explained above, our concentration system is very limited – we can focus on only one target at a time. That's not a problem if you choose the correct target, as Paul McGinley or Michael Johnson did. But if you find that your mind wanders a lot, you may have to learn to switch quickly from one type of focus to another. Indeed, successful athletes have mastered this skill to such a degree that they appear to be concentrating equally well on several jobs at the same time. Instead, in reality what they are doing is switching their focus rapidly to meet the demands of a changing sport situation.

Zinzan Brooke, the former All-Black rugby forward, revealed a remarkable ability to change his attentional focus with devastating effect during a test match against Australia in 1997. Fielding a high ball on his own 10-metre line (using a narrow external focus of attention), he became aware of a team-mate in a favourable position (using a broad-external focus) and passed to him. This player then ran almost the length of the pitch before scoring a try.

Zinzan Brooke (courtesy of Inpho Photography)

'Losing' concentration?

Why is it so hard to stay in the present moment – and so easy to lose your focus? Unfortunately our concentration system is rather fragile because our minds were not designed to pay attention to *anything* for very long. This happens for two reasons. First, we have a very limited concentration span. To illustrate, have you ever found yourself going into a room in your house to look for something but forgetting what it was as soon as you entered the door? If you forget your intentions that easily, what hope do you have of remaining focused for an entire game in the face of pressure and distractions?

Another explanation for our inability to stay in the moment is that, for evolutionary reasons, we're highly distractible. For our ancestors, becoming absorbed in a task was potentially dangerous, as it increased their vulnerability to attacks from predators. Therefore, we are distractible because we have learned to do several things simultaneously – including constantly monitoring our environment for possible signs of threat. And that brings us to the myth of 'losing' your concentration.

Earlier, we said that concentration resembles a mental spotlight that we shine at things in which we are interested. If so, then it is never *really* lost – but merely redirected at some target that is irrelevant to the task that we are trying to perform. This happens quite often in everyday life. Take the case of reading. Have you ever had the experience of suddenly discovering that you've been reading the same sentence in a book over and over again without comprehension because your mind was 'miles away'? If so, then you have distracted yourself by allowing a thought, daydream or feeling to become the target of your mental spotlight.

In summary, we allow our minds to drift because our concentration span is limited and because our minds are inherently distractible. So, what kinds of distractions do you encounter in sport?

Distractions

Although distractions come in all shapes and sizes, they can be divided into two main categories (external and internal) according to their origin.

External distractions are environmental factors that divert your attention away from its intended target. By contrast, internal distractions include a vast array of your thoughts, feelings and/or bodily sensations (e.g. pain, fatigue) that may impede your efforts to concentrate on the job at hand. Let's explore these two categories in more detail now.

External distractions	**Internal distractions**
Crowd noise/spectator behaviour	Thinking too far ahead
Weather conditions	Reflecting on how you are feeling
Gamesmanship	Analysing mistakes

External distractions

Typical external distractions include factors such as crowd noise or movements and changes in background noise levels. Two golf examples of this category come to mind. First, when golfer Retief Goosen was leading in the US Open championship in 2004 in Shinnecock Hills, some unruly member of the gallery jeered: 'All yours to lose, now, Retief! Go on, three putt, make it interesting!'[7]

Fortunately, Goosen ignored these jibes, held his focus, and won the tournament. But sometimes distractions affect players who are at the peak of their powers.

Retief Goosen (courtesy of Inpho Photography)

For example, noise of a different sort affected Tiger Woods. When he was playing in the 2002 American Express World Championship in Mount Juliet, Ireland, he was leading the field with one hole to go. Playing that final hole, and trying to become only the second golfer ever to win a tournament without registering a single bogey, he was suddenly distracted by the 'click' of a camera as he prepared to play his second shot to the green. This distraction cost him a bogey and a place in the record books – although he still won the tournament! Nevertheless, he was very angry afterward:

> It was the most important shot of the week. Of all the times to take a photo. . . . I didn't want to end the tournament with a shot like the one I hit.[8]

Many other external distractions have occurred in top-level sport. For example, in soccer, teams visiting the Turkish football club, Galatasaray, in the Ali Sami Yen stadium in Istanbul, have complained of being greeted by hostile supporters letting off fireworks and waving threatening banners bearing such messages as 'Welcome to hell!' Not surprisingly, these intimidating gestures make it difficult for visiting teams to focus properly before and during matches.

Supporters have distracted athletes more directly as well. To illustrate, consider a bizarre event that occurred during the marathon race in the 2004 Olympic

Games in Athens. The Brazilian athlete Vanderlei De Lima was leading the field about 36 km into the race when a spectator (an eccentric Irish priest, who was subsequently defrocked) jumped out at him from the footpath and wrestled him to the ground. Naturally, De Lima was stunned by this assault and ended up in third place behind Stefano Baldini of Italy. Bad weather can also be distracting. For instance, if you're a golfer, playing on links courses in particular can be difficult because of unpredictable gusts of wind blowing in from the sea.

Another classic external distraction is gamesmanship by opponents. At corner-kicks in football, the opposing team's forwards often stand in front of the goalkeeper to prevent him/her from tracking the flight of the incoming ball. Of course, gamesmanship is not confined to physical contact sports. Seve Ballesteros earned a reputation in golf as a tactical 'cougher'. On one occasion, Paul Azinger (USA) alleged that Ballesteros coughed strategically as a form of gamesmanship during the 1991 Ryder Cup match against Europe. In his defence, Ballesteros claimed that he had suffered from a 'dust allergy' during the match in question! More recently, Ian Poulter complained about Ballesteros's coughing antics when he said, 'Initially, it came when I wasn't expecting it but I soon expected it all the time.'[9]

To make matters worse, when the coughing stopped, Ballesteros allegedly shuffled his feet while his opponent was putting.

Regrettably, gamesmanship is rife in competitive sport – especially in individual games such as tennis and snooker. The tennis star Maria Sharapova was accused of 'legalised cheating' by a prominent coach (John Newcombe) because of her habit of grunting and screaming during rallies – a tactic that prevented opponents from hearing the ball coming off the strings of her racket. Interestingly, her screams have been recorded as being louder than a pneumatic drill!

Similarly, a controversy over alleged gamesmanship occurred when snooker player Peter Ebdon defeated Ronnie O'Sullivan 13–11 in the quarter-finals of the 2005 World Snooker Championship in Sheffield by playing extremely slowly. To give you an idea of the snail's pace adopted by Ebdon, in the 20th frame, he took 5 minutes 30 seconds to complete a break of 12 – which is 10 seconds *slower* than O'Sullivan had taken to complete a maximum 147 break at the same venue in 1997! Furthermore, Ebdon took 3 minutes 5 seconds for a single shot in the opening frame of the final session. This slow play left O'Sullivan feeling so frustrated that he spent most of the time slumped in his chair – and even asked a spectator for the time at one stage during the second frame of the evening.

Internal distractions

Internal distractions include any thoughts, emotions (e.g. anger) and/or bodily sensations (e.g. pain, fatigue) that prevent you from concentrating fully on the job at hand. One of the most common of these distractions comes from thinking either

Maria Sharapova (courtesy of Inpho Photography)

about past mistakes or too far ahead – wondering about what will happen in the future rather than focusing on what you have to do right now. Other such distractions include thinking about the result of a match long before it's over, worrying about what other people might say or do, and feeling tired or upset emotionally.

Sometimes, these distractions combine to upset athletes. To illustrate, consider how the Republic of Ireland soccer team narrowly failed to qualify automatically for the 'Euro 2000' international football tournament. They led Macedonia 1–0 in Skopje, Macedonia, as the match was in the third minute of injury time. An Irish player asked the referee how long was left and was told that there were only about 10 seconds to go. Suddenly, a corner-kick was awarded to the home team. As the ball swung into the Irish penalty area, none of the Irish players noticed a

Doug Sanders (courtesy of Inpho Photography)

Macedonian defender running from midfield. He headed the ball into the Irish net for an equaliser. How can international soccer players suddenly forget to 'mark up' for a corner-kick? The explanation was simple. Asking the referee how long was left was a major mental lapse and distracted the Irish player who should have been marking the Macedonian 'runner'. Fatigue compounded this error. Interestingly, research shows that more goals are scored in the final 15 minutes of a game than at any other time in a soccer match.

Another example of a very costly internal distraction occurred in the case of the golfer Doug Sanders, who missed a putt of less than three feet to win the 1970 British Open championship in St Andrews, Scotland. This error prevented him from winning his first major tournament and cost him millions of dollars in lost prize money and endorsements. Remarkably, Sanders' mistake was precipitated by thinking too far ahead and making a victory speech before the putt had been taken:

> I made the mistake about thinking which section of the crowd I was going to bow to! I had the victory speech prepared before the battle was over. . . . I would give up every victory I had to have won that title. It's amazing how many different things to my normal routine I did on the 18th hole. There's something for psychologists there, the way that the final hole of a major championship can alter the way a man thinks.[10]

A remarkable aspect of Sanders' statement is his awareness of how he allowed his normal routine to change under pressure but was apparently unable to rectify this problem. The same thing happened to the British golfer Greg Owen when victory was in sight during the 2006 Bay Hill Invitational tournament in Florida. Leading by two shots on the 17th hole, and doubtlessly rehearsing his victory speech, Owen three-putted from three feet and got so annoyed with himself that he subsequently bogied the last hole to finish a stroke behind the eventual winner, Rod Pampling (Australia). Sadly, this missed putt cost Owen £230,000 (sterling) – a big price to pay for losing his focus. Afterwards, he admitted ruefully:

> I had one of the biggest tournaments in my pocket and I threw it away. . . . I can't say I got nervous on that putt . . . I got quick on it, I lost concentration.[11]

Interestingly, 'getting quick' on a shot is another example of how your routine can change under pressure. It's a classic symptom of thinking too far ahead – which is why top players deliberately use pre-shot routines in an effort to slow them down (see later in the chapter).

Thinking too far ahead can also affect jockeys in horse-racing. To illustrate, a young and talented Irish jockey named Roger Loughran learned a concentration lesson that he'll never forget when riding his horse Central House in the Dial-a-bet Chase at Leopardstown in late December 2005. Leading narrowly with about 90 metres to go, Loughran misperceived a stick on the finishing straight as the winning post and sat up in premature celebration – punching the air in front of a crowd of 20,000. Unfortunately, by the time he realised that he had made a mistake, Loughran had allowed two other riders to pass him. So, he ended up finishing third, not first, in the race, and to add insult to injury he was also banned for failing to ride through the finish.

Rather unkindly, this lapse in concentration was described by the tabloid press as being a bad case of 'premature jockelation' (!) – and was estimated to have cost punters a seven-figure sum. Interestingly, a similar perceptual problem happened in the Grand National race in 1956 when the horse Devon Loch, ridden by Dick Francis, was 10 lengths ahead with 50 yards to go but suddenly slipped on the flat – apparently because it had mistaken the shadow of a fence for the finishing post and had pulled up accordingly. These examples highlight the hazards of losing your focus at the wrong time in sport.

At this stage, you might find it helpful to explore your own distractions.

Now that we have explored types of distractions that you might experience, let's consider how to develop more effective concentration skills.

Exploring your distractions

- What things tend to upset your focus *before* a game/match? Give an example of the experience or situation and try to describe how it makes you feel and how it affects your performance. Was this distraction external or internal?
- What distractions bother you *during* the event itself? Again, try to describe how a distraction makes you feel and how it affects your performance. Was this distraction external or internal?
- Looking back at these two experiences/situations, how would you like to have reacted to them? Remember – you can't change an external distraction but you *can* change how you react to it.

Building good concentration

As we have indicated earlier, a good way to establish the building blocks of effective concentration is to explore the minds of athletes who have achieved peak perform- ance in their sport. Research suggests that there are at least five components of effective concentration in sport.

You have to decide to concentrate – it won't just happen by chance

The first building block of effective concentration concerns 'conscious attention', which we introduced earlier in this chapter. The idea here is that you have to *decide* to invest mental effort in your performance. Put simply, you have to prepare to concentrate rather than simply hope that it will happen by chance. Interestingly, this link between *deciding* to concentrate and subsequently performing to your full potential is well known in sport. For example, Oliver Kahn, the former German international and Bayern Munich goalkeeper, claimed, 'If you don't prepare your- self mentally it's impossible to maintain consistently high standards'.[12]

Similarly, Ronan O'Gara, the Irish and Lions' rugby out-half, admitted, 'I have to be focused. I have to do my mental preparation. I have to feel that I'm ready.'[13]

A practical tip on getting ready for competitive matches is to visualise a 'switch-on' signal for your concentration in the place where your sporting action will take place. For example, you could imagine turning on your concentration switch when you change in your locker room before a match. Similarly, you could associate 'switching off' your concentration with stepping into the shower afterwards. This idea of learning to switch on your concentration when you need it most is what Garry Sobers, the famous cricket star, had in mind when he said:

> Concentration's like a shower. You don't turn it on until you want to bathe. . . . You don't walk out of the shower and leave it running. You turn it off, you turn it on. . . . It has to be fresh and ready when you need it.[14]

In summary, as you get ready in the locker room, you should take a moment to clear your mind and switch on your concentration for the match itself.

Be single-minded: focus on one thought at a time

The second building block of effective concentration is the 'one-thought' principle – the idea that you can focus consciously on only one thing at a time. This single-mindedness sometimes produces unusual theories among sporting champions. For example, Retief Goosen, who won the 2004 US Open golf championship in New York, revealed that he plays his best when pressure situations force him to concentrate on what he has to do:

> I've reached a point where I feel like I can only play my best golf when I'm really under the cosh. When you're under pressure, it's a sort of 'must' thing. You must focus and you must make the putt. That's what I feel.[15]

Your mind is focused when you're doing what you're thinking

The third principle of good concentration is the idea that your mind is truly focused when there is no difference between what you are thinking about and what you are doing. For example, after Roger Bannister had run the first sub-4-minute mile in May 1954 in Oxford, he said, 'There was no pain, only a great unity of movement and aim.'[16]

We discovered this idea earlier in the chapter when analysing Michael Johnson's quotation about clearing his mind and concentrating on the jobs he had to do. To increase your chances of achieving this state of mind, you have to concentrate on actions that are specific, relevant and, above all, under your own control.

Keep your mind on track: refocus when necessary

The fourth concentration principle is that, as you are likely to encounter many distractions in your sport, you need to remind yourself to refocus regularly so that your mind stays focused. One way of doing this is to write personal symbols on your sports gear as reminders of your concentration goals.

Focus outwards when you get nervous

The final building block of effective concentration is that, if you get nervous, you must make sure to focus *outwards* on actions – and not *inwards* on doubts. Some athletes are so good at this skill that they play every shot as if it were the only one that mattered. For example, a story tells of the time that Jack Nicklaus, the famous golf champion, was one hole down with one to play in a match. Having hit a bad drive, he produced an amazing recovery shot to win the hole and draw the match. When asked afterward how he had managed to concentrate under such pressure, he uttered the immortal words: 'The ball doesn't know the score!'[17]

Practical concentration techniques

Lots of techniques are available to help athletes to focus properly. The ones that we have found to work best are those that narrow the gap between what you're thinking and what you're doing. Let's explore each of these techniques now.

Set goals – focus on actions, not results

The first practical tip on improving your concentration is to set performance or action goals for yourself every time you compete. These goals (e.g. 'keep up with play' or 'get your first serve in') are jobs that you can do no matter what the score is or who you're playing against. By focusing on actions that are under your control, you're less likely to be distracted than if you concentrate on the possible result of your match.

Use routines

The second concentration technique has already been outlined in Chapter 4 – use a consistent routine before you perform key skills. Routines take you from thinking about something to doing it. They are valuable because they help you to focus on the job you have to do, one step at a time. For example, if you are a tennis player, you may like to bounce the ball a certain number of times before you serve (maybe saying 'bounce', 'hit' at the same time to keep the right rhythm). Also, by concentrating on each step of your routine, you're encouraging yourself to stay in the present moment.

Developing a pre-shot routine in golf

Step 1

First, you have to *assess* the situation or 'check it out'. The task here is to gather all relevant information before planning your shot. In particular, you should pay attention to such key factors as the lie of the ball, the length of the grass, the direction and speed of any wind blowing, the distance between your ball and your target, and the existence of any special hazards.

Step 2

Having gathered this information, you must *plan* your shot. In this step, you have to decide on the type of shot you'd like to play, the most suitable club for that shot, and the best target for this shot. A useful tip here is to *stand behind the ball* while you grip the club and choose a specific target. The important thing is to be decisive, and once the decision is made, to draw a line. If you are still deciding when you are taking the shot, the outcome may be disappointing.

Step 3

The next step involves 'seeing' and 'feeling' the shot that you would like to play. Visualise this shot in your mind's eye as vividly as possible. For example, can you see the shape of the shot? Can you see it landing and bouncing close to your target? Once you've pictured it, get into the 'ready' position and align your club and body to the target. Then, take your preferred number of practice swings to establish the correct rhythm for the shot. As you rehearse your swing, feel the smooth *tempo* of the shot.

Step 4

The final step involves making yourself comfortable as you address the ball, clearing your mind of all thoughts, making any final adjustments to your stance, waggling your club, glancing at the target again, and then – letting your shot flow. This final stage of the routine is often quite difficult because it requires a lot of *trust* to move from thinking about your shot to actually playing it. To clear the mind of thought during the execution of the shot itself, it may be helpful to say to yourself a word that characterises the action – *flow* and *easy* are common examples.

Routines are the most popular concentration strategies used by top athletes. For example, the British Olympic champion Kelly Holmes revealed the routine that led her to double-gold medal success at the 2004 Olympic Games in Athens:

After the first heat of the 800m, the races were always around the same time so I stuck to the same routine. I left for the track at the same time, I kept wearing my Team GB dog-tag around my neck, and it became my lucky charm, kissing it. When I went to the warm-up track, I would listen to Alicia Keyes singing 'If I ain't got you' and applied the words to the gold medal I wanted. I sang it as I warmed up and it brought tears to my eyes because I was dreaming of a gold medal. When I eventually got it, I kept the same routine for the 1500m. I cried before I left to run the 800m final because it was either going to be my dream or it would go all wrong and I cried again before the 1500m – I have been an emotional wreck.[18]

Routines can be combined very successfully with other concentration techniques. For example, the Irish rugby player Ronan O'Gara used imagery and trigger words as part of his pre-kick routine before kicking the winning penalty in the 2006 final of the European Cup against Biarritz in Cardiff:

It was obvious how important it was, but I just had to get into my routine and block everything else out. Usually, there's a mark in the centre of the crossbar and I focus on that. Thomond Park has a black dot, at Lansdowne Road it's green. I imagine a little hoop between the sticks, like a gymnasium hoop, and I picture the ball going through that. I stepped back and the buzz words in my mind were, 'Stay tall and follow through.'[19]

Use 'trigger words'

The third focusing technique involves the use of trigger words or short, vivid and positively phrased verbal reminders designed to help you focus on a specific target or perform a relevant action. To illustrate, during the 2002 Wimbledon ladies' singles tennis final between the Williams sisters, Serena Williams (who defeated Venus 7–6, 6–3) read prepared notes to herself during the 'change-over' time between games. Afterwards, she explained that she had written certain trigger words as instructional cues to remind her to 'hit in front of you' or 'stay low'. For similar reasons, the rugby out-half Jonny Wilkinson used trigger words such as 'alert, stay bouncing, head up', 'make 100% tackles', and 'focus low, drive the legs' when playing for England in the 2003 World Cup final against Australia. And as we have just explained, Ronan O'Gara used the phrase 'stay tall and follow through' before his penalty kicks.

Visualise what you want to do next

The fourth concentration strategy involves the use of mental imagery – 'seeing' and 'feeling' yourself performing a given skill in your mind's eye before you actually do it (see Chapter 6 for practical advice on using imagery). Imagery helps you to prepare for various possible scenarios, thereby ensuring that you will not be distracted by unexpected events. It can also help you to distinguish between 'on' and 'off' zones in competitive sport situations. For example, if you're a racquets player, you could mark an imaginary 'performance zone' at the back of the court where you can switch on and off, as required.

Imagery is widely used in sport as a concentration technique. For example, Jonny Wilkinson uses images of certain targets to concentrate while kicking.

Sometimes, he imagines he's a golfer and that his foot is a 7-iron. Another image is that of either a woman holding a can of Coke or a jeering mouth behind the goal, and he imagines that he attempts either to hit the can or send the ball down its throat (see also Chapter 6). As he said:

> The idea was that, instead of aiming at the posts, you were aiming at something specific 30 yards back. That way, we changed the emphasis of where I was aiming and it made me really kick through the ball.[20]

Similarly, the golfer Darren Clarke revealed how much he relies on mental imagery:

> Visualizing things is massively important. If you don't visualize, then you allow other negative thoughts to enter your head. Not visualizing is almost like having a satellite navigation system in your car, but not entering your destination into it. The machinery can only work if you put everything in there.[21]

Relax and centre your body

Physical relaxation techniques represent the fifth strategy for helping you to concentrate more effectively. For example, lowering your shoulders, doing gentle neck-rolling exercises, flapping out the tension from your arms and legs, and taking slow, deep breaths can lower your centre of gravity and reduce the likelihood of error. Indeed, one of the biggest mistakes made by novices in sports such as golf and tennis is to hold their breath in while they prepare for a shot. When this happens, their muscles tense up and their swing is affected.

By contrast, exhaling while relaxing your muscles is widely used as a focusing technique in sport by stars such as Jonny Wilkinson:

> As I got more into kicking, I became more involved in looking at other aspects, and one area I looked at was focusing from the inside, slowing down the breathing, relaxation, 'centering', which is a way of channeling my power and energy from my core, just behind my navel, down my left leg and into my left foot to get that explosive power.[22]

Simulation training: try a dress rehearsal

The last concentration strategy is simulation training or dress rehearsal, which is based on the assumption that you can learn to concentrate more effectively in real-life pressure situations by training under conditions that recreate them in practice. For example, the late Earl Woods, the father and first coach of Tiger

Woods, used various dress rehearsal methods with Tiger when he was a boy. Indeed, at one stage, Woods senior claimed,

> All the strategies and tactics of distraction I'd learned I threw at that kid and he would just grit his teeth and play . . . and if anyone tries pulling a trick on him these days he just smiles and says, 'My dad used to do that years ago.'[23]

Simulation techniques are also widely used by soccer coaches at present. To illustrate, Javier Aguirre, the former coach of the Mexican national soccer team, instructed his players to practise penalty-taking after every friendly match that they played in the year leading up to the 2002 World Cup in an effort to prepare for the possibility of penalty shoot-outs in that competition. Likewise, the former England manager Sven-Goran Eriksson is also reported to have used dress rehearsal methods by requiring his penalty takers to practise walking from the centre circle to the penalty area in an effort to simulate real match conditions. A list of possible simulation techniques for counteracting distractions in soccer is provided in Table 5.1.

TABLE 5.1 Simulation training in soccer: practical suggestions

Distraction	Possible simulation technique
Crowd noise	Playing pre-recorded CDs of crowd noise during training sessions in order to familiarise players with expected distractions during away matches
Gamesmanship	Arranging for team-mates to simulate opponents' gamesmanship during training sessions or practice matches
Fatigue	Alternating normal training sessions with short bouts of high-intensity exercise to induce tiredness
Heat/humidity	Arranging for players to train and play while wearing layers of extra clothing to simulate hot-weather effects
Unfavourable refereeing decisions	Designing 'modified' games containing deliberately biased umpiring decisions
Pressure	Simulating pressure situations in training (e.g. practising with your team losing 1–0 with 5 minutes to go)

Unfortunately, even the most ingenious simulations cannot fully replicate the arousal experienced by most athletes in actual competition. For example, Ronan O'Gara admitted that although you can practise taking penalty kicks in training,

It's completely different in a match where my heartbeat is probably 115 beats a minute whereas in training it's about 90–100.[24]

There is a solution to this problem, however. If you're a kicker, you could run up and down for a few minutes in training before taking penalties. This short bout of high-intensity exercise should increase your heart rate sufficiently to simulate what it would be like to have to take a kick during actual match conditions.

Chapter 6

Imagining

The line-kicking had been in my mind all week. . . . I couldn't go three minutes without visualising drilling the ball, kicking into the corners and finding touch.[1]
Irish and Lions rugby out-half Ronan O'Gara (2005) on his use of imagery to practise his kicking skills

Introduction

HAVE YOU EVER VISUALISED yourself 'in your mind's eye' hitting a great golf shot or threading a perfect pass to a team-mate just before you actually played it? If so, then you're in good company because many world-class athletes use their imagination to preview and rehearse what they want to do next. Put simply, they believe that what your mind can conceive, your body can achieve. And we share that belief. Therefore, by combining insights from such sports stars with the latest research findings in the field, we'll explain why your imaginative ability to 'see' or 'feel' a skill before you perform it is vital for success in sport. In short, the purpose of the present chapter is to show you how to use your mind's eye to give your sporting skills a winning edge.

Ronan O'Gara (courtesy of Inpho Photography)

Imagery: what you 'see' is (nearly always) what you get

Athletes, coaches and psychologists have known for a long time that mental imagery is a powerful weapon – if it is used properly, and positively, it can boost your skills and performance. In general, the images that top athletes strive to create are ones that involve the different senses that are required by the skill in question. For example, in golf, when Tiger Woods claimed that 'you have to see the shots and feel them through your hands',[2] he highlighted the importance of combining visual and kinaesthetic (feeling-oriented) imagery before striking the ball. Imagery from these same two senses featured in an account by Peter Stringer, the Munster, Irish and Lions rugby scrum-half, of his persistent attempt to 'see' and 'feel' himself scoring a try to earn his province a victory over Biarritz in the 2006 European Cup Final – something that he actually achieved:

> Sometimes as well, I try to get the feeling of what it would be like to dive over the line unchallenged and score a try, the feeling of touching the ball off the ground and my body landing a split second later. In my head, I want to feel what it's like because I've never done that. . . . So, I had to keep replaying it in my head in bed . . . that feeling of hitting the ground. I kept trying to imagine it, because I would think to myself, 'If I don't get the feeling now I'm not going to score the try.[3]

Similar use of visualisation is evident among other famous athletes such as Roger Bannister (who ran the world's first sub-4-minute mile in 1954), George Best (the legendary soccer star) and the rugby out-half Jonny Wilkinson (who won the 2003 World Cup with England). To illustrate, consider how Roger Bannister mentally prepared himself for his world record attempt:

> Each night in the week before the race there came a moment when I saw myself at the starting line. My whole body would grow nervous and tremble. I ran the race over in my mind. Then I would calm myself and sometimes get off to sleep.[4]

Roger Bannister breaks 4-minute mile (courtesy of Inpho Photography)

Clearly, mental imagery, or the ability to 'see', 'hear' and 'feel' information in the mind that is not currently being perceived by the senses, was a vital part of Bannister's mental preparation for competition. Over the past decade, imagery techniques have become extremely popular in sport psychology for several reasons. First, an obvious appeal of imagery is that you can engage in it anywhere (on the practice field, in the locker room, on a bus) and at any time – even when you're physically injured. Second, imagery is a versatile tool that can be used to improve not only physical but also mental skills (such as concentration; see Chapter 5) as well as technical ones (such as the putting stroke in golf – see later in the present chapter). Finally, imagery effects have a solid theoretical basis in psychology and are well validated by research in this field.

Unfortunately, what advocates of imagery don't always tell you is that you have to be very careful about what exactly you imagine. For example, consider the danger of visualising the wrong target in golf, something that is especially likely to occur whenever you're anxious about a shot that you face.

Let's imagine that you're a golfer standing on the tee box of a tricky dog-leg hole. Having identified a spot to aim your drive at, you suddenly notice a large water hazard to the right of the fairway. Because you're a little worried about the consequences of making a mistake, however, your only thought as you stand over the ball is, 'I hope I don't hit that lake'. Sadly, that's exactly what happens a moment later as you slice your drive and watch helplessly as your ball plops into the water. In this case, you've made the classic mistake of engaging in negative visualisation before you perform a skill – imagining a target that you want to *avoid* (the ball hitting the lake) rather than one that you want to hit (reaching the spot on the fairway). Interestingly, this example also shows us that your mind does not always distinguish between positive and negative targets. Thus, in golf, as in other target sports, the last image that you have in your mind before you strike the ball is the one that's most important in guiding your aim. The lesson is clear: your imagery must be *positive* in order to improve your performance in sport.

In our experience, mental imagery (or more precisely, the way in which we actually use it) has some other drawbacks as well. For example, you should not confuse deliberate mental rehearsal with aimless daydreaming. Although both of these processes use imagery, the difference is that whereas daydreams tend to dwell on speculative outcomes (e.g. holding the World Cup trophy aloft as captain of your national team) visualisation involves imaginatively previewing intended actions (such as practising a free-kick).

Another problem with imagery is that people often use it retrospectively rather than prospectively. To explain, the habit of picturing a negative experience in your mind after it has happened is rarely helpful. Replaying a silly mistake or a missed opportunity in your mind's eye after a match is not only frustrating but also rather pointless unless you can use this experience to correct some flaws in your game.

The learning point here is that imagery is more likely to be effective when it's used in *preview* rather than review mode. A third problem concerns the fact that engaging in mental practice in public is not always a wise move, as it may invite ridicule from onlookers. For example, when the Portsmouth and England goal-keeper David James uses mental rehearsal in his car in traffic jams on the way to the training ground, he often receives puzzled glances from other drivers:

> I have had a few strange looks when people see my head nodding from side to side but I firmly believe that it is part of the repetitive process that every sportsman requires.[5]

Interestingly, James has improved his goalkeeping skills considerably as a result of his regular practice of imagery. For example, in April 2007, he set a new Premier-ship record when he produced his 142nd 'clean sheet' after a scoreless draw between Portsmouth and Aston Villa.

Despite these problems afflicting certain types of imagery usage, visualisation is a popular and effective performance-enhancement technique in sport. However, before we show you how to use it to your advantage, let's try to explain what happens in our mind's eye when we imagine something.

David James (courtesy of Inpho Photography)

Inside the mind's eye: what really happens in your magic theatre

Although we take mental imagery for granted, we should really marvel at this remarkable skill because it allows us to create virtual experiences of the world – in other words, to 'see', 'hear' and 'feel' things (sensations, movements, people, places and situations) that aren't actually happening at present. To illustrate, when you close your eyes and imagine yourself kicking a ball, you experience sensations that seem real even though you're not actually moving your limbs. Therefore, imagery is often portrayed as a kind of private film theatre where you can look at mental pictures with your mind's eye whenever you wish. This magic theatre idea is often evoked in sport when athletes describe their imagery experiences. For example, Jack Nicklaus, arguably the most successful golfer of all time, famously revealed that he always used to imagine a shot before he hit it: 'I never hit a shot, even in practice, without having a sharp, in-focus picture of it in my head.'[6]

Similarly, Luke Donald, the British golfer, claimed recently that he relies on imagery to such an extent that he thinks in pictures not words: 'I can't explain how I'm going to hit a shot 230 yards straight [but] . . . I can picture it in my mind.'[7]

Likewise, Leonardo, the former soccer star who won the World Cup with Brazil in 1994, said,

> I still dream before I run onto the pitch about how I'm going to play. . . . I spend all day thinking about it. I play it over and over like a film in my mind.[8]

Interestingly, some athletes go to extraordinary lengths to make their mental pictures as vivid as possible. For example, a famous Swiss double-Olympic bob-sleigh champion named Gustav Weder was so meticulous in his imagery homework that he took photographs of the Winter Olympic course and mentally rehearsed on it every day before the competition began.[9]

Nicklaus, Donald and Leonardo all emphasise the visual aspects of imagery. But do we really look at pictures in our mind when we imagine something? And what exactly happens in our brains during imagery experiences? Although it seems appealing, the 'pictures in the mind' metaphor of imagery is a little misleading because not all images are visual in nature. For example, if you are a track-and-field athlete, you should be able to imagine the sound of a starting pistol (an auditory image). Similarly, if you close your eyes, you can probably imagine the sound of a crowd cheering (an auditory image). Also, you should be able to imagine the feel and texture of a basketball (a tactile image), the taste of chlorine in the swimming pool (a gustatory image), the smell of wintergreen in the changing room (an olfactory image), or the muscular sensations that you'd experience while cycling up a steep hill (a kinaesthetic image).

These examples show that you can experience imagery in any of your senses – even though research by Stephen Kosslyn at Harvard University shows that about

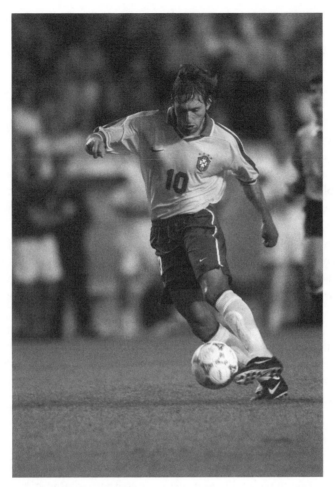

Leonardo (courtesy of Inpho Photography)

two-thirds of people's mental images are largely visual in nature.[10] Of course, this finding is not really surprising, as we rely greatly on vision in everyday life. To illustrate, have you ever found yourself wandering around a congested car park trying to remember where you parked your car? In such cases, you're probably trying to recreate a mental map of where you thought you had left your vehicle. But imagery is certainly not confined to the visual sense – in fact most of our imaginary experiences are multisensory. For example, you can combine visual and auditory images when you imagine seeing a short golf putt rolling towards the hole and making a rattling sound as it disappears from view. This example leads us to an important question. How exactly do we generate images in our minds?

In order to answer this question, we need to remind ourselves that imagery involves perception without sensation – or, put differently, running perception backwards. To explain, whereas perception occurs whenever we interpret sensory input, imagery arises when we interpret memorised information. In other words, you need to know what sinking a putt involves before you can conjure it up from your imagination at will. Based on the idea that imagery resembles perception in certain ways, we would expect that similar parts of the brain should 'light up' when we imagine things as when we actually perceive them. In this way, visual imagery should be associated with neural activity in the cortical areas that are specialised for visual perception.

Until recently, this hypothesis remained untested simply because no technology was available to allow researchers to measure what happens in the brain during people's cognitive activities. Over the past decade, however, advances in neuroscience have helped us to understand and measure such brain activation. By a variety of neuroimaging techniques, research has shown that the occipital cortex or visual centre of the brain (which is located at the back of the head) is triggered when people are asked to imagine things visually.[11] Similarly, when dancers or athletes are asked to visualise their skills, the parts of the brain that become active are those that are involved in planning and executing the relevant movements.

Overall, these brain-imaging studies show that, contrary to what most people believe, mental imagery is not a single ability but actually a collection of different mental processes that are controlled by different brain regions. Now that we have explained some of what happens in your mind's eye, let's consider some of the key characteristics of mental images.

Images differ in vividness

To begin with, images differ from each other in their vividness, clarity or realism. A 'vivid' image is one that clearly resembles the experience that it mimics. The greater the number of senses that you use to create an image, the more vivid the resulting experience. A simple way of increasing your imagery vividness skills is to examine an object from your sport (e.g. a rugby ball) using all your senses. Pay careful attention to what it looks like (what colour is it?; does it have a logo?), what it feels like (is it rough or smooth?), how heavy it is, and whether or not it has a distinctive smell.

Images differ in controllability

A second way in which images differ from each other is in controllability or the ease with which you can manipulate them for a specific purpose. The following box gives a test of your controllability skills.

The feather test

Can you imagine a feather falling from the ceiling, slowly wafting this way and that before gently landing on your desk? Now, try to imagine this feather reversing its path – floating back up towards the ceiling like a balloon, as if carried higher and higher by currents of air. If you found these images easy to create, you probably have good control over your visualisation.

And images differ in the feelings and emotions they evoke

A third feature of mental images is that they tend to evoke feelings (imagine how hard it would be to lift a packed filing cabinet) and emotions (recall how Roger Bannister trembled with anticipation when he imagined himself competing in an important race). Can you visualise yourself as a novice rock-climber standing on the ledge of a cliff face, not knowing what to do next? This mental picture should make you feel a little queasy. By contrast, can you imagine yourself scoring the winning goal for your country in the World Cup Final? Hopefully, this time, you should feel a surge of euphoria.

To summarise this section, mental images have a number of important characteristics. First, the process of forming a mental image uses a great deal of the same brain machinery or neural circuitry that we use in perception. In a way, it could be said that imagery occurs when we run perception backwards. Secondly, they are multisensory experiences that enable us to bring to mind sensations of absent people, objects, events and/or skills. Finally, images vary both in vividness and controllability. But what exactly are the practical implications of these ideas? In the box below we provide some practical tips on using mental imagery.

Using imagery: practical tips

Practise!

Remember that mental imagery is a skill that must be practised regularly for mastery – just like any other skill. For example, if you are a basketball player practising free throws, try to close your eyes for a second to 'see' and 'feel' each shot before you play it.

Be positive

When using your imagination, try to develop the habit of visualising a positive target (something to aim at) rather than a negative one (something that you want to avoid). For example, if you are a canoeist, try to picture your line through the gate. Remember, what you see is what you'll get.

Visualise specific actions rather than general results

In order to avoid daydreaming, it is better to visualise actions rather than results or scores. For example, in bowls, try to picture the shot that you want to play next rather than the score that you'd like to have for that end.

Use all your senses when forming your image

To increase the vividness of your images, try to combine as many of your senses as are relevant to the skill that you'd like to practise. For example, if you're mentally rehearsing a penalty kick in rugby, you should be able to 'feel' the turf under your feet and the weight of the ball as you place it on the ground. You should also be able to 'hear' the sound of the ball as you strike it and to 'see' its flight as you curl it between the posts.

Use imagery in practice sessions

Visualisation works best when it is alternated with periods of physical practice. So, you should develop the habit of spending a moment or two mentally rehearsing a skill or movement just before you go to start a training session.

Getting things in perspective

So far, we've introduced mental imagery, outlined what happens in your mind's eye when you imagine something, and sketched some properties of images. However, not everyone visualises things in the same way. To illustrate, when you imagine kicking a ball, do you see yourself on a screen as if you're watching someone else performing the skill, or do you feel as though you're actually kicking the ball yourself? There is an interesting difference between these perspectives, as we'll now explain.

Briefly, when you create a mental image of a skill, you have a choice of two perspectives to adopt. On the one hand, you could visualise yourself performing this skill as if you were watching a video replay on a screen. This approach is called 'external' imagery because it involves viewing your actions from outside your body, and it depends mainly on the visual sense.

On the other hand, you could combine various sensory experiences to create a feeling of what it would be like to perform the skill yourself – not watch someone else do it. In this case, you are using 'internal' or within-body imagery. Let's clarify this distinction by a golfing example. If you were visualising yourself playing golf on a wet and windy day from an *internal* perspective, you should not only be able to picture yourself hitting the ball, but you should also feel the weight of the club in your hands as well as the wind and rain on your face. In this case, the multisensory experience of imagery increases its vividness. If you find it difficult to imagine a skill from an internal perspective, it may help to pay attention to the feelings that are generated in each of your senses as you practise this skill.

Having explained this distinction at a theoretical level, let's now illustrate the difference between external and internal imagery perspectives by a practical example. The one we've chosen is adapted from an exercise devised by Tony Morris, Michael Spittle and Anthony Watt[12].

Imagery at the pool

In order to explore two different ways of looking at things in your mind's eye, let's imagine that you are a swimmer about to compete in a 100 metres freestyle race.

External imagery

Imagine standing on the blocks along with the other competitors, who are lined up on either side of you. You can see yourself as if you were on a large video screen, looking confident and relaxed. Although the other swimmers are standing to your left and right, your eyes are focused on the water in the pool, which looks blue and inviting. You adjust your cap and goggles and prepare for the starter's command. When you hear 'On your marks!', you bend forward – poised and ready for a powerful start. At the sound of the beep, you dive like an arrow into the pool. You are completely immersed in the water and hear nothing. All you can see is your streamlined shape under the water. You break the surface, kick hard and glide through the pool, using strong and powerful strokes. You're aware that the other swimmers are beginning to fall behind as you surge towards the wall. As you reach it, you start the turn. Flipping over, you can see yourself pushing hard against the wall as your body is submerged. The shape of your streamlined body is visible under the surface. As your head breaks the surface again, you can see that you're still in the lead. Looking totally focused, you glide through the water using powerful strokes.

Internal imagery

Imagine standing on the blocks along with the other competitors, who are lined up on either side of you. You feel that you are really there. You look around at the other competitors and are fully aware of all the sights and sounds around the pool. You can smell the chlorine at the pool and the water seems inviting. You adjust your cap and goggles until they feel just right and bounce up and down on your toes as you wait for the starter's command. When you hear 'On your marks!', you bend forward slowly and prepare your body for a powerful start. At the sound of the beep, you dive like an arrow into the pool. As soon as you hit the water, your body feels completely immersed. Your body feels streamlined and you kick hard. When you break the surface, you kick hard again and you can feel your powerful strokes helping you to glide through the pool. You're aware that the other swimmers are beginning to fall behind as you surge towards the wall. As you reach it, you start the turn. Flipping over, you can feel yourself pushing hard against the wall as your body is submerged. You start the turn, throwing your legs over your head and pushing your streamlined body tight and hard. As your head breaks the surface, you can see that you're still in the lead. Feeling totally focused, you glide through the water, using powerful strokes.

(Based on Morris, Spittle and Watt, 2005.)

Which imagery perspective is better?

An obvious question that arises from this exercise is, which of the two imagery perspectives is better? There is no clear answer to this question for two main reasons.

First, most athletes tend to switch their perspective as they become more proficient in their chosen sport. Indeed, research shows that about 25 per cent of expert canoeists can 'feel' the muscular movements involved in paddling – even when they're viewing themselves from an external imagery perspective.[13]

Second, each perspective has its own strengths and weaknesses. For example, the benefit of an external perspective is that it allows you to inspect your actions from different positions, thereby enabling you to correct obvious errors in your technique.

Of course, this assumes that your image-control skills are good enough to allow you to zoom in on the relevant aspects of the skill in question – something that cannot be taken for granted. On the other hand, the benefit of using an internal imagery perspective is that it should enhance the vividness or realism of the imaginary action. Furthermore, different sport skills may require different types of imagery. In particular, external imagery may be helpful for skills in activities such as gymnastics or rock-climbing in which body 'form' or shape is important. This perspective may also be useful for open skills such as making a tackle in soccer. On the other hand, internal imagery may be more suitable for skills that depend on perceptual sequencing such as canoe-slalom paddling or catching the ball in rugby. Also, an internal imagery perspective may be best for closed skills that are largely self-paced such as dart throwing or the free throw in basketball.

Now that we have outlined the main difference between external and internal imagery, let's summarise research findings on imagery in sport. After that, we'll give you a few practical tips on how to use imagery to practise your sport skills mentally.

Imagery in sport: guidelines from research

Based on hundreds of studies of imagery in sport, a number of conclusions have emerged, and these are summarised below.

Visual and kinaesthetic imagery are most common

First, visual and kinaesthetic (feeling-oriented) imagery seem to be more popular than other kinds of visualisation among athletes. This finding is not really surprising because most athletic activities demand some degree of eye–hand coordination and 'feel'. To illustrate the latter requirement, consider what the Spanish tennis star Rafael Nadal said after he had defeated Lleyton Hewitt at the 2006 French Open to set a new record of 57 consecutive wins on clay courts: 'Today I think I played my best match. I could feel the ball.'[14]

Imagery is used more frequently by successful athletes than unsuccessful ones

Second, research shows that successful athletes tend to use imagery more often than less successful athletes. Again, this discovery is not really surprising as it's been reported that 90 per cent of a sample of athletes at the US Olympic Training Centre claimed to use imagery regularly.

Imagery is common before competition

Third, athletes tend to use imagery more in pre-competitive than in training situations. This trend indicates that sports performers visualise more for performance enhancement in competition than for skill improvement in practice.

Imagery can be motivational

Fourth, athletes appear to use imagery for both motivational and cognitive purposes. Although the precise motivational value of imagery has not been fully established, there is no doubt that imagery can make it easier for you to visualise your goals, and to feel positive about having the capacity to achieve those goals.

Rafael Nadal (courtesy of Inpho Photography)

Imagery content is not clear-cut

Fifth, studies of the content of athletes' imagery show that performance is better when they visualise a positive target rather than a negative one. Despite this advice, many sports performers are plagued by negative images involving dreaded mistakes and the possibility of encountering bad luck.

Using imagery

Athletes can use imagery for a variety of purposes, including skill learning and practice (as in mentally rehearsing skills such as goal kicking or free throwing), developing tactical and game skills (going over a game plan in your mind for a forthcoming match), preparation for competition (using imagery to familiarise yourself with a match venue), attempting to improve psychological skills (using visualisation to increase your confidence or to reduce your anxiety), and engaging in pain reduction (imagining a pleasant situation to distract yourself from the gruelling pain of running a marathon). Let us explain in greater detail.

Mental practice

As we mentioned earlier, you can use imagery to rehearse mentally sport skills (e.g. tennis serve, golf drive) by 'seeing' and 'feeling' yourself performing these actions in your imagination before doing them in reality. We'll give you some practical tips on this application of imagery in the next section.

Developing strategies and plans

You can also use imagery for strategic reasons such as formulating a game plan before a competitive event or trying to counteract opponents' tactics during a match.

Preparing for competition

Imagery is being used increasingly as a form of 'dress rehearsal' for the big day. For example, the former England cricket batsman Mike Atherton used to practise in his mind's eye in an effort to improve his ability to anticipate distractions:

> What I find really good for me is to just spend a few solitary moments out on the pitch either the day before or on the morning of the match which is when I do the visualisation stuff – what's going to come, who's going to bowl, how they are going to bowl, what tactics they will use, what's going to be said to try and get under my skin so that nothing can come as a surprise . . . the visualisation is vital.[15]

Increasing motivation

Elsewhere in the book, we've explained the motivational value of specifying goals as clearly as possible. You can do this very well through the use of imagery; for example, imagining yourself feeling tired but happy after a long training run could give you a motivational boost for an upcoming marathon.

Reducing anxiety

Imagery can also help you to feel relaxed and to behave calmly in anticipated stressful situations. Richard Faulds (the British shooter) created the image of an 'ice-man' prior to winning the 2000 Olympic gold medal for trapshooting: 'The image is the ice-man. You walk like an ice-man and think like an ice-man.'[16]

Increasing confidence

Many athletes report that a relationship exists between imagery and confidence. This link is nicely illustrated by the champion golfer Nick Faldo. Speaking of the time in the early 1990s when he won three majors, he said:

> In each of those weeks, I had total confidence in what I was doing. I was picking a shot, visualizing it and trusting myself to pull it off. I could stand up there and do precisely what I intended to do.[17]

Nick Faldo (courtesy of Inpho Photography)

Improving concentration

As we explained in Chapter 5, mental imagery is used widely by athletes as a concentration strategy. For example, Jonny Wilkinson, the English rugby place-kicker, regularly imagines that he's a golfer and that his foot is a 7-iron.[18] Another image that he favours is that of a jeering mouth behind the goal. He holds this image in mind and attempts to send the ball down its throat (see Chapter 5).

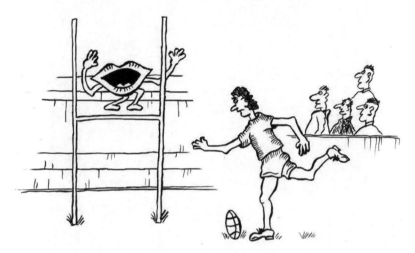

The goal mouth!

Yet another image is knocking a can of Coke out of the hand of a woman called Doris who sits in a particular seat in the stand behind the goal. Although such imagery seems bizarre, it has a clear logical function – to remind him to kick *through* the ball, not at it.

Recovery from injury and managing pain

One of the latest roles for imagery is as a tool for physical rehabilitation. When Steve Backley (the British javelin thrower who won medals at three successive Olympic Games between 1992 and 2000) was unable to walk or train after he had sprained an ankle some years ago, he began to use imagery as part of his re-habilitation. Sitting in a chair, he imagined himself throwing the javelin in each of the world's top sports stadia. Astonishingly, he estimated afterwards that he had mentally 'hurled' over 1,000 javelins during that period of injury. Even more remarkably, when he returned to competition a few weeks later, he continued where he had left off before the injury and achieved his Olympic goals.

From these examples, you can see that imagery has many possible applications in sport, but this versatility should make you cautious because many of the

Steve Backley (courtesy of Inpho Photography)

alleged uses of imagery have not been verified adequately. However, there is one use of imagery that is both popular and well validated – mental practice (MP).

Mental practice (MP): practical tips

As we indicated earlier in this chapter, MP involves rehearsing skills in your mind's eye before actually performing them. Although it may seem like a modern invention, MP is not a new technique at all. In fact, psychological interest in MP is as old as the discipline of psychology itself. Over a century ago, William James suggested, rather counter-intuitively, that you actually learn to skate in the summer and to swim in the winter – because of the way in which you anticipate experiences in your imagination.[19] Since that era, the effects of MP on skilled performance have been studied extensively by psychologists.[20] From these studies, a number of conclusions have emerged:

1. **MP can improve your skilled performance.** Relative to not practising at all, MP improves skilled performance. Not surprisingly, MP is less effective than physical practice in helping people to master sport skills – presumably because it doesn't provide any actual muscular feedback to the practitioner.
2. **MP works best when combined with physical practice.** When combined and alternated with physical practice, MP tends to produce better skill learning than that resulting from either MP or physical practice alone.
3. **MP is helpful for cognitive skills.** MP improves the performance of cognitive sport skills (that is those that involve some degree of sequential planning such as skiing, paddling, motor sports or equestrian events) more than motor skills or strength tasks.
4. **MP is more suitable for skilful than novice athletes.** In general, MP tends to be more effective for those who are already proficient in the skills that they are trying to improve. Novices do not benefit from MP as much as experts because their mental 'blueprint' of the skill in question is not very well established.
5. **MP is more effective for people with good imagery skills.** Available evidence suggests that those who are adept at generating and controlling vivid images tend to benefit more from visualisation than do people who lack such imagery abilities.
6. **MP effects decline fairly quickly.** Although there are only a few studies on this topic, it seems that the positive effects of MP on skilled performance tend to decline quite sharply over time.

In summary, there is now abundant evidence that MP is a powerful and effective technique for improving the learning and performance of a variety of sport skills. These skills include not only 'closed' actions (that is ones which are self-paced) such as golf putting, throwing darts or place-kicking but also 'open' or reactive ones (which depend on other factors such as tackling in soccer or rugby). But how exactly does MP work?

Although many theories of MP have been proposed since the 1930s, the psychological mechanisms that underlie it are still unclear. Nevertheless, three main theories hold sway – the 'neuromuscular' model, the cognitive account, and the 'bioinformational' approach.[21]

Briefly, the neuromuscular model proposes that imagining an action causes faint activity in the muscles that are used to perform the skill in question.

This faint activity helps you to practise the skill as if you were actually doing it. By contrast, cognitive theories claim that MP helps you to pay attention to and remember key elements of the skill being rehearsed. In other words, it works by changing your mental 'blueprint' of a skill or movement. Finally, the 'bio-informational' theory claims that MP effects reflect a complex interaction between three factors – the environment in which the movement in question is performed ('stimulus' information), what is felt as the movement occurs ('response' information), and the perceived importance of this skill to the performer ('meaning' information).

At this stage, however, let's leave the theories aside and examine instead how MP works. Perhaps the best way of doing this is by taking you through a visualisation exercise in golf putting (see below).

Golf putting . . . in your mind's eye

The purpose of this exercise is to help you to 'see' and 'feel' your putting stroke in your mind's eye. By learning to visualise this stroke, you can practise it even when you're not playing golf. Please make sure that you are sitting comfortably with your eyes closed and that you will not be disturbed for the next few minutes.

Imagine standing on the green of a particular hole at your local golf course on a bright summer morning. The flag is lying to the side of the green, casting a small shadow from the sun, and you are all alone. Your ball is lying about a metre from the hole and you are standing comfortably beside it. As you look at the ball, you can see it glistening in the sunshine and feel the weight of your putter in your hand. You can also feel the springy grass underneath your feet. Walking slowly to one side, you stand behind the ball and crouch down to assess the situation – noting a slight slope to the left. After a few seconds, you begin to see the best line for your putt, and to make absolutely sure, you imagine drawing a white line between the hole and your ball. Slowly, you allow your eyes to gaze back and forth along this white line – back and forth, back and forth. Your target for this line is a slightly yellowish blade of grass which lies about a foot from where your ball lies. You look at this blade of grass to remind you of the line you have chosen. Then you stand up slowly and approach the ball. Standing directly over the ball, you lower your shoulders, get comfortable, and adjust your feet so that you're standing square to your putting line. Your set-up feels nice and relaxed and you breathe out gently – slowly and deliberately. Then, keeping your head still, you take two or three gentle practice swings – feeling your shoulders, arms and putter working together as a solid unit. Feel the smooth follow-through of your practice swing each time. Now, you're ready. So, you glance at the hole one more time, focus on the yellow blade of grass, and then release your swing. Slowly and gently, you guide the ball down the line.

Having examined the theory of MP and given you an example of how it works in golf, let's now turn to the practical question of how you can apply this technique to your own sports.

MP: four steps to success

MP involves four steps. First, you have to prepare your mind by relaxing as much as possible. Second, you have to create the mental image of the skill that you wish to practise. Third, you should try to recall a successful performance of that skill by 'replaying' it in your mind. Finally, you should programme this visualisation into your mental preparation by combining it with a pre-performance routine.

Before you begin these steps, however, you must be quite clear and specific about the specific skill or situation that you'd like to rehearse in your mind's eye. So, let's start by pausing for a moment to pick a specific skill or situation that you would like to practise in your mind. Describe it in the box.

Mental practice (MP) in action

The skill/situation which I want to practise is —— .

When did you last perform this skill correctly?

(We ask this question so that you will bring to mind a specific example of yourself performing this skill successfully.)

Now that we've picked a skill to work on, let's explore the four steps of MP.

Step 1: relax

People visualise best when they are relaxed. That's one of the reasons why you often find yourself daydreaming as you sit comfortably in a bus or train. In general, imagery occurs spontaneously in our minds when we feel relaxed. One of the best ways to relax your body is through the deep (with your diaphragm rather than your chest)-breathing exercise. Before you begin this exercise, sit down in a quiet place and close your eyes. Now, slowly 'centre' your body by lowering your shoulders gently. Then, gently flap out any tension that may be present in your arms and legs. After that, take 10 deep breaths – making sure that you're pushing your stomach *out* slowly when you breathe in and pulling *in* your stomach gently when you breathe out. Over time, you can train your body to relax even better by saying the word 'relax' to yourself as you breathe deeply. One way of doing this is to say '**re**' when you breathe **in** – and '**lax**' as you breathe **out**. Remember – re-lax.

Step 2: create your image

Now that you feel relaxed, you will find it easier to create the situation or skill that you wish to visualise.

Think of and picture a skill or movement that you wish to improve in your next training/practice session. Close your eyes and imagine the venue where you will be performing this skill. Now try to see yourself doing this skill. Take a few minutes to imagine this scene as vividly as possible – notice details of the sights, sounds and bodily sensations that you are experiencing.

Step 3: rehearse

Now see and feel yourself performing the skill slowly, smoothly and correctly.

Notice how calm and confident you feel as you perform the movements in your mind. At first, it may help to slow down the movements – as though you're watching a slow-motion video of yourself playing the skill perfectly.

As you get better at visualisation, however, you should form images in 'real time' (that is, at the same speed as in real life). Watch yourself performing this skill over and over again for a moment or two.

Step 4: make routine

Combining visualisation with a pre-performance routine is a technique for improving your concentration. As we explained in Chapter 4, a pre-performance routine is simply a series of actions that prepares you for your stroke/skill. It is like the steps of a stairs that takes you to your favourite place – your quiet zone where you will be free from distractions. At the beginning and end of your routine, visualise clearly what you want to achieve in your performance.

Chapter 7

Improving

There's nothing wrong with getting knocked down,
as long as you get right back up.
                    Attributed to Muhammad Ali

The man who makes no mistakes does not usually
make anything.
                    Edward John Phelps, 1889[1]

Ever tried. Ever failed. No matter. Try again. Fail
again. Fail better.
                    Samuel Beckett, 'Worstward Ho', 1983[2]

If you're looking for average, then try not to make
mistakes but if you're looking to be great, you've got
to make loads of mistakes.
                    Pádraig Harrington, 2006[3]

Introduction

ALTHOUGH IT IS DIFFICULT to accept defeat or failure in
any aspect of life, it is surprisingly easy to develop the
habit of seeing such setbacks as someone else's fault. This
tendency to blame other people for our own misfortunes is
so prevalent in sport that it has even induced Brad Gilbert,

137

Muhammad Ali (courtesy of Inpho Photography)

the renowned tennis coach, to joke about his role as a professional scapegoat for his players. Although he has guided champions including André Agassi, Andy Roddick and, more recently, Andy Murray, Gilbert is honest enough to admit that, in his experience, coaches are the first ones to be blamed or sacked when things go wrong.[4]

Make no mistake, shifting responsibility in this way is self-defeating in the long run. Ironically, if you play the 'blame game' regularly as a performer, *you're* the one who will lose out in the end because you have denied yourself something very valuable – the possibility of learning from the feedback (however unpleasant) that any setback provides and moving forward or improving.

With this in mind, the purpose of this chapter is twofold. First, we'll show you how to develop a helpful way of 'framing', or looking constructively at, setbacks in sport so that you can either learn from them or use them to motivate you in some way. Second, we'll arm you with some practical advice on developing effective mistake-management techniques.

At the outset, let's clarify an important point. Mistakes aren't always bad for us in sport, especially if we can use them to our advantage. An example of this latter possibility comes from the world of snooker. Briefly, in the 1997 Thailand Open, Nigel Bond staged a remarkable comeback to defeat the world champion at that time, Stephen Hendry. The most surprising aspect of this comeback, however, was that it was triggered by an error! To explain, because Bond had thought that the match was a best of *eleven* rather than nine frames, he was not unduly perturbed by Hendry's early lead in the game and played in a relaxed frame of mind, not realising how close he was to defeat.

Strictly speaking, it wasn't really a mistake that helped Bond's performance. It was actually his ability to stay calm when he fell behind that made all the difference. Interestingly, research suggests that mistakes can help players to improve their skills.[5] This happens when players realise that their mistakes mark the boundaries of what is currently possible for them. By implication, the number and type of mistakes we make define the limits of our performance at any given time.

The idea that mistakes define boundaries has at least one practical implication. Briefly, if you receive positive feedback on almost everything you do in sport, you won't improve your skills very much because you're working too close to your comfort zone. To avoid 'coasting' on talent alone, you have to be adventurous – and be ready to push out the boundaries of your performance. This point was highlighted by the golfer Pádraig Harrington, the winner of the European Order of Merit for 2006 and the 2007 Open Championship, when he said:

> You can't be great at anything unless you explore it right to the edge and if you're going to the edge, mistakes will definitely follow. That's the way it is. If you're looking for the comfort of not making mistakes and not failing, you'll finish up mediocre. . . . But reaching greatness requires falling off the edge a load of times and having the courage to get back up and get on with it.[6]

And that brings us to the main theme of this chapter – the idea that to achieve success in sport you must be able to put your mistakes behind you and simply 'get on with it', as Harrington advises. A good example of this type of mental toughness in action comes from the manner in which Tiger Woods won the 2004 WGC Matchplay Tournament despite playing relatively poorly in the final against Davis Love. Although Woods struggled with erratic driving throughout this match, his excellent mistake-management skills enabled him to recover from the trouble that he had created for himself. And so, he was able to grind out a victory – or 'win ugly', as Brad Gilbert would say.

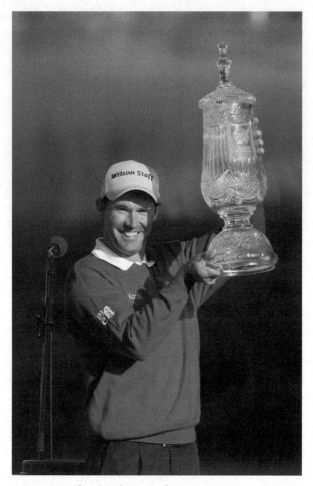

Pádraig Harrington (courtesy of Inpho Photography)

Getting on with it

In general, the ability to bounce back from setbacks requires three important psychological steps.

First, you need to develop the *right attitude* to setbacks from the beginning. Winners in sport tend to 'frame' their errors as temporary misfortunes that are caused by factors that can be changed in the future – not fatal diseases! In other words, mistakes challenge us to work harder on our skills. Unfortunately, most of us fail to grasp this challenge because we tend to seek excuses for our errors.

Second, you need to *check your assumptions* from time to time. This step involves looking in the mirror (see Chapter 3) and addressing some deep-seated beliefs about your sporting performance. Do you expect to play flawlessly all the time? If so, then your impossible standards are setting you up for a hard fall. Remember that in competitive sport, your performance is always a compromise between what you'd really like to achieve and what is possible in the prevailing circumstances. To illustrate, let's imagine that you're a good tennis player who loves to play an attacking serve-and-volley style in every match. That's a nice aspiration but is clearly unrealistic on certain occasions. For example, you'll have to make compromises when the weather is windy and your serve is affected – not to mention matches in which your opponent slows the game down in an effort to break your momentum. In these situations, you have to learn to ignore your mistakes as you attempt to grind out a win – just as Tiger Woods did against Davis Love in 2004.

The third requirement in dealing with setbacks is that you need a toolbox of practical *mistake-management techniques* to use when things go wrong. These techniques are designed to help you to let go of errors so that you don't dwell on them unnecessarily. They're helpful in preventing us from engaging in 'snowballing' – a form of chained thinking in which we allow one negative idea to trigger another one like a snowball rolling downhill.[7] You might say, 'If I miss a tackle early in the game, I always play badly.' This thought could make you so anxious that you concede a foul in your first challenge of the match – which then leads you to lose confidence and 'hide' on the pitch for a while. The main benefit of mistake-management techniques is that they stop the 'snowball' from gathering momentum by preventing you from indulging in fortune-telling and by helping you to snap back into the present. Not surprisingly, the importance of mistake-management skills is especially evident in top level sport.

For example, Bill Beswick, the sport psychologist to the England soccer team under Steve McClaren, believes that without specific training in mistake-management techniques, players are especially vulnerable to lapses in control and performance on the pitch.[8] Later in the chapter, we'll provide some practical tips to help you in this aspect of your game.

Before we finish this section, we should also note that mistakes contribute to the dramatic appeal of competitive sport. In fact, you could argue that from a spectator's perspective, the real drama of watching top sports stars in action comes not from admiring their robotic perfection but from anticipating how they will react to setbacks during the event itself. And that leads us to the obvious question – why are setbacks inevitable in sport?

Prepare to make mistakes

Everyone makes mistakes. So, when Tiger Woods (playing for the US team) hit his first drive into a lake in the 2006 Ryder Cup match against Europe at the K-Club

(Kildare, Ireland), inadvertently he was reminded that setbacks are part and parcel of competitive sport, because no matter how skilful you are as a performer, you will slip up occasionally. For example, consider the mishaps by top-level athletes in the 'Whoops!' box.

Whoops!

- The top French tennis player Cedric Pioline once served *four consecutive double faults* in a single game at Wimbledon (in the 2000 championship) – something that rarely happens even to a novice.[9]
- The American 50 metres rifle shooter Matthew Emmons squandered the opportunity to win a second gold medal at the 2004 Olympic Games in Athens when he fired at the *wrong target* on his last shot.[10]
- And the Ethiopian athlete Kenenisa Bekele (a 10,000 metres Olympic champion and one of the world's best distance runners) famously lost a race because he actually *miscounted* the number of laps he had completed in the 2005 Boston Indoor Games. To explain, although indoor 3,000 metres races take place over 15 laps, Bekele raced for only 14 laps. Pausing after this lap in the mistaken belief that the race was over, he slowed down and allowed Ireland's Alistair Cragg to pass him and win the race.[11]

Although Woods, Pioline, Emmons and Bekele were able to put their mistakes behind them and get on with their careers, Andres Escobar, the Colombian soccer star, was not so fortunate. Tragically, his sporting error actually cost him his life. He scored an own goal in his country's loss to the host nation, USA, in the 1994 World Cup finals. This mistake led to large-scale gambling losses among some Colombians. Venting their fury on him, these gamblers shot Escobar dead when he arrived home after the football tournament.

Why are mistakes inevitable in sport? Several reasons spring to mind. To begin with the most obvious one, it is impossible to play flawlessly all the time because nobody's perfect. Even Muhammad Ali, one of the greatest athletes of all time, experienced defeats both before and *after* he became a world champion. But he never lost his confidence as a boxer because he knew that one loss doesn't make you a loser. In his own words:

> Only a man who knows what it is like to be defeated can reach down to the bottom of his soul and come up with the extra ounce of power it takes to win when the match is even.[12]

Secondly, the pressures and distractions of competition induce errors among even the world's best performers. A third reason why mistakes abound in sport is

Andres Escobar (courtesy of Inpho Photography)

because it's very difficult to anticipate the way in which opponents may play or react in a game – and errors can creep in as you try to adjust to what they're doing.

...But don't fear them!

Although it's important to strive for a perfect performance every time you play sport, it is very unhelpful to castigate yourself for failing to achieve it. Nevertheless, some people set impossibly high standards for themselves all the time. Let's explore this issue in more detail.

'Perfectionism' probably involves two separate but related habits: a tendency to set excessively high standards for your own performance and a habit of criticising yourself harshly for failing to achieve them. Underlying these unhealthy habits lies an uncompromising 'all or nothing' belief – the assumption that if you don't perform perfectly all of the time, you're a failure. There is no middle ground for the perfectionist.

As you would expect, this type of thinking causes lots of problems for you as a sports performer. For example, it encourages you to associate mistakes with failure and to become preoccupied with avoiding errors at all costs. And by influencing you to dwell on your mistakes, perfectionism makes you lose sight of the skills that you performed well in a given situation.

Not surprisingly, the more extreme your level of perfectionism, the less tolerance you will show for even the most trivial of errors. The result of this 'over-concern' for mistakes is that perfectionist performers end up being motivated more by a fear of failure than by the hope for success. The trouble with this outlook is that it leads to unnecessary anxiety. Put simply, people who are scared of making mistakes tend to become unusually nervous in competitive situations, and their performance suffers a result. Again, in the words of Muhammad Ali, 'He who is not prepared to take risks will accomplish nothing in life.'[13]

So, take risks, be prepared to make mistakes – but how exactly do mistakes affect sports performers?

The psychology of mistakes

Mistakes affect athletes in a number of ways; some obvious, others more subtle. On the obvious side, they can alter the result of a sporting contest – if your team concedes a needless penalty kick in injury time in a match where the scores are level, you are likely to lose the game. Less obviously, mistakes affect the way in which athletes think, feel and behave in competitive situations.

Thinking

To begin with, mistakes can make you think differently about your game – if you make a bad blunder early in a match, you may decide that it's not your day and begin to imagine that other mistakes are predestined to occur later. This kind of superstitious thinking is very common in sport. Often, the first link in the chain of such thinking is a negative voice that we hear inside our heads scolding us for making mistakes ('That's awful – you're playing like a loser'). By contrast, top players have developed mistake-management skills that enable them to ignore such negative 'self-talk' and to focus instead on thinking clearly about what to do next. This approach is illustrated nicely by Pádraig Harrington, who observed: 'I know I can't swing it well every day but there is no reason why I can't think well every day.'[14]

Mistakes can also affect you emotionally – they can dent your confidence and make you feel frustrated and angry. Indeed, of all the emotional reactions caused by mistakes, anger is probably the most commonly experienced. So, how does it affect your performance in sport?

Although anger may have certain temporary physical benefits (for example, it can increase your physical strength and intensity), it invariably impairs rather than enhances people's performance over time. This is particularly true in sports (such as golf) that require a combination of skills such as precise eye–hand coordination, fine perceptual judgement and delicate motor movements.

Nevertheless, anger is widespread in sport. For example, even in the sedate world of golf, some players have been known to lose their temper with dramatic consequences on the course. An American golfer named Danny Goodman (who competed on the European Tour in the early 1980s) is said to have once decapitated his clubs by driving his car all over them after he had failed to make the cut in a tournament in Germany![15] However, his emotional reactions to mistakes seem positively restrained compared to those of a compatriot from an earlier era – the infamous Lefty Stackhouse. This latter golfer competed in the 1940s and had a ferocious temper that occasionally resulted in him punching himself![16] Not surprisingly, this unusual mistake-management routine was not very effective in helping him to achieve tournament success.

In general, winners in sport tend to have a mood profile characterised by lower levels of anger and depression than less successful counterparts. This is known as the iceberg profile[17] because negative mood scores are all below the average (or waterline), while the score for vigour is elevated. Curiously, however, there is an ambivalent attitude to anger in sport. For example, supporters of the 'let rip' approach often cite John McEnroe as someone who appeared to play *better* tennis when enraged by some perceived injustice on court than when calm. This brings us to consider a practical question for players and coaches – if you reduce the anger, do you impair a player's performance?

You can't take it away from him – or can you?

Many top coaches are wary of calming athletes' anger in case it reduces their drive, competitiveness and performance on the field of play. After the England soccer star Wayne Rooney had been sent off for stamping on Ricardo Carvalho in the 2006 World Cup quarter-final match against Portugal, his manager, Sven-Göran Eriksson remarked, 'Of course, he has a temperament [sic] but you have to live with that. You can't take that away from him because he would never be the same player.'[18]

Wayne Rooney (courtesy of Inpho Photography)

Eriksson's view raises an old problem in sport. If you control your temper, do you lose your edge as a player? Many players and managers believe that you do. For example, Ronnie O'Sullivan, the brilliant but mercurial snooker player, believes that venting your emotions is a good thing in sport because it shows your 'character'. Indeed, after O'Sullivan had been criticised for making an obscene gesture at the 2004 Embassy World Championship, he said:

> I'll keep showing my feelings by swearing and gesturing at the pockets . . . I'm not switching off my emotions for anyone and if I swear at a pocket while playing it's because I'm annoyed and showing some character. What's wrong with that?[19]

Well, to answer O'Sullivan's rhetorical question, all we have to do is to look at athletes whose performance *improved* when they learned to curb their temper and transform their anger into self-control. For example, consider the case of Bjorn Borg, the former tennis star with the ice-cool temperament who won eleven grand slam titles in his career. Remarkably, he revealed that he had been a volatile player in his early years: 'When I was twelve, I behaved badly on court, swearing, cheating, throwing rackets – so my club suspended me for six months. When I came back, I didn't open my mouth . . . I felt that I played my best tennis being focused.'[20] Clearly, as you can see, Borg wasn't always as cool as the iceberg that he became in later years! And so, hot anger can be turned into cool concentration.

Doing

The third way in which mistakes affect athletes is by influencing their behaviour during a game. For example, a soccer player who makes a silly mistake in a match may subsequently hide on the pitch, avoiding passes from team-mates or shirking defensive or attacking responsibilities. Based on such experience, many players have developed strategies for trying to correct this problem. One common approach is to try to wipe clean the mistake by taking a decisive action shortly afterwards. This 'overcompensation' effect is well known to coaches and players – and may lead to bigger problems, as riskier options are attempted. For example, according to Keith Wood, the former Ireland and Lions rugby captain:

> There was a time when, if I made an error, I wanted to immediately make up for it by doing something spectacular. Inevitably, I would make a further error and compound the situation. Now I have developed a routine whereby I repeat a mantra word to myself. This clears my mind, and I then focus on next doing a simple thing well.[21]

In summary, we've seen that mistakes can affect players at the level of thinking, feeling and doing. Let's combine these three levels now to explore how Alan, a fictitious badminton player, has been trained to react better to his unforced errors on court (box).

Mistake management in action

Alan is a young, extremely talented badminton player who has recently been selected for the national squads for his age group. Unfortunately, his volatile temperament is holding him back from further progress. This flaw is particularly evident in Alan's reaction to mistakes. For example, Michael, his coach, has noticed that when Alan makes an unforced error, his first reaction is to throw his racket on the ground or to hit the net. This display of temper has not only earned him penalty points in several national tournaments but also puts him in the wrong frame of mind for the next point during games. Michael is also worried about how easily Alan criticises himself aloud and uses swear words on court – reactions that send all the wrong messages to his opponents. After some advice from a sport psychologist, Michael tries to replace Alan's faulty habits with the following mistake-management strategies on court.

Whenever he makes an error, Alan imitates or 'shadows' the shot that he should have played. This helps him to correct the mistake and override the memory of it when he prepares to play a similar shot later in the game.

Another mistake-management strategy used by Alan is to acknowledge the mistake, turn his back on it to symbolise putting it in the past, and then turn around again to face his opponent, either to serve or receive.

Finally, Alan has been taught to release his frustration after a mistake either by standing still for a moment or by smiling. This helps to defuse his tension and annoyance.

The latest news about Alan is that he's working very hard on his game and has become a lot more consistent on court. He's still prone to losing his temper from time to time, but, overall, Alan and the national coach are very pleased with his progress.

Putting it behind you

Earlier in the chapter, we explained that even the best make mistakes from time to time. That may not be much consolation to you, however, as you struggle with the basics of your own sport. But what might make a difference to you is the idea that mistakes, by themselves, are rarely decisive in any game. Instead, what really matters is how quickly and how efficiently you can manage to put errors behind you and get on with the game. As the former champion golfer Gary Player remarked, 'The toughest thing for people to learn in golf is to accept bad holes and then to forget about them.'[22] Clearly, the way in which you react to, and recover from, mistakes tells us a lot about your mental toughness. For example, according to Graeme Souness, the former Liverpool soccer player and Premiership manager: 'You can judge people's character in the little things – like the way they react to a tackle from behind or if they miss a goal-chance.'[23]

Mistakes, or the way in which we react to them, provide a window to an athlete's mind. Endorsing this idea, the sport psychologist Bill Beswick claimed that when he watches a soccer match he is probably the only person in the stadium not looking at the ball.[24] Instead, his eyes are focused on how his team's players react to setbacks. Do they wave their hands and appeal to the referee when they lose the ball

Keith Wood (courtesy of Inpho Photography)

in a tackle?; do they lash out and try to foul the player who won the ball?; or do they track back, chase down their opponent, and try to retrieve the ball fairly? Each of these reactions tells us something valuable about a player's mental strengths. But what if you are afraid to make a mistake in the first place?

Understanding errors and mistakes

So far, we have been using the words 'error' and 'mistake' interchangeably, but there is an important if rather subtle technical difference between them.[25] Specifically, whereas errors are unintended or undesirable actions (that is, skills that are appropriate to a given situation but that are executed in a faulty manner – such as serving a double fault in tennis), mistakes are best defined as inappropriate actions stemming from faulty perception, judgement or analysis (such as passing the ball to an opponent rather than a team-mate in basketball). Another way of looking at errors is to regard them as situations where there is a discrepancy between planning and execution of a given skill. Let's explain what we mean by this statement.

If you practise any task extensively, it will become automatic or capable of being performed without thinking. At first glance, this phenomenon of automaticity seems like a good thing because it means that you will be able to perform a highly practised skill quicker and more efficiently than previously. It also means that your mind has been freed to pay attention to other things. However, a disadvantage of automaticity is that it removes the need for you to check consciously what's going on as you perform the skill in question. In other words, a lot of automatic behaviour consists of habits that are hard to change. Clearly, *not* thinking about what you're doing can sometimes lead to error. So, what kinds of errors have been identified?

Several ways of classifying errors have been proposed.[26] For example, there is a difference between errors of omission (leaving out something) and those of commission (adding something inappropriate). Let's explore this distinction in more detail.

Errors of *omission* are situations in which you should have performed a certain action but did not. For example, if you forget to sign your card after playing a round of golf, you have committed this type of error. That's exactly what happened to the golfer Pádraig Harrington, who was disqualified for not signing his card in the Benson & Hedges Open Tournament at the Belfry in 2000 after the third round, when he led the field by five strokes. Typically, errors of omission happen because an old habit has replaced an intended action. After all, golfers don't usually fill in or sign cards when they're playing practice rounds. Therefore, a habit of walking off the last green without your pen and card in hand could easily override the correct 'card-signing' routine after a round of competitive golf. On the other hand, an error of *commission* occurs when you perform an action that you should not have executed. For example, if you are a soccer defender and you handle a ball going over your head, you've committed this type of error.

Another way of classifying sporting mishaps is to put them into some kind of theoretical framework according to what may have caused them. For example, we can distinguish between skill-based and rule-based errors.

Skill-based errors happen when you absentmindedly fail to monitor the outcome of a highly practised action and, as a result, repeat it needlessly. For example, if you're a golfer, you probably have an established green-reading routine that involves squatting down and looking at the ball and hole several times, from different angles, before deciding on the line of the putt. However, if your mind is not fully on the job, you may end up going through your routine on automatic pilot and not absorbing relevant information because you're thinking of something else. So, unless you deliberately remind yourself what the line of the putt is (for example, 'My line is slightly to the left of the hole'), you may end up having to repeat the routine because your mind was elsewhere.

Rule-based errors happen when the action occurs as planned, but the plan *itself* turns out to be wrong because it was based on faulty analysis. Imagine yourself as a soccer coach who forms a game plan for a match based on the apparent weaknesses of a specific player on the opposing team (for example, the goalkeeper who has a tendency to stay on the line rather than going for crosses and commanding the penalty area). If your entire game plan is based on exploiting this player's weakness, you may receive a nasty shock when you discover that this goalkeeper has not been selected by the team in question. Clearly, the error in this case lies in poor planning.

Despite their differences, errors and mistakes challenge us to learn from the feedback that they provide. So, in the remainder of this chapter, we'll explore how to analyse and learn from the setbacks that you experience in your sport.

Using errors to improve your game: asking the right questions

A key theme of this chapter is that mistakes provide feedback for the prepared mind. But in order to benefit from the feedback that errors provide, you must be able to analyse them properly. This means asking yourself a series of incisive questions in an effort to pinpoint precisely which aspect of your game let you down – and why.

To learn from setbacks, we need to remind ourselves of the four hypothetical quadrants of athletic performance – physical, technical, tactical and psychological. First, the physical side of your performance refers to concepts such as fitness, strength and stamina that can be measured objectively. The 'technical' side involves your level of skill or proficiency in your chosen sport. Next, we have the 'tactical' dimension, which refers to your awareness of the strategic aspects of your game. Included here are such skills as planning and decision-making. Finally, the 'psycho-logical' aspect of your performance refers to your mental fitness for competitive action.

Asking incisive questions about your performance is probably the best way to begin to analyse your errors and mistakes, and it provides a natural follow-up to the skills outlined in Chapter 3.

Analysing your golfing errors and mistakes

If you play golf, it is important to review your performance regularly. One of the best ways of doing this is to ask the following questions about your errors and mistakes.

1. What exactly happened when I made the error? The more precisely you can answer this question, the better. For example, in golf the statement, 'I missed a putt', is less helpful than 'I judged the distance of my putt wrongly and it fell short of the hole.'

2. When did my mistake happen? For example, did your putting let you down as you got more tired towards the end of the round? If so, then it may be helpful to note, 'I missed four short putts over the last seven holes.'

3. What was the result of my mistake? Usually, this consequence can be described quite easily. For example, 'I lost two shots on that hole because I three-putted from a short distance.'

4. How did I react to the mistake? A common reaction is to let the mistake linger in your mind so that it prevents you from playing properly afterwards. In this case, you might note, 'I got angry with myself and couldn't keep my mistake out of my mind as I played the next few holes.'

5. What parts of my game (physical, technical, tactical or psychological) should I review? If your errors tend to happen in the last few holes, perhaps you need to work on your physical fitness as well as your concentration.

Developing the right attitude to mistakes – the good, the bad and the ugly

As we indicated earlier, errors and mistakes in sport tend to produce a variety of reactions among athletes. These reactions include the good (trying to learn from them or using them as motivating factors), the bad (thinking superstitiously about them), and the ugly (losing emotional control and allowing the setback to affect your performance).

Interestingly, as we explained, the tennis coach Brad Gilbert coined the phrase 'winning ugly' to describe the strategy of grinding out results by doing what you have to do in order to secure a victory.[27] Borrowing from Gilbert, we've coined the phrase 'losing ugly'.

Losing ugly

For us, 'losing ugly' is the worst way of reacting to errors and mistakes because it regards them as highly personal signs of inescapable failure in the future. In other words, if you make a blunder, you're doomed. By contrast, a helpful way to look at setbacks is to regard them as temporary outcomes of a set of circumstances that can change. In our experience, a key characteristic of persistent, highly motivated people is that they see failure as a form of feedback that indicates those things that need to be changed in their lives. This attitude gives them the 'courage to fail' or push themselves beyond their comfort zones. And because successful people are not afraid to fail, they take the risks that constitute the building blocks of progress and improvement.

So far, we have seen that because mistakes make us feel uncomfortable, we rarely like to talk about them. But we can't make progress without making mistakes and analysing why they happened. Indeed, you could argue that if you never received any setbacks, you're being denied the opportunity to learn and improve. As Clive Woodward, coach of the England rugby team that won the 2003 World Cup, remarked, 'In order to win, you have to know how to lose. You have to know how to handle your setbacks in order to move forward.'[28]

In order to make progress, you need to have the courage to fail.

Do you have that courage?

Mistakes challenge you to improve your game. Therefore, a central theme of this chapter is the importance of learning from mistakes. And a key step in this process is having the 'courage to fail'. Interestingly, Frank Dick, the former British national athletics coach, claims that when such courage is missing, people play safe and invariably perform below their ability.[29] In his view, the fear of making mistakes is one of the biggest barriers to athletes' attempts to fulfil their potential. This fear stunts people's growth because it prevents them from taking risks. Clearly, without risk-taking, there can be no progress. But as well as having the courage to risk failure, it's important to be able to 'frame' your mistakes in a helpful way.

Framing your mistakes

As we have explained, most sports performers are sensitive and uncomfortable about discussing their mistakes. They take them as personal weaknesses that are embarrassing and that may make them feel inadequate in some way. But there is another way of looking at setbacks – one that allows you to learn from them. An example of such a belief is the idea that it's OK for players to make mistakes as long as they don't make the same ones over and over again. That is partly what Samuel Beckett meant when he urged us to 'try again, fail again'.

Some practical tips on reframing your setbacks are listed in the box.

Reframing your setbacks: eight practical tips

1. Stop taking failure so personally. Everyone makes mistakes – but not everyone blames themselves as a result.
2. Try to put your disappointments in perspective. In a year's time, you probably won't even remember why you were so upset about some silly mistake.
3. Stop torturing yourself about what might have been. Wishful (or 'counterfactual') thinking can't change anything and is a waste of time.

4. Stop focusing on the mistake you made. Concentrate instead on what you plan to do differently next time.

5. Try to learn from the way in which other people (especially winners who remain at the top) handle setbacks. You'll probably find that successful people try hard not to make the same mistake twice.

6. Ask yourself what advice you'd give someone else who made a similar mistake to yours. It's surprising how objective we can be when we're looking at other people's problems.

7. Ask yourself what aspects of the setback are due to factors that can change in the future. Successful people see setbacks as caused by things that they can change in time.

8. Try to identify at least one good thing (e.g. a lesson learned such as a change in perspective, a resolve to work harder on your game) that happened as a result of your setback.

So, what are the good and the bad ways of looking at mistakes in sport? Perhaps the best way to answer this question is by exploring what research tells us about the way in which we try to make sense of things that happen in our lives.

Explaining mistakes – look on the bright side!

Most of us are interested in seeking explanations for the things that go wrong in our lives. But the way in which you account for things that happened to you in the past (that is, your attributional style; see Chapter 2) can affect your chances of achieving success in the future. For example, consider two different ways of explaining the cause of a certain result. On the one hand, a badminton player may attribute her victory over an opponent to her own fighting spirit on court.

This is a motivational explanation for the result. On the other hand, the manager of a volleyball team that has been defeated in a match may attribute this result to a fluke (such as a deflected shot which was going wide) or to some other misfortune over which he had no control (such as an apparently unfair refereeing decision during the game). These examples show different attributional approaches in action. Whereas the badminton player's explanation for her victory invokes an internal, personal quality (her determination), the volleyball manager's explanation refers to external factors such as bad luck or poor refereeing.

Following from the discussion in Chapter 2 on what makes the winning mind, research shows that people have a tendency to favour a similar way of explaining things that happen to them in different situations in their lives. This style can be measured by a questionnaire called the Attributional Style Questionnaire (ASQ)[30]

Mia Audina (courtesy of Inpho Photography)

that requires you to identify the possible causes of various hypothetical situations. An interesting feature of this test is that it also asks you to rate these causes along three separate dimensions. These dimensions include 'locus of causality' (did I cause this event or was it due to someone else?), 'stability of causality' (is the cause likely to persist in the future or not?), and 'globality of causality' (is the cause likely to affect every aspect of my life or not?).

By analysing the pattern of your responses to the ASQ, pessimistic and optimistic styles can be identified. In general, pessimists tend to explain failures and setbacks in ways that are personal ('it was my fault'), permanent ('this situation is always going to be like this and there's very little I can do to change it'), and far-reaching ('this failure has ruined almost every aspect of my life'), whereas optimists tend to adopt the opposite approach.

155

Research reveals that winners in sport tend to offer rather different explanations for their performance than do losers.[31] Typically, winners tend to favour attributions to internal and personally controllable factors such as the amount of practice they have engaged in before the event. Remarkably, as we indicated earlier, these attributions can be predictive of future athletic success. For example, if a young sprinter attributes a sequence of poor performances to a lack of ability (a relatively stable internal factor) rather than to the high quality of the competitors (a variable external factor), she may become disillusioned and lose heart.

Swimming against the tide

Studies on the relationship between people's explanatory style and their athletic performance have generated some interesting findings. Martin Seligman, and his colleagues administered the ASQ to collegiate swimmers prior to the start of their competitive season.[32] Before the start of the swimming season, Seligman and his team gave the test to 50 swimmers in a university. Then, they rated each of the swimmers on how they thought they were likely to perform over the season. The following three main findings emerged:

1. Swimmers with a pessimistic explanatory style were more likely to perform below the level of coaches' expectations during the season than were swimmers with a more optimistic outlook. In fact, the pessimists on the ASQ had about twice as many unexpectedly poor swims as their optimistic colleagues.
2. Pessimistic swimmers were less likely to 'bounce back' from simulated defeats than were optimistic counterparts. After a rigged defeat (produced by false feedback; swimmers were told that their swim times were slower by up to five seconds than they actually were), the performance of pessimistic swimmers deteriorated whereas that of relative optimists did not.
3. The explanatory style scores of the swimmers were significantly predictive of swimming performance even after coaches' judgements of ability to overcome a setback had been removed from the analysis.

Given the importance of explanatory style in sport, let's see whether you're an optimist or a pessimist. Try the exercise in the box below.

Glass half-full or half-empty?

In order to find out if you're an optimist or a pessimist, we ask you to answer some questions. First, think of a match that you lost recently. Do you think that you were personally responsible for the result or was it due to some external circumstances? This question relates to 'personalisation' (that is, an internal or external cause).

Second, do you think that the cause of this result will persist in the future? Finally, how much will this event affect other areas of your life? This question assesses the pervasiveness of the cause. The more aspects of your life you think will be affected, the more pervasive is the cause in question.

Analysis

If you attributed the event to yourself (question 1) and to factors that will not change in the future (question 2), and if you believe that the cause affects many different aspects of your life (question 3), then you probably have a *pessimistic* explanatory style. If so, you tend to explain setbacks by saying, 'I've only myself to blame' (personalisation), 'It's going to happen again and again' (permanence), and 'It's going to ruin my whole life' (pervasiveness).

In general, pessimists believe that negative experiences are their fault, will never change and are catastrophic. Optimists, on the other hand, tend to interpret setbacks as being caused by temporary circumstances that can be changed in the future – given sufficient effort on their part.

Can you change your approach?

We hope that by now you will have thought long and hard about your preferred attributional style. You can *change* this style, however, by learning to think differently about what caused your setbacks. For example, in general, coaches can help athletes to become more self-reliant by helping them to decrease their tendency to use external attributions after poor performances and instead to use certain kinds of internal attributions. Thus a golfer may confide in her coach that she had been lucky to get away with a bunker shot that barely skimmed the rim of the bunker before landing on the green. This attribution to an external unstable factor (e.g. luck) may erode a player's confidence over time. But if the golfer could be trained to rephrase this attribution to an 'internal' source (e.g. 'If I concentrate on getting more uplift on my sand shots, I will become a much better bunker player'), then she will probably be more motivated to practise her bunker play in future.

To help you move forward positively, let's summarise some key ideas from this chapter in the form of practical tips on mistake management.

Five practical tips on mistake management

From the beginning, we have emphasised the importance of putting mistakes and misfortune behind you as quickly and as efficiently as possible. The reason we place such importance on this mental skill is that competitive sport is full of examples of athletes and teams who recovered from seemingly impossible deficits to win crucial matches.[33] For example, Dennis Taylor won the world snooker championship in 1985 (by 18–17) despite trailing Steve Davis by 7 frames to 0 at one stage. More recently, Liverpool defeated AC Milan in a penalty shoot-out in the 2005 Champions' League final even though they were 3–0 down at half-time.

Inspired by such recoveries from adversity, the box below shows five practical tips on positive mistake management.

Five practical tips

1. Try to learn from your mistakes – don't ignore them. Most athletes think that if they ignore their mistakes, they will go away. This is not true because the mistakes are habits that will resurface if not corrected.
2. Don't be too hard on yourself when you make a mistake.
3. Keep a log of one thing that you're proud of and one mistake that you made after every competitive game. By identifying patterns in your errors over time, you'll be able to seek advice from coaches about how to improve your technical skills.
4. Observe how top athletes in your sport deal with their mistakes and try to learn from them.
5. Try to develop a short mistake-management routine for your sport.

The last word

Having covered a lot of theoretical ideas in this chapter, let's leave the last word on mistakes to the golfer Pádraig Harrington:

> Unless you're prepared to make mistakes and put your head on the line, you're going to get nothing and it'll be worth nothing. . . . You will have many mistakes and failures and the higher up you get, the more magnified those failures will be. But they're all worth it in the end because when the good days come, they're made all the better by the memory of those mistakes and failures. . . . If you're looking for average, then try not to make mistakes but if you're looking to be great, you've got to make loads of mistakes.[34]

Chapter 8

'Teaming'

TEAM: Together Everyone Achieves More

There may be no I in TEAM – but there is ME!

Introduction

UP UNTIL NOW, OUR journey through sport psychology has focused on the individual and how that person can harness skills to realise his or her sporting potential. This is core business for sport psychology, and yet individual activity can only represent part of our story, for sport is, at heart, a social activity and is based around teams.

By definition, many sports are group activities involving complex interactions between team members, and even in more solitary athletic endeavours, it is very rare

We won! (courtesy of Inpho Photography)

for group work not to feature in some way. This is true in competitive sport of whatever kind. Take golf. At first glance it seems to epitomise individual sporting pursuits. After all, it's just you against the course. But on closer inspection, we discover that top golfers travel and work with a large support team of advisers including caddies, managers, physiotherapists, swing coaches, putting specialists and psychologists. For example, Pádraig Harrington, the 2007 Open winner, had a back-up team of seven – a caddie, an agent, a coach, a psychologist, a fitness consultant, a sport scientist and a physiotherapist.

Therefore, popular portrayals of the loneliness of the long-distance runner, explorer, mountaineer or sailor can be misleading because behind the scenes, invariably, there will be a team involved in setting the person off down the road – and in subsequently keeping them on track. Two examples may help to illustrate this point. The first is from mountaineering.

Alone

In January 2006 one of the greatest mountaineers of all time, Jean-Christophe Lafaille, died during his attempt to make the first solo winter climb of an 8,000-metre mountain, the Himalayan peak Makalu. The task Lafaille had set himself was remarkable by any standards. No team or individual had succeeded in climbing

Makalu in winter, let alone without oxygen. Without question, he died alone, yet only hours before he passed away Jean-Christophe had contacted Katia, his wife and team manager, and their four-year-old son via his satellite telephone, a call he made several times a day on each of his solo expeditions.

From another sport, sailing, Ellen MacArthur is the first to acknowledge that her single-handed voyages across the world's oceans reflect a team effort, with a constant exchange of information with her shore team before, during and after each challenge. Her words, at the news conference after breaking the single-handed, round-the-world record in 2005, speak volumes for the role played by teamwork:

Ellen MacArthur (courtesy of Inpho Photography)

A record is nothing if not shared. I'm proud of the record but I'm even more proud to be working with the best team in the world. When I was out there I was never ever alone, there was always a team of people behind me, in mind if not in body.[1]

In most sports, teamwork is seen as something to be encouraged, and it is difficult to bring to mind many sports where this is not the case, horse racing being one of the very few exceptions. (If two jockeys riding for the same stable are thought to be adopting 'team tactics' to allow one chosen horse to win, both jockeys can face a ban. In the UK this is a minimum of 14 days.)

In view of the significance of teamwork in sport, it is right and proper that we should turn our attention away from the individual and towards the collective – to see how individual talent and potential can be drawn together effectively within the context of a team.

What is a team?

Most of us have a great deal of experience of, and confidence in, teams of various kinds – whether they are formed in sport or at work (e.g. committees). But what are the characteristics of a 'team'? And is our confidence in them justified? In our experience, teams do not necessarily bring out the best in individual members. On the contrary, time and again teams are beset by social forces that stand in the way of optimal performance. For example, research shows that when people work collectively on a common task, they tend to generate *less* total effort than if they each worked alone – a phenomenon called 'social loafing'[2] (see later in the chapter). Yet our faith in teams remains unshaken. With this caution in mind, let's first explore what teams are, before considering what they could be.

Let's be honest, we all know what a team is – at least at a superficial level. After all, as we live, work and play in teams from playground to tea dance, you might think that there is little to be gained by exploring the theoretical literature on the subject. However, casual experience is no substitute for careful analysis, so it's important that we grasp this golden opportunity to consider the qualities that make teams good, bad or plain ugly.

In the literature,[3] teams have been characterised typically by five features – interaction, structure, cohesion (both related to the task at hand and social issues in the team), goals and identity. Almost any sport team, from the most organised professional side to the most ramshackle five-a-side soccer outfit, will normally qualify on all five counts – but sometimes only just. And so, when working out what has gone wrong with a team, these features offer a useful diagnostic framework.

To show what we mean, think of a team that you are involved with at the moment before reflecting on the prompts in the box. By reflecting on your answers to the questions in the box, you should be able to start building a team profile, marking out the special characteristics of your team. Note that cohesion is best thought of as two-dimensional – task and social. Task cohesion is concerned with how well the team work together as a playing unit, while social cohesion is about how well they get on together as a social group. These are independent factors and should never be confused or compounded – one definitely predicts success, but the other is often predicted by success. No prizes for guessing which is which.

Understanding your team

Interaction

During play:
Do the players communicate effectively? What interferes with effective communication? Is communication generally positive or negative? Who talks and who listens? Is body language positive or negative?

In the changing room:
Do team members talk openly? Are they generally quiet or vocal? Who takes the lead? Who makes useful contributions? Is there much banter and how is it taken?

During training:
How do team members interact during training? Who speaks and who doesn't, and with whom? Do players volunteer information freely?

Socially:
Do the team members mix socially – where, when and how frequently? Who socialises and who doesn't? Are there cliques? Do younger and older players mix freely? Who takes the lead and who follows?

Overall, how would you score the team on interaction?
(0 = very poor; 5 = midpoint; 10 = excellent)

Structure

How long has the team been together? Are there well-defined team roles, both formal and informal? Has the team 'matured' as a working unit? Are those with assigned roles (captain, vice-captain) good communicators? Who is respected? Who is listened to? Who cracks jokes? Who is usually the centre of affairs? Is there a pecking order within the team? Are the team members punctual? Is attendance at training good or patchy?

Overall, how would you score the team on structure?
(0 = very poor; 5 = midpoint; 10 = excellent)

Task cohesion

Would an observer say the team members play 'together'? Does the team seem to bring out the best in individual players? Do they give the impression during play itself that they know what to do and how to do it as a unit? Would you describe them as a 'tight' team on the pitch? Is training competitive – is there a healthy edge or are they relaxed?

Overall, how would you score the team on task cohesion?
(0 = very poor; 5 = midpoint; 10 = excellent)

Social cohesion

Off the pitch, are they a tight group? Are they respectful of each other? Are they exclusive? Do they seem comfortable in each other's company? Are they too comfortable? Do they choose to socialise together?

Overall, how would you score the team on social cohesion?
(0 = very poor; 5 = midpoint; 10 = excellent)

Goals

Has the team well-defined short-, medium- and long-term goals? Are they implicit (unwritten but acknowledged) or explicit (well formulated and agreed)? Does everyone always seem to pull in the same direction? Are there different agenda at work in the team? Are there dissenting voices or whispers either within the team or among the backroom staff? Does the team stay 'on message' during a game? Is the collective goal stronger than individual goals or priorities? How committed are they to the cause?

Overall, how would you score the team on goals?
(0 = very poor; 5 = midpoint; 10 = excellent)

Identity

Does the team have an identity (for example, has it defined its strengths and weaknesses)? Is the team defined by its own qualities or those of others? Is the history of the club or previous teams a help or a hindrance in terms of the team's own identity? Do the key players (e.g. captain) reinforce the identity of the team through what they do and what they say?

Overall, how would you score the team on identity?
(0 = very poor; 5 = midpoint; 10 = excellent)

Before going further, it is also important to bear in mind that no two teams are ever the same – or what is more, *should* ever try to be the same. In practical terms, this means the management of every team must be tailored to the particular qualities of the players and that group of individuals. To illustrate, one team may have a strong sense of identity, a clear, explicit goal, and well-defined structures, and yet interaction between players is poor and the team lacks both task and social cohesion. Another team may communicate well and task cohesion may be sound, yet the sense of identity is not well developed and different agendas may be driving individual members towards very different goals. Without labouring the point, it is worthwhile exploring the precise qualities of the group of players with whom you are working before moving forward too hastily.

The looking-glass

Taking these five team dimensions into consideration, you can begin to mirror-gaze on the qualities of the team itself. Avoid the temptation of labelling the team crudely as being either 'good' or 'bad'. Instead there must be greater precision in defining the various qualities that are before you. Only through a systematic evaluation of each one of the five elements of 'teamness' will you produce a sound foundation for the work to come.

Also be aware that even within one team there may be several subunits or teams, especially when a common goal is not shared or task cohesion is weak. For example, the bench and the court teams in sports such as basketball may operate to very different agendas and may respond quite differently to the team's successes and failures. Thus, if you were a substitute and the player whom you were supposed to replace was having such a great game that you weren't required, would you be happy? Even within a starting team, there may be different dynamics depending on position and role. Within a rugby XV, the team climate that is needed to optimise the performance of backs and forwards may differ dramatically: forwards must work together as a unit at all times, while backs may have more space for creativity and flair. Therefore, to treat the collective as a 'team' may ignore more subtle dynamics that lie beneath.

In a related way, the extent of players' role clarity within a team has a different impact on performance depending on the position in question. With defensive roles, role clarity will usually correlate positively with performance. In other words, you need to know what to do and how to do it in order to be able to perform as part of an organised and effective defensive unit – to stifle opposition attacks and build offensive moves through established channels. By contrast, with more attacking or offensive roles, there may be a negative correlation between role clarity and performance. Too much clarity could inhibit creativity and flair – for example, being told precisely what you have to do and how to do it may not help you find that novel and creative key to unlocking a tricky defence.

So a reflection on roles and role clarity cannot ignore group dynamics and must take into account factors including playing position, as well as the players' temperaments. With this in mind, it is not difficult to see why so many of the players that managers would automatically describe as 'difficult' are those who are playing in positions where role conflict goes hand in hand with creativity and good performance. The soccer star George Best is one example of a creative, attacking genius (he 'wrote poetry' with his feet) who could run rings around defenders and team managers with equal dexterity, and who tried the patience of many managers and team-mates to the breaking point and beyond. As one famous example, when asked to explain his many absences from team practices with Manchester United, George allegedly remarked, 'I used to go missing a lot ... Miss Canada, Miss United Kingdom, Miss World!'

The team in its place

After we have developed a profile of the team, the next step must be to consider the situations and circumstances within which the team must operate. There will be the demands made by the particular sport and then there is the environment in which the team must operate. Sports can be classified in many ways, but there are crucial aspects that will influence the significance of the team issues already identified. These include the following questions.

First, does the sport involve activity that is *unitary* (where the task cannot be broken down and where group members typically work together on a single task (for example, a rowing eight), or is it *divisible* (where the task can be broken down to smaller units and where each team member can be assigned to particular tasks, e.g. a horse-riding team or sailing crew)?

Second, in which ways does team performance relate to *quantity* or *quality* of contribution? Some sports emphasise quantity of contribution (known as *'maximisation'* tasks; e.g. tug-of-war, weightlifting), while some focus on greater quality of contribution (*'optimisation'* tasks; e.g. snooker, darts, shooting, golf). Very generally, the former usually involve gross motor skills while the latter depend on fine motor coordination. In the real world, every sport combines the two to varying degrees, but recognising the quantity/quality ratio in your sport can be helpful in deciding the climate or atmosphere that will maximise the chances of team success.

Third, does the team performance depend on interaction or co-action? On the one hand, there are *interactive sports* involving coordination between team members (e.g. soccer, rugby, netball, basketball, hockey), while, on the other hand, there are *co-active sports* that involve team members performing individually but in a team context (e.g. golf, bowls, archery, skiing, shooting, darts, snooker). Very few sports are exclusively one or the other. Instead almost all sports combine unique interactive and co-active elements through different phases of play. Sports such as baseball or cricket are intriguing in this way, as both demand high levels of both co-action and interaction. For example, fielding is principally an interactive team activity, but batting and bowling are primarily co-active.

Without naming names, certain players in both these sports have been renowned as exceptional individual co-actors or athletes who never quite made the grade when it came to team or interactive elements of the game. To illustrate this point, the following extract is taken from the official English cricket website describing one of the greatest English batsmen of all times, Geoffrey Boycott:

> As opener he saw his first task as scoring heavily enough to protect his teams against defeat, and in Test cricket and the County Championship – the matches that counted in the first-class averages – he was as sparing with the attacking strokes as, in retirement, he is strident in his opinions on the game. How valuable he was to England is shown by the fact that only 20 of his 108 Tests ended in defeat, mainly when he failed. His most productive strokes, off the back foot through the covers (his speciality) and the on-drive, were majestic in their power and placement. But he was not the man to press home an advantage. A loner, and an insatiable net-player, he was short of friends inside the game; indeed there were many who heartily disliked him because of his self-centredness.[4]

Geoffrey Boycott (courtesy of Inpho Photography)

Boycott may not have won many plaudits as a team player, but as a batsman he was second to none and his contribution to England's team performance was immense. As sports differ so widely in their nature, it is inevitable that the significance of team factors in determining success also varies.

Not surprisingly, the more that a sport requires team members to be inter-dependent *(interactive sports)*, the more significant team cohesion is likely to be. In sports where athletes may represent the same team but individual performance does not depend on teamwork *(co-acting sports)*, cohesion is less significant in determining success. Some sports may be both highly interactive and co-active (e.g. rowing, tug-of-war), whereas some may be highly interactive but involve less identifiable co-action (e.g. volleyball). Others may be low on both dimensions (e.g. marathon running, chess), and yet others may be co-active but not interactive (e.g. archery, bowls).

As a reflection on all three questions in combination, the team atmosphere and general dynamic of the group that is likely to maximise performance vary dramatically between sports. Never imagine that there is a simple formula for success or that the formula remains constant. Instead, at any moment the team character must reflect the particular demands of the situation, and the key to success will often lie in identifying or profiling the circumstance and then tailoring the team to these demands.

Successful teams: fit for purpose

There is no such thing as a 'good' team, but there are teams that are fit for purpose, that are equipped to meet the demands of their sport and any challenges put before them, large or small. As a broad foundation for success, a team that is fit for purpose should aspire to create an environment where individual players can flourish and express their individual talents, and where the team's per-formance becomes greater than the sum of its parts. Great teams, and great managers, do more than simply bringing together talented individuals; they bring 'value-addedness' and are able to create performances that are better than an objective assessment of individual players and their talents would suggest are possible.

One way of achieving this value-addedness is through clever communication. Here's what Gordon Strachan (manager of Glasgow Celtic FC) has learned from experience:

> What you say or don't say to players is so important. You tell certain ones how brilliant and strong they are, when really you know they are mentally weak and might let you down. It is all about getting the best out of them.[5]

Team huddle (courtesy of Inpho Photography)

Realising both these aspirations presents a challenge of considerable pro-portions, especially as research suggests that small groups rarely perform at the level of their average member, let alone their best member. It is here that good team management becomes critical. The mechanics of team management will be dealt with in the next chapter, but for now it is important to recognise that management should not just be about setting and reaching performance targets but should also be concerned with nurturing satisfaction with the team process or dynamic. Short-term performance is important (and in many professional sports is the only guarantee of continued employment for a manager), but without the added 'feel-good' factor, long-term loyalty (and hence performance) will suffer. Most well-managed teams are characterised by a healthy balance between team performance and team satisfaction, but let either one of these factors predominate and the well-being of the team will suffer.

If you bring to mind teams in your chosen sport that have achieved success and consider both what they have in common and what makes them different, very often you will find no common themes or profiles emerging. Each team faces its own distinctive challenges and meets these challenges in unique ways. As with the elusive search for a profile of the individual champion, it's not surprising that the team literature has struggled to find a winning team formula. Instead it has been

169

able to identify critical variables that relate to success, and these are briefly outlined below.

Team cohesion

From an early age we are taught to value teamwork and we learn what it means to be good team players. As a consequence, we soon develop implicit beliefs about what teamwork is and what makes for a good team. High on this list is the idea that a tight, cohesive team is a good team. Many coaches, inspired by many sport psychologists, come to see the building of a good 'team spirit' as their number one priority. The world of sport constantly echoes and reinforces the significance of team spirit but often without taking stock of what this may actually mean.

Successful teams will talk about the important role that team spirit has played in their success, yet the jury is still out as to whether the chicken comes before the egg, or the egg before the chicken. That is, has cohesiveness created success or did the success create this impression? Interestingly, if anything, the available research more strongly supports the latter – success tends to breed team cohesion, but the impact of cohesion on success is much more open to debate. Without doubt, task cohesion is critical – the team that plays and works together is the team that wins together. However, task cohesion and social cohesion are distinct; in other words, the team that drinks together is not always the team that wins together – but rest assured, they will have come up with very effective ways of explaining why they lost!

Undoubtedly, if the team has bonded together around a common goal and with a common purpose, this will enhance commitment, but the management of social cohesion should always be mindful of the dangers of too much teamwork – especially where this detracts from effective performance.

Healthy conflict and rivalries within a team can spur that team to success and individual players to want to achieve great things. This philosophy can be taken to extremes. Take the example of Leicester Tigers Rugby Club, consistently one of the most successful teams in Europe. During training, fights between players would appear to be commonplace, if not encouraged:

> The fascinating thing about Leicester is not so much the way they handle big games as how they behave in the privacy of their midweek practice sessions. The players all have different theories as to why the Tigers are hunting an unprecedented treble tomorrow but it is amazing how often conversation turns to training-ground fisticuffs. Welcome to a club whose idea of perfect harmony is to ensure players compete from dawn to dusk and, where necessary, punch one another's lights out.[6]

In the words of the captain, Martin Corry, these altercations are a healthy sign of commitment: 'They're not something to be proud about but they show that people care. That's the most important thing.'[7]

On the other hand, being a member of a tight team may encourage members to perform not to the best of their ability but at the same level as everyone else. The more cohesive the team, the less likely it may be that members will want to appear to be different, and when the pressure comes on, the more likely it is that team members will turn inwards and seek solace and comfort from their team-mates. This will not always help individual players to dig deep into their mental and physical resources but instead will make players feel comfortable with their mediocrity.

To marry cohesion effectively with success certain positive steps must be taken. First, team goals must be clearly defined. Second, the expectations of individual players must be high; if goals are fuzzy and expectations are low or are focused on solidarity at all costs (for example, not showing other players up), then performance will suffer. Third, the focus must be squarely on task-related issues. Players may be different, with varied social lives and operating in diverse social worlds, and they should be allowed or even encouraged to be different away from the pitch or training ground. Remember, good teams thrive on difference; poor teams stifle individuality.

Team continuity and maturity

Any group or team will take time to develop into an effective working unit, and it will come as no surprise to learn that research consistently shows a positive relationship between the length of time that a team has played together and its level of success – but only to a point. Beyond that point the climate that has developed in the team will determine whether the team continues to strive to achieve or whether it begins to lose its cutting edge.

In the 1960s, an American psychologist called Bruce Tuckman unwittingly may have laid a false trail when describing group development as a series of stages.[8] According to his model, the group initially gets together and works through the formal orientation stage (forming). Next, there may well be heightened tension associated with competition for status and influence in the team (storming), before things settle down as norms, rules and standards of behaviour eventually stabilise (norming). Finally, the group will have matured to a stage where it can work together as a unit (performing) and will continue to perform consistently until members go their separate ways (adjourning).

Clearly, this process takes time, and when players change, any group or team has to work through the process afresh and performance will invariably suffer during this period of readjustment. However, what the model fails to consider is what happens beyond early stages of development – what climate will help a team to continue to perform well in the medium to long term, beyond norming?

Waving not drowning: positive conflict

It is here that 'waving' should make an appearance. To explain, a stable team can become a lazy or complacent team, and in these circumstances team maturity and continuity can lead to underperformance. Waving is about allowing healthy levels of conflict to ebb and flow in the team within defined limits. Knowing when to heat things up (thawing) and cool things down (freezing) is critical in developing the long-term health of the team but has often been ignored, at considerable cost.

As should be apparent by now, in the world of team sports, 'conflict' should never be thought of as a dirty word but as an essential ingredient in a healthy team. Therefore, conflict is not to be avoided but managed positively. Teams that function most positively are not those whose members are continually supporting each other, patting each other on the back, and discouraging dissent and non-conformity. The most stable and productive teams are those where there is a healthy level of conflict, where players feel that they can express their own opinions and honestly and openly disagree with others, and where they have space to plough their own unique furrows.

In contrast, often the worst teams, in sport as in business, are those that try to eliminate conflict. In such situations, where disagreement is avoided in case it upsets the interpersonal dynamics of a group, a phenomenon known as 'groupthink' can develop. Groupthink characterises groups where everyone is in agreement and where everyone strives hard to be like the others and agree with everyone else.[9] Teams that suffer from groupthink underperform and actively suppress individual talent. Teams that avoid groupthink become comfortable with managed conflict between team members in an environment where people can express themselves without fear of being chastised.

Team identity

This concept rarely attracts attention in sport psychology although within social psychology it is taken as central to understanding intergroup relations. Research confirms the common-sense view that a strong sense of identity is closely tied to positive feelings of group solidarity, self-esteem and confidence. Many sport teams ignore this simple message at their cost. For example, instead of building a team around a strong sense of who they are, the temptation can be to borrow an identity from another team or nation, or to rely on history repeating itself in the club colours. In these circumstances, history can become a burden, especially where the new team differs in critical ways from its predecessors, including its style of play.

While history can help to instil a sense of belonging, each team must forge its own identity, and the nature of this identity must be tailored to the characteristics of that group of people and must be made explicit. One simple technique is to ask players collectively to come up with a number of short buzz words that define what the team is, and to use these words as a constant reminder through the good times as well as the not so good.

Creating a sense of identity that is real and powerful is not difficult, but timing is critical to the enterprise. If it comes too soon in a team's development, there may be confusion over what the team is – and if it comes too late, the team may have already defined itself in a way that will not necessarily improve or sustain its performance.

Another common identity problem encountered with many teams is that the team defines itself not by what it is but by what it *isn't*, or by what it ought to be. A practical consequence can be that such teams play reactively rather than proactively. In other words, they wait to see how the opposition plays before responding, rather than dictating terms and stamping their mark on the game. In preparation for competition, this tendency may extend to focusing attention exclusively on ways of dealing with the opposition – instead of how to play your own game. Clearly, match preparation must involve both the reactive and the proactive, but without a strong and positive sense of identity there is a danger that play reverts to planning how to avoid defeat instead of how to win, and preparing for failure reaps its due rewards. Interestingly, Brian Clough, one of England's most successful if enigmatic soccer managers, attached great importance to focusing more on his own team than on his opponents:

> I worked, taught, coached, cajoled – call it what you want – all with the aim of getting the most out of my lot because, provided I achieved that, I knew that the opposition would have too much on their plate to surprise us.[10]

Team building – the way to go?

For many organisations in sport, as in business, team building is feted as 'the way to go', but it may be worthwhile to reflect on the pros and cons before proceeding – with caution. In the wrong hands, team building has the potential to do more harm than good unless it is well managed and has deliberate objectives that tally with the identity of the team and what the team has to do to achieve success.

Over recent years, many professional sports teams have felt that unless they have been away on the obligatory team-building or bonding holiday before the start of the season, they have missed a trick. Why? No one seems to be absolutely sure, but since everyone else is doing it, it must work. What was often ignored in the process, however, was the potential cost when teams fell out or where different activities occupied people's minds at the expense of forging a unit that actually played well together.

As one extreme example, Leicester City's notorious mid-season 'jolly' to Spain in 2004 springs to mind. Eight players were taken into custody by Spanish police (and subsequently released) following allegations of rape by two women. Sadly, this was not the first time the team had hit the headlines for its overseas antics. Four years previously, the entire squad had been asked to leave the same Costa del Sol resort because of a well-documented catalogue of unruly and anti-social antics.

To understand why such trips may or may not be useful, it is necessary to return to earlier discussions for a moment. There may be opportunities for forming and storming, or getting to know one another as individuals, and the exercise may help establish a sense of identity. But against these benefits, is the experience likely to achieve long-term objectives in terms of playing together as an effective unit? According to some commentators, team building enhances loyalty to the team and coach, and harnesses support among team members. Granted, such jaunts will allow players to become acquainted, but could this have been achieved just as easily, and at a fraction of the cost, in a less exotic context – the changing room? Some soccer coaches remain sceptical of the value of mindless team-building activities. For example, Howard Wilkinson, the former manager of Leeds United and Sunderland, believes that there's a big difference between social interaction and team spirit:

> Going out and getting drunk generates a feel-good factor which is different to real team spirit. I think real team spirit is much more enduring – that feel-good factor cracks under pressure.[11]

Clearly, the dangers as well as the benefits of team-building activities need to be carefully weighed before rushing out to your local travel agent.

Some teams have taken the team-building experience to an entirely different plane by replacing 'jolly' with another hackneyed and dangerous message, 'No pain, no gain'. Boot camps for teams prior to major tournaments became fashionable in the 1990s, but again hard evidence to support their benefits is difficult to find. By contrast, the anecdotal evidence cataloguing the harm and hurt that these experiences have delivered is easy to unearth. One of the most notorious was the camp used by the South African rugby union team in their disastrous build-up to the 2003 World Cup.

Kamp Staaldraad

Set in the South African bush, Kamp Staaldraad ('Camp Barbed Wire') was a last-ditch attempt to bring the team together following a series of unplanned upsets. Among the more bizarre episodes, players were allegedly:

- made to stand naked in a freezing lake and pump up rugby balls underwater (those who tried to climb out were forced back literally at gunpoint).

- ordered to climb into a foxhole naked and sing the South African national anthem while ice-cold water was poured over their heads (recordings of 'God Save the Queen' (England's national anthem) and the New Zealand All Blacks pre-match haka were played at full volume).
- forced to crawl naked across gravel.
- made to spend a night in the bush, including killing animals and cooking meals.

Unfortunately, the consequence of Kamp Staaldraad was lots of pain but very little gain, as the Springboks were eliminated in the quarter finals of the competition after a series of inept performances, after which their coach, Rudolph Straeuli, duly resigned. A short quotation from a contemporary commentary on this particular team-building experience is interesting: 'Many rugby observers also pointed out that trying to eliminate all individuality from a team could be counterproductive, as there are many times during a rugby match when individual initiative can make the difference between victory and defeat.'[12]

In summary, team building may have some benefits in certain circumstances and especially as a quick 'get to know you' exercise when a young team is first coming together or forming an identity. However, it may be worthwhile bearing in mind the following measured comments by an eminent social psychologist, Donelson Forsyth, before jetting off to either La Manga or Kamp Staaldraad:

> A team approach does not, however, ensure success. Cohesive groups can be strikingly unproductive if the group's norms do not call for high productivity. Also, some kind of team interventions appear to be more useful than others. Interventions that increase members' control over and involvement in work, for example, are more powerful than interventions that focus on morale boosting or envisioning goals.[13]

What makes a good team member?

The histories of both professional and amateur sport reveal clear evidence that certain individuals are more at home in individual sports, while others perform better in a team environment. For some, it may be the sense of belonging associated with a team that drives them to greater heights, while for others personal mastery and control through individual achievement are what matters. Even within sports such as bowls, tennis or badminton, some players perform at their best in singles competitions while others shine in the team events. In track athletics and swimming, there have been athletes who have only ever revealed their true potential in relays rather than individual events. One famous example was the 400 metres athlete of the 1980s, Phil Brown, who could always be relied on to produce a spectacular time as part of a very successful GB relay team but never came close to matching these achievements in individual events.

Why motivation and performance are influenced in this way is still not clearly understood, but almost certainly a number of variables ought to be taken into account. Also, it is worth remembering that performance and motivation are not directly related, and so it may be that a team happens to provide the correct motivational environment for those who, without knowing it, find that individual events take them beyond their individual zone of optimum functioning (IZOF). Without retreading old ground from earlier chapters, especially Chapter 4, we may say that the team is safer and is less likely to trigger stress levels that are above the optimum.

In addition, if an athlete is burdened with a fear of failure or of being evaluated by others (Chapter 3), the team is ideal for providing him or her with a safer environment in which to perform. A related psychological construct may be 'diffusion of responsibility' – in other words, a trouble shared is a trouble halved. The burden of expectation is reduced dramatically when you are one of many on a team. In a similar vein, some players welcome the freedom provided by 'coming in off the bench' as a substitute in a team sport. Again, fear of failure is lowered and inhibitions likewise are reduced.

A second factor to bear in mind is the culture or society that provides the backcloth for the team. One way in which social scientists have categorised societies is along the dimension of 'collectivism–individualism'. That is, certain cultures and societies place a high value on individualism (most obviously the USA), while other countries (most obviously former Eastern bloc countries such as China) value collective action and downplay the significance of individual ambition. From its pioneering infancy to the present day, the USA has placed great store by individual and personal achievement, often portrayed as 'against all odds'. In stark contrast, China, especially since the time of the communist revolution under Mao Tse-tung, has valued collectivism and the strength of the group above any one person.

Players from collective cultures may find themselves more at ease and inspired in team events, while those from societies that value individualism may struggle with the competing motives of the individual and the collective. Golf's biennial Ryder Cup competition between the USA and Europe provides a fascinating glimpse into such issues, where the American players often seem ill at ease with the team basis of the competition, while many of the European team genuinely seem to thrive in this environment, relishing the experience as refreshing and different from the daily grind of the professional tour.

Shortly before the 2002 match, Sam Torrance (manager of the European team), sought advice from Alex Ferguson (manager of Manchester United FC) in an effort to forge 'togetherness' among his players. Apparently, Ferguson's simple message was to treat everyone in the team in the same way. This advice was duly implemented by Torrance and appreciated by his team. As one of the players, Pádraig Harrington, said, 'everybody got the same treatment, there were no stars in the team'.[14] By contrast, Curtis Strange, the captain of the US team, gave preferential treatment to Tiger Woods by allowing him to practise on his own before the match even though the other players were required to practise together. This episode highlights the argument that the preparation of national teams should acknowledge cultural differences rather than assuming that the players will be swept along on a euphoric but alien tide of teamness generated by the emotion of the competition.

Those who value collectivism may argue that personal ambition is the eighth deadly sin, while collective ambition is one of the noblest of human virtues. This may be an exaggeration, but without doubt the inspiration of team success does not burn as deeply in some as in others, and an acknowledgement of this fact can go a long way towards helping establish a motivational climate that will 'work' for a diverse group of players, whatever their sources of motivation, personal or team.

The third variable to consider is the qualities that we look for in team players. This is deceptively easy, individuals. As the previous discussions should suggest, good teams are not made up of clones or robots who are not allowed to be them-selves, but instead it is necessary to create an environment in which individuality is valued but bound in a team context where individual goals can still matter – but not as much as the team's. Individual ambition may be important, but in a good team it should never be allowed to stand in the way of collective ambition.

Home and away: teams in context

The circumstances that influence team performance have been subject to close scrutiny within sport psychology. One topic in particular has come under the microscope – the effects of home advantage on team performance. Intuitively we would assume that playing at home brings an automatic advantage, but research reveals a more complicated picture. In one notable study, the results of several thousand professional games played in the USA were analysed to discover if home advantage existed.[15] The authors did indeed find some evidence of home advantage in baseball (53 per cent home wins), ice hockey (64 per cent), American football (60 per cent) and basketball (64 per cent), although the report went on to caution against setting too much store by home influence. In fact, the authors found the effect was most pronounced for teams already riding on a tide of success, high-quality teams appearing to be boosted by home support. In contrast, poorer teams may actually play better away from the confines of home. What is more, home advantage often disappears in the latter stages of competitions, unless the team happens to be defending a title.

177

US Ryder Cup Team (courtesy of Inpho Photography)

Euro 2006 Ryder Cup Team (courtesy of Inpho Photography)

What is meant by 'home' is also interesting. Home may not actually be home at all but the perception of home. For example, one study of a US college basketball team that had to play at five different home venues while its stadium was being rebuilt, revealed home advantage in all five 'home' venues. Home may be where the fans are, but even this statement must be qualified for the nature of home support is critical. Some supporters are notoriously fickle and place such a burden of expectation on their teams that players often play with greater freedom when away from home. On the other side of the coin, verbally aggressive home crowds have been shown to have a powerful inhibitory effect on away teams and can success-fully be used to create a fortress mentality, a powerful tactic that has been used by many coaches and managers over the years.

Looking beyond the final score to play itself, other research suggests that venue can influence performance in more subtle ways, including team discipline. In sports including soccer, American football and basketball, it has been found that the incidence of reactive or dysfunctional aggression, as noted in indices such as foul counts, relates positively to the distance from home.

Even the nature and size of the crowd, as well as the design of the venue, play their part, crowd density rather than actual size being critical. The special atmosphere created by certain grounds is legendary in particular sports, and is a factor that must be taken into account when preparing any team. For example, within US college basketball, Duke University is famous for the fervour of its

Packed stadium (courtesy of Inpho Photography)

supporters, and the wall of noise and colour that they are able to sustain through-out a home game.

Drawing all this research together, it would appear that venue and crowd, home and away, can have a significant effect on performance and results,[16] if they are not well managed. At the same time, from a performance perspective, is it sensible to allow these factors to have an unregulated effect, or would it be more prudent to prepare teams to play wherever they happen to be and to have in place routines that ensure what happens on the pitch is isolated from these factors – while making sure your opposition is still bombarded with the slings and arrows of outrageous fans? The answer is likely to lie in accommodating both issues, using the venue card when it yields benefits (the 'fortress' mentality) but also having tech-niques for insulating players from these effects when they could interfere (same game, same rules, different venue).

Many hands – light work or spoiled broth?

So many proverbs refer to the effects of others on our behaviour that it should come as no surprise to learn that we do indeed behave differently in the presence of other people than when we are alone. Three experiments dating from the early 1900s first alerted the world to the significance of these effects in the context of sport. The first compared the times of cyclists who were training alone, with club mates, or in competition.[17] Norman Triplett found a steady improvement across the three conditions, with the poorest times alone and the fastest in competition. The second study by a French agricultural engineer called Max Ringelmann involved measuring the force exerted by up to six people pulling on a rope in comparison to the same people acting alone. Repeatedly he found that in the team situation individuals performed at only around half what they had shown they were capable of when in isolation. In the third study, by Ernst Meumann, the weight lifted by men exercising in a gym by themselves was contrasted with the weight they lifted when the author returned to watch them pump iron. Consistently their per-formance improved when being watched, although they were not conscious of the effect.[18]

Social facilitation describes what is happening in all three examples. We work harder in the presence of a team or an audience than when we are alone, especially when we know we are being evaluated. Later work found that the effect was most positive for well-learned, routine tasks but was negative for new or complicated tasks where quality as well as quantity counts. Who are most likely to be adversely affected by social facilitation? Those who are learning or gaining experience. In fact, the good become better, and the bad become worse, as was shown dramatic-ally in an experiment carried out in a pool hall some years ago. Players were secretly rated as being above or below average by their potting accuracy, and then a group

Tug of war (courtesy of Inpho Photography)

casually stood and watched them play. Those players who were above average significantly increased their percentage of successful shots; those who were below average missed even more.[19]

The implications of this work are considerable. First, it may be better to insulate athletes from evaluation while learning new skills. Second, once the routines are well drilled, it is important to simulate match conditions during training; otherwise the crowd may later interfere with effective execution during competition itself. Third, as a team moves forward in a tournament and the likelihood of performing in front of larger crowds increases, it is important to make sure that preparation for each game takes due account of this likelihood; for example, by stepping down, not stepping up, the build-up to each game.

The second social phenomenon worth mentioning is known as social loafing. The research evidence here is unequivocal – when we are working in a group or team, and especially when we know that our individual contribution cannot be identified, we subconsciously take our foot off the gas pedal or accelerator, often without even being aware that it is happening. Along with personal responsibility, many factors influence the extent of social loafing including the strength of team identity, the degree of task cohesion, and the extent of trust and interdependence between team members.[20] Again the implications are considerable. In particular, it is vital that there can be no hiding place for the individual within the collective, and players must be given feedback on individual as well as team performance constantly to remind them that they are being personally monitored.

Historically, both social facilitation and social loafing have been described separately, but over recent years there has been a tendency to describe these team influences in conjunction. In summary, the combined effects are as shown in the box.

It all depends!

- **When** the presence of others increases evaluation of our performance, easy or well-learned tasks improve because we are more highly motivated ('social facilitation').
- **But** the execution of more difficult or creative skills may be impaired because of an increase in stress ('social inhibition').
- **When** the presence of others shields us from personal evaluation, performance on easy tasks may become worse because we do not care, especially when goals are not well defined ('social loafing').
- **But** performance on difficult tasks may improve because we are less anxious in a team setting ('social security').

In conclusion

A great deal of time and effort has gone into writing about the nature of teams, but when all is said and done there is no need to overcomplicate. Teams should be constructed and managed primarily to provide an environment where individual talent can flourish and where the collective can become greater than the sum of its parts. As Phil Jackson, former coach of the Chicago Bulls basketball team (six-times NBA champions) put it, 'Good teams become great ones when the members trust each other enough to surrender the "me" for the "we".'[21]

The detritus that collects around teams often muddies the water, making us lose sight of these core principles. But you have to act with these principles in mind if you want to make a difference to a team, or, as Cloughie (Brian Clough) once observed, 'You don't change a stagnant pool by staring at the water; you have to disturb it – eliminate the pollution and introduce the elements that can make it fresh again.'[22]

While this may sound easy, the person-management skills which must be employed to achieve this goal and to keep a team on track and hungry for success are considerable, and this inevitably brings us to the final stage of our journey, how to create and sustain such an environment.

Chapter 9

Leading

It is better to lead from behind and to put others in front, especially when you celebrate victory when nice things occur. You take the front line when there is danger. Then people will appreciate your leadership.

Nelson Mandela, South African President

A leader is best when people barely know he exists, when his work is done, his aim fulfilled, they will say: we did it ourselves.

Laotzu, Chinese philosopher and founder of Taoism, 600–531 BC

A good leader inspires people to have confidence in the leader, a great leader inspires people to have confidence in themselves.

Unattributed

Introduction

What makes a good leader? Sad to say, there is no easy answer because good leaders come in many different shapes and sizes, and searching for a simple formula for success is likely to be a monumental waste of effort. To

Nelson Mandela (courtesy of Inpho Photography)

illustrate, take a sport such as professional soccer or American football and list the five most successful managers or captains of all time. Now briefly describe the psychological profile of each person using whatever words spring readily to mind.

Whatever people you come up with will almost certainly differ radically from each other in their style, personality and temperament – ranging from the astute yet distant tactician to the passionate, all-consuming teamster. There may be some you like or admire more than others, but in terms of success, a single winning formula is elusive if not illusory. Opposite, two statements by players about two of the most successful European soccer club managers illustrate this diversity of style well.

Compare and contrast

Manager A

' —— is a smart fellow and intelligence is the key. He is persuasive, he speaks well, he can marshal an argument and he is a very decent tactician. Of course he is also an outstanding man manager. You never knew exactly where you were with him. He would be your best friend when you met him in the corridor one day and the next he would ignore you. It kept you on your toes. He gives you a challenge and if you meet it you become one of his lieutenants and you feel you will play with him forever.'[4]

Manager B

'He gave me a lot of confidence. He made any player feel like a great player. If you feel like one, then you'll play like one. Even when we lost, the boss would prove that it was all a mistake – the winning goal was offside, one of our blokes was fouled – that sort of thing. Another thing is that there were no non-triers in a —— team. He wouldn't tolerate any lax attitudes – no matter who you were. We didn't have any stars really – everyone was treated the same.'[5]

From the 1900s onward, psychologists have tried in vain to define what makes a good leader and reluctantly have come to the conclusion that the search has been pointless. Instead, attention has turned away from certain personality types and towards the functions that leaders must perform – as well as towards the circumstances which challenge them to fulfil the potential of those in their charge.

As a starting point, it is worth remembering that the primary task of good leadership is not to boost the leader's ego or to exert power and influence for its own sake but to maximise the potential of those being led. In the cut-throat world of competitive sport, one US college basketball coach is credited with achieving this goal year after year with a consistency that has become legendary within, and famous beyond, his own sport. That man is John Wooden.

Wooden deeds

John Wooden was brought up in near poverty on a small holding in Indiana, from where he went on to gain a scholarship to Purdue University, gaining along the way the nickname, 'the Indiana Rubber Man', for his suicidal dives on court. He went on to become an All-American player before turning to coaching. He is best remembered for coaching the UCLA Bruins from 1948 to 1975, catapulting the team from the weakest in the Pacific college conference to the pinnacle of their sport, with an unsurpassed record, including 88 consecutive victories, 10 NCAA championships (including seven in a row), 38 Consecutive NCAA tournament victories, and four years in which the team went undefeated for the entire season.

In later years, Wooden was portrayed as a wise, old sage, but during his early years at UCLA, his passion was less contained, as he regularly launched verbal barrages at officials and opposing players – incidents which he later regretted. The following excerpt, taken from a fan's online tribute, eloquently sums up the man and his achievements:

When all is said and done concerning college basketball coaches, one name will stand alone over all the others: John Wooden. The 'Wizard of Westwood'

John Wooden (reproduced with kind permission of CoachWooden.com)

was the epitome of coaching, embedding in his players the importance of teamwork and consistency on the hardwood. He also stressed the value of perfecting defensive and offensive fundamentals, as his teams seemed not to have any conceivable flaws. Not too keen on flamboyance, Coach Wooden was a modest man who did not seek the limelight; and at the same time, showed the utmost grace and decency to all UCLA's opponents – win or lose. As for his coaching record, neither an 80.6% winning percentage and winning ten NCAA championships define the man completely. Rather, it is the respect he still garners today from those who are in or simply follow college basketball, which defines him best. Undoubtedly, John Wooden was the greatest coach ever in any sport, and is the measuring stick for which all other great coaches of all sports will be measured until the end of time.[1]

How was John Wooden able to bring out the best in those he coached – not once but over several decades? The 'ten commandments' or quotations from the man himself, presented below, begin to reveal his winning formula. This approach did not depend on charismatic oratory, cheap tricks or gimmickry but on the promotion of a philosophy that sits very comfortably with so many of the principles described throughout this book (thus, his 'second commandment' echoes the importance of learning from your mistakes; see Chapter 7). His words speak for themselves[2,3]:

Wooden words

- Don't let what you cannot do interfere with what you can do.
- If you're not making mistakes, then you're not doing anything.
- Be more concerned with your character than your reputation, because your character is what you really are, while your reputation is merely what others think you are.
- Do not let either praise or criticism affect you. Let it wash off.
- Ability may get you to the top, but it takes character to keep you there.
- Don't measure yourself by what you have accomplished, but what you should have accomplished with your ability.
- In anything, failure to prepare is preparing to fail.
- Be quick, but don't hurry.
- A player who makes a team great is more valuable than a great player.
- Talent is God-given. Be humble. Fame is man-given. Be grateful. Conceit is self-given. Be careful.

Looking beyond success

John Wooden began with nothing and created a basketball dynasty. But team success is not the only way of assessing good leadership in sport. Taken in isolation, it is not always a good yardstick. A far more useful measure is 'value-addedness' – what ingredients did that person have at his or her disposal and what was achieved with those resources?

In reality, some of the greatest sports coaches or managers are unknown beyond their own small worlds. These are the unsung local heroes who, against all odds, have created an environment where potential talent is realised and where the team became greater than the sum of its parts.

Equally, great captains are often characterised by achieving great things but with limited resources at their disposal, or helping to mould the values and ethics of a team during its formative years – sometimes referred to as 'cultural architects'. In truth, the annals of sport include many so-called 'great' and famous captains who were no more than exceptionally lucky to be around a team that had reached its prime and where captaincy was no longer an essential commodity – they just happened to be in the right place at the right time. This accidental heroism contrasts with truly great captains who were able to inspire their teams to achieve great things with modest resources and often against all odds.

Beyond the credibility gap

It is interesting that despite all the evidence to the contrary, one essential selection criterion for both managers and captains appears to be simply how good they are, or more correctly, *were* as players – the T-shirt factor or the 'been there, done that' badge of honour. From a practical perspective, there is a performance threshold that must be reached before a player can be considered for captaincy. The simple question here is this: can the player hold down a place on the team? Beyond this issue, playing ability alone is not likely to relate to captaincy skills and may even have a negative influence if other players feel they can shirk responsibility by hiding behind the leading light. Many of the greatest captains in sport have not been great players. But for the manager, the task of selecting an effective captain becomes the challenge of finding the person who can best embody the values and identity of the team, whether formed or to be formed. Who can find the square peg for the square hole?

Perhaps Clive Woodward's greatest achievement, as manager of England's World Cup-winning rugby team in 2003, was to choose Martin Johnson as captain, a man who epitomised the rugged, no-nonsense, forward-oriented English game at that time. Interestingly, Woodward revealed that he used five criteria in choosing Johnson as a captain of England.[6] First, the player had to be the best in his position

Martin Johnson (courtesy of Inpho Photography)

in the squad. Second, he had to have shown a capacity for thinking clearly under pressure. Third, he had to be someone who would command the respect of all of his team-mates. Fourth, he had to be 'at one' with the coach in conveying his messages to the team. Finally, he had to have some previous experience of the job or have shown leadership skills at a level just below international competition.

Many of the greatest coaches and managers may not have had great physical prowess or talent as players but were able to bring unique qualities to their management roles. To illustrate, in professional soccer, research[7] shows that of the 26 managers who coached winning teams in the Premiership (formerly the First Division) in England between 1945 and 2000, only *five* had won more than six caps for their countries. Remarkably, such highly successful managers as Bob Paisley and Bill Shankly (both of Liverpool) and Sir Alex Ferguson (manager of Manchester United and arguably the most successful club manager in England over the past 50 years) were never capped by their native country, Scotland. Similarly, Arsene Wenger (Arsenal) never played for France and José Mourinho was never capped for Portugal. Amusingly, when asked if being a great player was a pre-requisite for being a great manager, Arrigo Sacchi (who won the Italian League and two European Cups with AC Milan even though he had never even played professional soccer) is alleged to have replied: 'What's the problem here? . . . If you want to be a good jockey, it's not necessary to have been a horse earlier in your career!'[8]

The point here is that to understand the game and all its intricacies there is a need for some experience of the sport, but it is probably safest to view this in selection terms more as a desirable competence than an essential criterion.

The question of credibility appears to drive the constant search for those who have achieved, and yet the significance of this criterion is at best short-lived. The past soon becomes forgotten if the square peg doesn't fit the round hole.

Ten steps to sporting leadership

From what we have said so far, it's clear that leaders cannot simply be pulled off the shelf. Although they vary in personality, they must be the right horse for the right course. But are there any defining ingredients that must come together in sporting leaders? Having sifted through the literature, we have identified the following steps to sporting leadership.

1. It has to matter

Of all the defining qualities of sporting leaders, there is one that cannot be ignored or sidestepped: commitment – it has to matter. Without such commitment, a person's capacity genuinely to inspire others to the cause will be extremely limited. This does not always equate with 'charisma' or skills of oratory or well-honed man-management styles, but it *does* have to matter. Some people have taken this to the limits, and at times too much commitment can be as dangerous as too little. After all, in comparison with other life domains, sport has its place but that can still be a significant place.

The legendary Liverpool Football Club manager Bill Shankly (1913–1981) once (in)famously remarked, 'Some people think football is a matter of life and death. I assure you, it's much more serious than that.' A great quotation but in our heart of hearts we know, and he surely knew, that it isn't true. More significant is the fact that he ever said it in the first place and was then able to inspire others to greatness because of his personal, unbridled, naive passion for his sport and for his club, Liverpool FC.

Is there a need to pass beyond a stage of acknowledging that when all is said and done, in actual fact it doesn't really matter? After all, it is *only* sport and in comparison with many things in life, including death, it is of less consequence. Strangely, having come to terms with the fact it doesn't really matter as much as you thought, it can matter all the more because of that honest acknowledgement of the purity of the endeavour – in other words, pure sport. That is a key theme in our book and one that we return to time and time again: you have to care. And that is not to say that other parts of life then pale into insignificance, but that genuine passion can be reserved for something that shouldn't really matter but does.

Not everyone can display the naked passion of a Shankly nor should they aspire to. To try to be someone that you are not will take you down an uncomfortable road to nowhere. Some may prefer the quiet rage, others the ice man, and still others the extrovert or flamboyant showman. There is no magic formula but somewhere within you the flame has to burn. An obvious consequence of this idea is that when a coach or manager reaches a time of life when the flame burns less brightly, that may be the time to reflect on a life beyond active involvement in sport.

2. Letting go

Many coaches and managers bring incredible levels of commitment to their sport, and then assume that all those they work with must also carry the same flame and with the same fervour. Passion matters – but then we encounter a paradox – for good leaders also must know how to let go and when to let go. As Zen masters tell us, in the martial arts, to gain control, you have to know when to give up control.

In any walk of life involving supervision and the imparting of skills and knowledge, the true sign of a job well done is aspiring to voluntary redundancy. Again, we have emphasised this point in our earlier discussion of the value of sport psychology (see Chapter 1). The gentle hand on the tiller can never disappear completely, but for long periods of the voyage the autopilot should become just as effective. Knowing that this endpoint is a happy consequence of good leadership should not be forgotten. Too many leaders find letting go of the reins difficult, but any well-managed team or athlete must aim to reach a point in their development where the manager, coach or even captain should be prepared quietly to relinquish the driving seat – for stages of the journey at least.

In certain respects, a sporting leader can be thought of as a sensitive thermostat, responding to temperature changes with appropriate actions but also acknowledging that one of the most important management styles involves knowing when not to manage at all!

3. Reflecting

As the previous point makes clear, a good leader in sport must have the capacity not only to look *out* (to devise tactics, analyse and assess) but also to look *in* constantly to reflect and adjust. Fortunately, the performance skills already described in Chapter 3 are directly transferable to coaching and management.

Profiling in particular gives you the tools for systematically evaluating your strengths and weaknesses, with goal setting then providing the techniques for bringing about positive change. In the spirit of Chapter 3, the list of profiling attributes you decide on must be personal, but as a starting point you could refer to the following checklist. This was developed spontaneously during a workshop for top-level coaches across many team and individual sports. When asked to define the

TABLE 9.1 Profiling a coach

Personal qualities	Interpersonal skills	Technical skills	Knowledge
Energetic	Delegator	Goal setter	Sport-specific
Visionary	Effective manager	Analyst	Tactical awareness
Confident	Networker	Counsellor	Biomechanics
Enthusiastic	Listener	Innovator	Physiology
Honest	Communicator	Planner	Psychology
Resilient	Empathiser	Decision-maker	Nutrition
Punctual		Tactician	Political sense
Positive thinker		Administrator	Medical
Self-disciplined		Selector	Knowing when to walk
Committed			Sceptical enquirer
Patient			
Adaptable			
'Personality'			
Stress manager			
Questioning			

characteristics of a good coach, they identified the skills and characteristics shown in Table 9.1.

Unless you are also gifted with the ability to walk on water, it is unlikely you could ever hope to possess all these skills or qualities. But knowing what you can't do as well as what you can do equips you with the knowledge of which gaps need be filled and how to fill them.

In general terms, psychologically, we are most comfortable and least challenged when surrounded by those who are like us and who reinforce our views. Difference is more effortful but is far more rewarding and interesting. With this in mind, it is critical to have the courage to surround yourself with people who complement rather than match or reinforce you – those who fill gaps rather than reinforce defences. Many of the most successful management teams in sport have been built on this principle of complementarity and difference. Put another way, beware the 'yes' men and women!

4. Adapting

The late Brian Clough was a soccer legend, plucking Derby County and Nottingham Forest from obscurity to the dizzy heights of national and international league and cup success. Euphemistically, his management style is perhaps best described as idiosyncratic, being liberally laced with the capacity to surprise – especially in his team-preparation techniques. In one famous example, before Nottingham Forest's victory over Malmo in the 1979 European Cup, Clough supplied bottles of beer to his players on the bus that took his team to the stadium before the match! This unconventional idea stemmed from a well-founded belief that athletes perform best in a relaxed frame of mind. Indeed, his coaching philosophy is epitomised by his statement that

> Nottingham Forest would be represented by good players who were relaxed. . . . That's why we had beer on the coach. . . . Forest's footballers weren't uptight footballers when they took to the field.[9]

Along with his other management-half, Peter Taylor, Clough was able to mould young players into formidable teams, and on the strength of his proven achievements was invited to take over from Don Revie at Leeds United on Revie's surprise departure.

The Leeds team was mature and had achieved incredible success over several years. Many of the players were seasoned internationals who did not respond well to Clough's ill-judged confrontational style of management when he met the

Clough and Shankly (courtesy of Inpho Photography/Getty Images)

Leeds players. Within 44 days the relationship had ended. As he said many years afterwards,

> I was confronted by a seething, resentful, spiteful dressing room when I arrived on my first morning. . . . Leeds had done it all. . . . They weren't threatened, any of them, because they felt they were bigger than me.[10]

A salutary lesson for Clough and for any aspiring team manager – new brooms may sweep clean but they can also break in the process.

Clough and Taylor made a superb management team in the right situation, but that talent did not transfer well. The capacity to change and adapt is a core principle of good leadership, and it is a dangerous strategy to assume that reputation alone will afford you the capacity to impose a style; it may work, but it is high risk with no guarantee of success. A more sensible approach may be 'softly softly', or 'sussing out' what's happening by carefully assessing the situation and the personnel that you must deal with before deciding how best to proceed. Sometimes this may involve going with the existing flow until sufficient credit has accumulated, but sometimes imposing your will earlier if the situation is critical. Whatever else, this must be a careful, considered response, as opposed to a hasty reaction.

In a similar vein, adapting to the changing needs of the team or athlete is critical in continuing to foster a healthy relationship. Sport is littered with stories of successful coach–athlete relationship that have foundered during the *Sturm und Drang* (storm and strife) of adolescence, or even beyond, for no other reason than the coach has failed to recognise that the athlete is, naturally and normally, growing up. The relationship and the coach must change or perish in the process.

Research shows that athletes look for different types of support and advice at different stages of their careers.[11] Young athletes look for considerable social support early on, but this need decreases as time goes by. In addition, too much emphasis on skills training can be demotivating for young people. Technical advice is most appropriate in mid-career, while more mature athletes will often prioritise personal support to help them through the stresses of major competitions.

There is little point in bombarding you with theory on this matter. Both sport and industrial psychology are littered with dozens of leadership theories and models. While each has a different focus and uses different language, all acknowledge that there is no magic formula for predicting who will be a good leader, and no single leadership, captaincy, management or coaching style can hope to be successful across a range of situations.

Instead, the only general advice that can be offered is that to be as effective as possible sports coaches, managers or captains must develop the ability to assess changing situations and then employ a leadership style in keeping with circumstance, meeting the needs of others and the demands of the situation. In the elegant words of the British prime minister, Benjamin Disraeli (1804–1881), 'I must follow the people, am I not their leader?' This is advice that you ignore at your peril.

5. Motivating

> Coaches who can outline plays on a blackboard are a dime a dozen. The ones who win get inside their players and motivate. (Vince Lombardi)

It should go without saying that a good leader must have the capacity to motivate, but don't imagine that this is a mystical art. It is a science that is understandable and the necessary skills are transferable. At the risk of repeating the messages of Chapter 2, it is important first to recognise that motivation is not just about a list of drivers or motivators but at its core is a process, a process that moves us, that gets us out of bed in the morning just as it spurs an athlete to dig deep into his or her dwindling physical reserves at the end of a gruelling competition.

A useful psychological model (Figure 9.1) for describing the process of motivation has already been outlined in Chapter 2. This describes the relationship between four factors. To be motivated, to want to expend energy, players must initially be able to recognise that increasing their effort can positively change performance (*expectancy*), the size of the effect being mediated by their ability, and the role or position that they are asked to play. Next, *instrumentality* refers to the player's belief that an improvement in performance will reflect in an increase in rewards. Without this recognition, it is unlikely that greater effort will be expended.

The term *outcome* does not simply refer to concrete rewards or benefits (such as cups, titles, money or status) but also includes intrinsic factors such as a sense of mastery, control, well-being, enjoyment and self-esteem. Available research suggests that too great an emphasis on extrinsic rewards can be demotivating in the longer term, while intrinsic motivation provides a more solid foundation for success. Furthermore, it is not absolute reward but what we receive relative to others – am I getting as much, more or less for what I do?

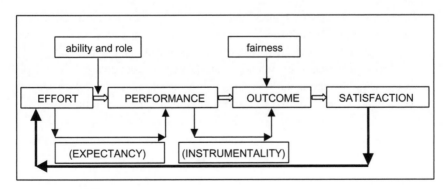

FIGURE 9.1 Modelling motivation

To apply this model successfully in everyday situations, the critical first step has to be getting to know your players or athletes and what makes them tick. Then it is possible to use this framework to understand problems and deliver effective messages. Perhaps players feel that outcomes or rewards do not depend on personal performance, that their place is secure, or that they will be dropped whatever they do – in other words their fate is already sealed. Perhaps players feel undervalued or believe that they are not able to improve performance however hard they try. Maybe the player's personal goals and rewards are no longer the same as those of the team or club, or the outcomes are not clearly defined.

Whatever is the case, by systematically applying this model, it is possible to pinpoint where the problem lies and suggest a positive way forward. It gives the coach, captain or manager the opportunity to understand what is going on in each player's mind and to understand their priorities, rewards and values – without doubt one of the keystones to successful coaching. As to the practical implications of this model for dealing with players, a number of the most important points are summarised in the box.

Positive coaching: five principles

1. *Know your players.* Coaches must ensure that they are aware of the priorities, valued rewards and goals of each player in order to maximise each individual's potential. No two players will have identical value systems, and allowance must be made for differences.
2. *Provide positive feedback.* Players must be provided with positive feedback on individual performance, on a job well done, in order to ensure maximum effort on future occasions.
3. *Relate effort to performance.* Players are likely to increase their effort only if they believe that this work will actually improve performance. By providing clear feedback on performance, the coach will improve the effort put into practice.
4. *Relate rewards to performance.* Players must be made aware that a change in performance will be reflected in either an increase or decrease in outcomes or rewards (either concrete or 'intrinsic') that they personally value.
5. *Be challenge oriented.* By setting challenging but reachable goals and providing clear feedback on attainment, high levels of performance may be maintained. Goals must not be too distant and must be attainable.

6. Decision-making

Moment by moment, leadership depends on making the right decisions at the right time, and often in the most trying circumstances. This could include devising and revising game plans, substitutions, training schedules, team selections, or longer-term strategies. Ultimately, a leader will be judged by the effectiveness of these decisions, and intuitively it may be assumed that decision-making is solely about the quality of the decision itself. However, this ignores a second crucial element, acceptance or the willingness to act on that decision.

Expeditions, as an extreme example, hinge on synergy between decision quality and decision acceptance, and many disasters are precipitated because one or both were not afforded due regard. On his ill-fated expedition to reach the South Pole, Captain Scott may have inspired his crew to unimaginable heroics by their uncritical acceptance of his decisions, but what about the quality of those decisions? On the other hand, Captain William Bligh may have been one of the greatest navigators and sailors of the eighteenth century, but by failing to marry the quality of his decisions with acceptance of those decisions by the crew of his ship, HMS *Bounty*, he created a recipe for mutiny.

Scott's ill-fated polar team (courtesy of PA Photos)

HMS *Bounty* (courtesy of PA Photos)

Successfully balancing decision quality with decision acceptance requires the adoption of a range of management styles, along with the key skill of identifying which style is best suited to which situation. There may be times when decision quality is critical and you are confident in the information available to you, and so you may adopt a more autocratic or authoritarian line. At other times where both quality and acceptance are significant, a more consultative or group style may come into play, or where acceptance is the overriding concern, delegation may be most successful. It all depends, and successful managers develop the ability to match the style with the situation.

When you are compelled to make a high-quality decision, other techniques can be employed to make sure that the decision is not contaminated by personal biases (see below). In some respects this decision-making technique merely builds on the cognitive process that we all use quite naturally when making judgements based on numerous bits of information. We accumulate the evidence and then assign different levels of importance to each factor before deciding on a course of action. Unfortunately, unless this process is systematic, there is a real danger that personal biases will creep in and certain elements will assume greater significance than they warrant.

Selecting a hockey player

To illustrate the technique in practice, imagine that you are a hockey coach and are selecting a team for an important league game. Many players are automatic selections and can be pencilled in without too much thought. However, there is one key defensive position that is open to two players. Both players have strengths and weaknesses, and it will be a difficult and potentially divisive choice unless handled sensitively.

To help decide and, what is more, to provide you with a concrete justification when the team is announced before the game, you first list all the attributes that are relevant to that position in the forthcoming match. Having listed these factors, you then assign a weight to each factor, from 1 (least important) to 10 (most important).

The two players are then scored on each attribute or factor out of 10 and their rating is then multiplied by the weighting to produce a score that is then totalled and can be compared, as in Table 9.2.

For this particular position, player A (393) gets the nod over player B (355). Critically, when you now approach both players, you can provide clear feedback as to why the choice was made and why you believe it was the correct decision. It will also provide the unsuccessful player with detailed feedback that can be translated into positive action for the future.

In the real world of sport, even this level of analysis will never completely eliminate the angst and anger attached to selection decision, and in many respects this cannot be avoided, as it is an indication that, if it hurts, it matters. However, at least you cannot be accused of acting on a whim.

7. Monitoring

Most of the skills and techniques already described ask the leader to look inward, to reflect. Introspection is important, but it must be counterbalanced with an aware-

TABLE 9.2 Selecting fairly

	Weight (W)	Player A		Player B	
		Rating (R)	W × R	Rating (R)	W × R
Speed	7	4	28	6	42
Distribution	6	7	42	6	36
Close stick work	4	5	20	3	12
Passing	3	8	24	7	21
Strength	8	9	72	2	16
Tackling	10	3	30	6	60
'Team member'	5	6	30	4	20
Age	2	8	16	4	08
Fitness	7	7	49	5	35
Competitiveness	8	8	64	8	64
Durability	3	6	18	7	21
Total			393		355

ness of what is going on outside, or monitoring. While the search for personality traits attached to leadership has been disappointing,[12] one attribute that often characterises good leaders is social perception or social intelligence. That is, being aware of others and having the skills to manage human relations. More generally, leaders typically have been characterised as being either socio-emotionally oriented (primarily concerned with good relations and maintaining harmony) or task oriented (concerned with the task at hand rather than good relations).

Whichever orientation you may incline to, it is imperative that the needs, expectations and feelings of others are accommodated in some way and then are reflected in your repertoire of management styles (directive, autocratic, democratic, consultative, delegative or laissez-faire).

Monitoring team dynamics can alert you to emerging issues, including processes of social influence. For example, although certain individuals may not have formal roles or titles, they may still be recognised by those around them as 'leaders', or at least influential, and it would be dangerous to ignore the influence that these players can wield on the team dynamic. Such individuals shouldn't be dismissed as disruptive influences and as a threat to authority, but instead it may be possible to harness their activities to the advantage of the team. This requires person-management skills that may not always sit comfortably with you, but the effort will be repaid.

To summarise, we list in the box three types of awareness that should be worked on.

Coaching awareness

- *Self-awareness*. Become aware of your preferred style of coaching/captaincy and try to expand and develop the range of approaches that you are able to use.
- *Social awareness*. As with motivation, a recognition of the characteristics of the teams and individuals you are working with is important. Also develop the skill of assessing changing situations quickly and adapting your approach accordingly. Try to balance the time that is spent on either technical skills or interpersonal concerns depending on the demands of the situation.
- *Exchange awareness*. Keep in mind that leadership is a two-way process. Followers allow themselves to be influenced and led only if they receive something in return.

8. Communicating

Reflecting and monitoring mean nothing if that information is not communicated effectively. For those new to coaching, management or captaincy, there is a temptation to adopt the communication style of a mentor or role model. This can be reassuring, but experience suggests that finding your own style sooner rather than later is likely to be more effective. Many of the best coaches and captains were far from great orators, preferring to speak with their actions or with a few, well-chosen words, and often leaving the limelight to those who are more comfortable in the glare of publicity. For example, Roy Keane (who managed Sunderland to Championship success in his first season in charge of the team, 2006–7) expects no more than 10 minutes' attention from his players:

> There might be a gut feeling, something that came to me during the week about our own team and our own performance. There might be something I might have heard before, but I try to add my own piece to it. We make players aware of the opposition. Five or 10 minutes of the opposition on DVD and then I talk to them. That's all you have really, 10 minutes.[13]

Traditionally coaches and players alike placed great store in the pre-match harangue or rant, supposedly rousing the troops to battle but more likely providing

Pre-match talk (courtesy of Inpho Photography)

little more than background noise (it is estimated that only around 5 per cent of pre-match talks can be recalled after the game!). Modern changing rooms bear little resemblance to the 'head-banging and hugging' locker rooms of old, with, at long last, an acknowledgement that each player must be afforded personal responsibility for preparing in a way that will optimise his or her own performance. Equally, half-time tirades have come to be replaced by more measured use of the available time, often incorporating a 'quiet time' for players to draw breath and reflect before gathering, and sharing information and instruction. In truth it is likely that many of the traditional rituals owed far more to relieving the coach's stress than preparing the players or athletes, and perhaps should be consigned to the waste bin of history. Also remember that a law of diminishing returns will apply – the first rant may have maximum impact, but the second may make less impression, and as for the third, fourth and fifth . . .

Content over style

The style of communication you employ should be your own, not borrowed. Instead, it is the *content* of the communication that is much more critical to motivating players and to influencing their performance. Through words and deeds, verbal and non-verbal, the coach and captain have the power to establish the climate for the team, a climate that can either allow players to develop or can inhibit expression and the display of skill. In order to maximise potential, a few simple rules, based on the previous chapters, are worth listing.

Golden rules

- *Set goals.* The highest levels of attainment will be reached when players are aware of what is expected of them, and where the goals which are set are difficult but possible. Describe performance in relation to objective standards or goals wherever feasible. These goals should be short-term, difficult but attainable.
- *Work to an agenda.* Have work schedules already to hand before sessions begin but be flexible enough to allow changes should circumstances demand. Communicate your requirements clearly in terms of training schedules and so on.
- *Provide positive feedback.* Let those players who reach these goals know that you are pleased. Positive reinforcement works; negative reinforcement is less effective. Use moderation and avoid lengthy comments. Be objective and avoid references to personalities.
- *Monitor performance.* Ensure that players are aware that you are constantly keeping an eye on their performance, in training and during competitions. This does not imply a constant dialogue but subtle reminders of your vigilance.

- *Emphasise quality.* Through monitoring, place the emphasis on quality of work rather than quantity. Again, feedback is important.
- *Allow honest mistakes.* With the emphasis on positive feedback it is important to allow players the freedom to make 'honest mistakes'. Constant criticism is bound to constrain expression and creativity.

9. Being fair

This issue speaks for itself. Sport itself rests on principles of fairness or fair competition. Without the foundation of fairness, the activity loses meaning for participants and spectators alike. Equally, it is impossible to continue to motivate and lead in an environment where fairness does not reside as a core value – lose fairness and trust will not be far behind.

One technique to ensure that fairness is sustained is to be conscious of principles of social exchange. All social relationships can be thought of as exchanges; we give and we receive, and we continue to invest in a relationship so long as we feel the books balance. What each person defines as a reward or a cost is unique, but it is rare to find a healthy relationship where all parties do not feel they benefit from the association. Over long-term relationships, awareness of social exchange (what did I give?, what did I get?) becomes less pronounced, but in new

It isn't fair (courtesy of iStockphoto)

relationships or when relationships have been damaged, exchange awareness is heightened. In these situations it is imperative that there is sensitivity to feelings of inequity when interacting with team members or athletes.

Taking this approach further, leadership itself can be characterised as a process of exchange. Leaders are given status and power, but in return those who are led expect to be rewarded, with fair treatment and with success. Once more, in the early stages of a relationship there is heightened awareness of costs and benefits, and it is dangerous to make assumptions that all is well without relying on regular feedback to check your perception against others.

10. Managing conflict

As Chapter 8 makes clear, in the context of team dynamics conflict is not a dirty word, and healthy conflict or competition is a necessary ingredient in the make-up of any successful team. In turn this means that a good leader must expect to be a good conflict manager, recognising the positive and the negative sides of conflict before responding in a way that meets the demands of the situation. Before jumping in with both feet, it is worthwhile reflecting on the nature of the conflict and deciding how to respond. When dealing with a conflict, either brewing or brewed, the following questions may help you come to grips with the issues more effectively.

Is the conflict genuine or false?

In other words, is this a genuine disagreement between two or more people, or is the conflict nothing more than a misunderstanding or communication breakdown. If it is the latter, the fix is usually more straightforward and involves correcting the misperceptions and bridging the communication gap before matters turn from bad to worse. However, if the breakdown in communication is merely symptomatic of a wider problem within the team, then this must be addressed at source.

Is the conflict positive or negative?

Many conflicts within teams or between coaches and athletes are positive, reflecting genuine differences of opinion, and these should be acknowledged as such and worked through accordingly. Unfortunately, when this positive label and approach is not applied quickly, there is the potential for spillage into other issues, and relationships can become quickly contaminated. At the same time, many positive conflicts may not need to be managed at all but actively encouraged if they create a climate that is productive and successful. Deciding the nature of the conflict, positive or negative, will help determine the nature of the intervention, if any.

Who is involved?

Determining just who are the key players is always important. For example, a major dispute within a club may have been sparked by a disagreement between two players, but others then become caught up, sometimes against their will. These innocent bystanders soon find there is no fence to sit on but are asked to take sides. Determining who are the main players and who are the support artists is essential.

What are the issues?

Often the history of the conflict will reveal an interesting sequence of events involving the interplay between many factors, including the following:

- *interests* (what I want, what you want)
- *understanding* (what I understand, what you understand)
- *values* (what is important to me, what is important to you)
- *styles* (the way I do things, the way you do things)
- *opinions* (what I think, what you think)
- *identities* (who I am, who you are).

Over time the root cause of the conflict may have been lost or clouded by later events. Unpicking the conflict and its history can be helpful in sequencing resolution techniques, often involving a strategy of dealing with the easiest issues first (and so creating a climate of conciliation), before moving on to tackle the major bones of contention. Ordinarily, only one of the factors outlined above presents itself as a major obstacle to resolution – values. If one or more players subscribe to a value system that is different from the system operating in the team or club, drastic measures may be called for to remedy the problem. If the conflict is based on any of the others, the solution is often easier to reach through a managed process of reconciliation.

Who is best placed to deal with this and how?

After you have taken time to work through the essential elements, the last stage involves working out a strategy for conflict resolution based on one or more conflict management styles (see below). You may decide to allow the situation to continue, perhaps if the degree of 'hurt' is still not great enough to guarantee engagement, or you may decide that it is better dealt with by others. Whatever decision you reach, it must be a strategic one, not influenced by emotion, in order to increase the likelihood of success.

Conflict-management styles

Having diagnosed, you are now in a position to apply the conflict-management style that is best suited to deal with this situation. The literature tends to agree that up to five styles can be used individually or in combination, and these are outlined briefly over the page. Common sense will often dictate which style to employ, but recognising that there are alternatives is useful, as is acknowledging that we are each inclined to use one style more often than others. If you are interested in finding out which styles you tend to use most often, try the following web link: www1.orange.co.uk/about/community/downloads/customercare/CONFLICT STYLESQUESTIONNAIREcc1.pdf

Managing conflict successfully

Forcing (competing)

When to use. Use forcing whenever quick, decisive action is vital, especially on important issues where unpopular courses of action need to be implemented fast – as in enforcing unpopular rules, discipline, health and safety. It is also a useful style on vital issues when you know you are right. Finally, it is a sad fact of life that bullies respond positively to being bullied, so this style can protect you from people who may try to abuse their power or take advantage of you.

Confronting (collaborating)

When to use. This style helps find a common solution when both sets of concerns are too important to be compromised, or when your objective is to learn (including testing your own assumptions and understanding the views of others). It is also useful for merging insights from people with different perspectives on a problem, thereby gaining commitment by incorporating their concerns into a joint decision. If hard feelings have been aroused in a relationship, this style will help to rebuild bridges.

Sharing (compromising)

When to use. Compromising works best when goals are not too important or worth the effort or potential disruption of more assertive modes. In particular this is true when two opponents with equal power are strongly committed to mutually exclusive goals. The style will help achieve temporary settlements of complex issues under time pressure, or serve as a fall-back when collaboration or competition fails to be successful.

Withdrawing (avoiding)

When to use. Use withdrawing when an issue is trivial and of only passing importance, or when other more important issues are pressing. Equally, use withdrawing when you perceive no chance of satisfying your concerns or the potential damage of confronting outweighs the benefits of its resolution. It helps buy time either when emotions are running high, allowing perspective and composure to be regained, or when the gathering of more information outweighs the advantages of an immediate solution. Finally, there may be situations where others can resolve the conflict more effectively, or when the issue seems tangential or symptomatic of another more basic issue.

Smoothing (accommodating)

When to use. Accommodate when you realise privately that you are wrong – it will allow a better position to be heard and will show that you are reasonable. It is especially valuable as a style when the issue is much more important to the other person than to yourself – for example, as a goodwill gesture to help maintain a cooperative relationship. By giving ground you can build up 'social credits' for later issues that are important to you ('you owe me one'), especially when you make clear that you have made a tactical decision to adopt this tactic. Accommodating preserves harmony in difficult times, and in the long term, it aids the development of subordinates by allowing them to experiment and learn from their own mistakes – letting go.

Common sense, aided by a structured decision-making process as outlined above, can normally succeed in turning difficult situations around. As a manager or coach, you will already be dealing daily with conflict, and often very effectively. This guidance may simply reinforce your existing good practices, or it may help prevent a drama turning into a crisis.

Chapter 10

Ending?

I travel not to go anywhere, but to go. I travel for
travel's sake. The great affair is to move.
Robert Louis Stevenson, from *Travels with a
Donkey in the Cevennes*, 1879

Introduction

By now you may think that it's all over, done and dusted –
that the fat lady's bellowed, so that there's nothing more to
be said or sung. That's understandable because, through
the preceding chapters, we have tried to offer you a com-
prehensive guide or Cook's tour through sport psychology.
But unlike other tours that you may have taken in your
life, this one doesn't have a definite end point. That's why
there's a question mark after the chapter title. Why? Two
reasons are important. First, until now, you've largely been
a passenger as we drove you through the landscape of sport
psychology. But at this stage, you have to take the wheel
and become the *driver* of your own future progress. In this
sense of accepting a new responsibility, your journey is
only really beginning. The second reason why this chapter
does not signal the end is that skill development is an active
cyclical process, not a passive linear one. You have to *make*

Some people are on the pitch! They think it's all over! It is now! (courtesy of Inpho Photography / Getty Images)

it happen – not wait for it to happen. A lesson from sport is worth repeating at this point: as soon as you passively wait for the final whistle or mindlessly play down the clock, you run the risk of undoing all your previous good work. As the old saying goes, don't count the time – make the time count! Remember that when the going gets tough, the tough keep doing what got them there in the first place. So, where does that leave you now?

Well, as a reminder, let's return to where we began with *Pure Sport*. Put simply, the voyage of exploration that we have tried to chart has one goal in mind – to help you realise your sporting or coaching potential. If you feel that you have come to the end of that journey and you have nothing left to discover, we will have failed. So long as you stay actively involved with sport, this journey should never end but should keep driving you forward and upward.

Across all sports, there have been too many examples of those who failed to realise their true potential because they mistakenly felt that they had already reached the terminus, journey's end, maybe having reached a significant milestone. Instead they should have acknowledged that it was just one more stop along the way. On any journey, there will be times when you may choose to stop and admire the view, but eventually the need to travel on should stir you to stride forward. Without that desire to journey and see what lies ahead, you are settling for a

Onwards and upwards (courtesy of iStockphoto)

comfortable life rather than a challenging one, and you should contemplate retirement.

If you flick back through the pages of the previous chapters, you should see that *nowhere* do we signal an end point but a whole series of new beginnings – techniques, skills and procedures that you continue to develop and carry with you on your sporting travels. To paraphrase clumsily the great writer and traveller, Robert Louis Stevenson, it is the *journey*, not the destination, that really matters.

Speaking of a journey, along the way you know that you will meet with good times and bad times, and that both matter to you – but neither too much. After all, without the one (i.e. failure), you can never hope to enjoy the other, success. What is more, you accept that you will continue to learn far more from your disasters than your triumphs, and, in the words of Rudyard Kipling's evocative poem 'If',

Remember to travel light!

you can learn to 'treat those two imposters just the same'.[1] Chapter 7 in particular should help you to use the bad times as well as the good times to your advantage.

To make your sporting journey as enjoyable as possible, it is imperative that you travel light. Experienced travellers know that you move most easily and quickly with the minimum of baggage. Let's face it, if you are carrying someone else's luggage and heading for a destination that was not your choice, then the journey can become tiresome and heavy. As a quick reminder, bring to mind these two questions from Chapter 2 – why are you doing it? (hopefully, for the twin goals of challenge and enjoyment), and who are you doing it for? (chiefly yourself). These remain the simple foundations on which to build and sustain a successful sporting career.

Your travel bag

With reference to Chapters 1 and 2, travelling light is critical but there are two small pieces of equipment that you may need to have with you on your adventure. The first is a mirror. This is not to check who is coming up behind you, nor to look too far around the next corner, but to use as a constant way of reminding yourself who you are and where you are. Lose sight of a realistic and honest sense of self-identity and trouble lies in store.

The second piece of equipment can be hidden well from view. Although it weighs very little, it will keep you moving ahead. It is 'the chip', or to be more precise, a chip on the shoulder. (It has been said that a well-balanced athlete often has a chip on both shoulders, but that's just greedy; one is plenty!) Don't regard this as a character flaw or mistakenly confuse it with arrogance or overconfidence. The chip is a positive indication that whatever has been achieved is never quite enough, and this drive then continues to fuel the hunger for more.

What is more, it can never be used as an excuse for sulking when the best-laid plans fail to come together. Reality tends to deliver cruel blows. But knowing the chip is on your shoulder is a sure sign that your journey has not come to an end but that you are willing to continue to move on, learning as you go. The maxim that we employ in Chapter 3 ('Feck it, do it, think about it') may sound crude, but it encapsulates the mindset of someone who is able to perform unburdened by doubt, who keeps analysis in its place (after the event), but who is always willing to learn before moving on, older and wiser. In this way, the journey itself becomes inspiring and energising, with you firmly in control at the centre of affairs.

Skills such as those associated with goal setting and profiling become crucial in helping you stay on track and equipping you with systematic ways of continuing to review and then improve. These can then dovetail with many of the techniques that we have outlined in Chapters 4, 5, 6 and 7 concerning stress management, imagery, concentration and self-talk. These techniques must be tailored to your own needs and circumstances but should provide you with a responsive portfolio that can help you to continue to explore your sporting potential.

To this point, the journey we have described is a solitary expedition, a journey of self-discovery and self-fulfilment. Not surprisingly, this is only one part of the equation because sport invariably involves teams, and it is at this point that a heavy qualification must be added to our commentary so as to accommodate the social alongside the individual.

There have been many great and talented athletes who never fully came to terms with the team element of their sport for one simple reason – individual ambition stood in the way of collective ambition. Everything we have described to date in terms of personal development can continue to flourish in a team environment so long as the individual is willing to buy unreservedly into a critical team value – collective ambition. In the words of one of the greatest coaches of all time, John Wooden, when describing Lewis Alcindor (later Kareem Abdul-Jabbar), one of the greatest basketball players of all time (and the NBA's highest points scorer, with 38,387 across his professional career):

> Lewis believed the team came first. . . . A great player who is not a team player is not a great player. Lewis Alcindor was a great team player. Why? Because his first priority was the success of the team, even at the expense of his own statistics.[2]

This idea of collective ambition is echoed by José Mourinho, the soccer manager who guided Porto to Champions' League success and who won numerous titles with Chelsea. In explaining his coaching philosophy, he said:

Kareem Abdul-Jabbar (courtesy of Inpho Photography)

> Everything is aimed at one thing – the quest for performance. The aim of my
> form of relationship is not that the players like me, the only objective is the
> performance of the group. I sacrifice the individual for the collective.[3]

Collective ambition is not a difficult concept to grasp. Indeed, in isolation none of
the messages in *Pure Sport* should be difficult either to understand or to translate
into realistic actions. To repeat ourselves, sport psychology is not rocket science
(although it does emphasise the need for target awareness, something which all
rockets require!), but it is extremely difficult to bring together consistently all of the
elements of peak performance.

A common mistake made by many sportspeople and coaches is being too
selective and reactive, cherry-picking only those elements that seem to be most

relevant at any time to remedy a problem that's suddenly become evident. In its worst form, this approach would involve bringing in a sport psychologist to address a team at a time of crisis – usually just before an important competitive event. Not surprisingly, these 'firefighting' tactics rarely work effectively for at least three reasons. For a start, they convey a message to players that optimal psychological preparation is not really their responsibility but is best achieved by an 'expert' outsider. This problem is especially likely to occur at the highest levels in sport where players have so much specialist assistance available to them (as in making travel and training plans and in packing gear bags) that they can unwittingly become helpless and indecisive. Second, calling in a sport psychologist at the last minute suggests that proper mental preparation is a 'quick fix' rather than a systematic philosophy. Finally, in our experience, any short-term benefits that may accrue from hearing a fresh voice prior to a big match are likely to disappear quickly unless players are persuaded to buy into the entire preparation package. And that package is precisely what we have tried to explore in this book. Put simply, we hope that *Pure Sport* has shown you how to identify and assemble the mental elements of sporting excellence. Piece by piece, we have tried to reveal the jigsaw that is commonly known as sport psychology but which actually encompasses the bringing together of certain thoughts, feelings and actions in the creation of a high-quality sporting performance. We leave the rest to you – enjoy the remainder of the chapter.

Frequently asked questions (FAQs)

Over the years, we have been called on by many people involved in sport to help them deal with difficult situations involving both individual athletes and the management of teams. As a conclusion to this chapter, we thought it may be useful to provide a brief flavour of some of these problems under the heading of 'Frequently asked questions' (FAQs), and also to sketch some possible solutions. In each case, we present a question that we are often asked and we then outline some practical issues that it raises. In keeping with the tone of this book, however, our advice comes with a strong health warning attached – proceed with caution. No two people or situations will ever be identical, and so there is little likelihood that one analysis or intervention will achieve magical results when practised on different people and situations. Instead weigh up the facts of each situation before tailoring your advice – horses for courses.

In passing, there is an unfortunate trend in popular books on sport psychology to endorse a 'one size fits all' intervention approach whereby the exact same psychological strategies (e.g. concentration techniques) are recommended uncritically for a variety of different athletic problems and situations. In our experience, these strategies have to be tailored to the needs of performers – bearing in mind such factors as the structure of their sport (for example, whether it is timed or untimed; whether play is continuous or 'stop start') and athletes' own informal theories about when and how they perform optimally. For example, if you're a golfer, the type and timing of 'trigger words' you use in order to concentrate effectively will differ from those you might use in soccer. And whether or not you use any concentration technique *at all* depends on the importance that you attach to mental preparation in the first place.

With these cautions in mind, we now present some ideas based on our practical experience to help you to translate theory into practice.

FAQs about individual performance

'I've lost confidence'

Admitting that you have lost your confidence is often a 'catch-all' excuse for all manner of issues relating to underperformance. In fact, it is probably the most common problem that sport psychologists are asked to deal with. In practice, the statement, 'I've lost confidence', usually serves to trigger discussion of a wide range of issues where psychology has started to impose itself unduly over action, and performance has suffered as a consequence. For example, if things have not been going well for you, you may be over-analysing and in the process, hampering your game (paralysis by analysis).

At one level, 'confidence' is easy to define. Put simply, it's the *belief* that you can play a certain shot or achieve a certain goal no matter what the prevailing circumstances are. Confident players think they can do it – no matter what situation they face. But at a deeper level, confidence is a complex phenomenon. Like any belief, it is shaped by circumstances and so may change in different situations. For example, few people are equally confident in all of their skills. If you're a golfer, you may be more confident with your driver than your wedge. Or if you're a baseliner in tennis, you're likely to be more confident at the back of the court than at the net. Clearly, the fact that confidence is skill- and situation-specific means that to improve it, you have to work *deliberately* harder on those aspects of your game that you least enjoy.

A perceived lack of confidence is usually the end product of a process that is likely to involve a combination of many of the issues we have addressed throughout the book (such as measuring your performance solely by results – a problem that can be overcome by goal setting; see Chapter 3). So, you should never fall into the trap of seeing a lack of form as a confidence issue set apart from other concerns. Instead, you should try to engage in a more objective and scientific evaluation of your performance in order to identify the reasons why your form has dropped temporarily. This habit of disciplined reflection will enable you to go back to basics, to identify strengths as well as weaknesses, and then use this foundation to develop a programme of rehabilitation, to gradually re-establish your form. Speaking of strengths, you need to remind yourself of your special skills or 'weapons' from time to time, especially if you have a tendency to judge yourself harshly. These skills are usually ones that you enjoy performing and are most confident about – and they establish a solid platform for the rest of your game.

Remember, talent never goes away but it *can* be mislaid. Potentially you will always be as good as your *best* game, and not your last game. If your form seems to have slipped, try not to burden yourself with high expectations of a flawless performance but set more realistic goals within a reasonable and attainable timescale. For example, if you're a soccer striker whose confidence has dropped because you haven't scored for a while, it might be helpful to set yourself a short-term target of getting a certain number of shots on target in your next game. Also, remember that too much confidence can be as dangerous as too little. There may be times when everything comes together, but a more realistic expectation is repeatable good performance (RGP), adjusting the bar as you progress. Successfully balancing the 3 Cs (confidence, commitment and control), and learning to enjoy the challenges of competition will provide a much more solid foundation for success than overblown confidence, summed up not as 'will win' but '*can* win'.

'I can't seem to rise to the big occasion'

The problem may not be as simple as you think. Perversely, in these circumstances it is almost invariably the case not that players are unmotivated but that they can't cope with the pressure of the big occasion. That is, they actually may be rising too high to the occasion and as a consequence are moving well outside the performance zone that normally works well for them – in other words, they are too stressed. At this point, an old maxim in sport is relevant: success comes in *cans*, not *can'ts*! Managing your anxiety (as through the techniques outlined in Chapter 4) may help to re-establish the critical point on the 'stress speedometer' that you need to be at in order to play at your best.

If you find it difficult to rise to the big occasion, it may be helpful to look at specific times in the past when you played to your full potential. Remember that if you did it before, you can do it again. By reflecting on what it felt like to be playing at that level, and by reminding yourself of how you prepared for your best performance, you can develop a pre-match routine that you can follow every time you compete. According to many commentators, one remarkable feature of Tiger Woods' preparation for major tournaments is just how unremarkable it is. He knows what works and so he doesn't change his routines. In other words, why change a winning formula?

One of the biggest mistakes any player can make is treating the majors as something special. In terms of preparation, Tiger Woods does not do that. Tiger gets a lot of credit for being able to get his game in its best shape for the biggest four weeks of the season, but the fact is that he warms up for every event as if it is a major. That is his 'secret'.[4]

For some people, this 'winning formula' may involve learning not to think too much about things outside their control such as the result of the match or how their opponents will play. What might help you to block out such negative thoughts are deliberate distractions (e.g. music, other activities) and planned 'time-outs'. Interestingly, many golfers hold conversations with their caddies as they walk between shots simply to prevent themselves from thinking negatively.

Alternatively, it sometimes happens that big occasions bring to the fore another problem – fear of failure. If you are worried about letting others down and are focused on the *result* rather than performance, then you need to switch your focus to specific, personal performance goals (e.g. 'I'm going to keep up with play' or 'I'm going to follow the player I'm marking no matter where he goes'). Before competition, make sure that you create space to do your own thing and don't be caught up in other people's preparation routines – they may work for them, but you know, deep down, that they do not work for you. At the same time, if you are spending too much time analysing and reflecting and this is causing anxiety, then deliberately see how you can turn off the spotlight, as for example, by helping others.

'I can't raise my game for anything other than the big occasion'

Sometimes, experienced athletes who have 'been there' and 'done that' over a long period of time may become a little complacent and lose the capacity to raise their game when it's necessary. If this problem applies to you, one way of rekindling your 'edge' for a forthcoming competitive event is to shift your focus away from outcome or result goals and towards personal performance targets. For example, if you're a footballer who has played hundreds of matches, it's difficult to sustain the work rate that you showed in your first game – unless you give yourself a 'personal-best' challenge. Put simply, this means trying your best to work harder and be more active in some area of your game today than you did yesterday. For example, can you win more tackles in your next game than you did in your last one? Explicit performance objectives expressed in activity levels are very useful in these circumstances because they remind us of our promise to ourselves. Alternatively, you may need to shift focus from internal to external, and so become more involved in the management and general well-being of other team-mates. This should have a positive effect on motivation and commitment, especially in situations where some players have developed the habit of being critical of less experienced team-mates.

'My head isn't right . . . I seem to drift in and out of games'

Younger players, in particular, often complain that they find it difficult to maintain concentration for the full game. As we explained in Chapter 5, this problem is perfectly normal, as our minds were not designed to pay attention to *anything* for very long. However, that chapter contains many practical techniques that will help you to break your playing time down into more manageable chunks through 'restructuring', to focus on one thought or action, and to switch your concentration from one target to another as required. Interestingly, many top coaches and captains use pre-match or half-time talks to emphasise the various stages in a game and to set specific targets that break the whole into smaller parts (recall World-Cup-winning rugby coach Clive Woodward's use of a strategy called 'second-half' thinking; Chapter 4). Even knowing that you are not required to maintain a single type of 'focus' (e.g. narrow, external) for the entire competition can help you to overcome the problem. After all, forewarned is forearmed.

'I can never reproduce in games what I have shown I'm capable of in practice'

This is a common problem among those who have not developed standard pre-match routines to ensure consistency of approach, or who have not come to terms with the stress levels that work well for them. Less commonly, this may be because the athlete is not interested in competition, but, if so, it is important to understand why (Chapters 2, 3 and 4). For those who cannot bridge the gap between practice and competition, the starting point must be quantifying or measuring how large the gap is before putting in place techniques for bridging. It is unlikely this will be achieved overnight but instead through a measured process that first minimises the difference between the two (that is, treating competition as no more than another practice session), before slowly but surely allowing the athlete to become more comfortable with the buzz of competition. This may take time but is not an insurmountable problem.

'I often seem to pick up injuries coming up to big games'

It is very common for top level athletes to report picking up niggling injuries in the build-up to important games. Sometimes, this trend is merely a by-product of increasing monitoring and a heightened sense of self-awareness that comes from wanting to ensure that everything is 'just right' for the big day. It's a bit like checking that every door and window of your house is locked before you go on holiday. In itself, this anxiety should not be a major cause for concern – especially where the player has performed well under similar circumstances in the past. On other occasions, reports of an injury may act as a psychological insurance policy or ready-made excuse that can be pulled out of the drawer if performance turns out to be below par – a phenomenon known as 'self-handicapping'.[5] The idea that 'I didn't play well because I had an injury' contrasts sharply with the 'no excuses' mantra of *Pure Sport*.

A related problem may occur if fear of failure creates a mindset whereby athletes do not want to meet the challenge and use the injury as an excuse for crying-off ('blobbing out'). This problem may call for a more significant

219

intervention to change the orientation to competition from 'I'll die if I lose' to 'I'll do my best to win'. If the injuries are stress-related, there may be greater cause for concern. For example, an athlete may constantly overtrain to compensate for a lack of confidence, and injuries may emerge as a consequence of this excessive regimen.

'I never play well when — is watching; I'll never be as good as —'

These statements are related and, in our experience, indicate that the people concerned have placed too great an emphasis on *external* reference points in evaluating their own performance. They indicate the thinking of people who are burdened by a high fear of failure. The solution is straightforward but can take time – to make the athlete more self-contained and self-evaluative. For example, if certain athletes, are constantly looking for ego stroking by others, deliberately put in place performance-evaluation procedures that they must complete immediately after competition. In this way, they will eventually come to rely more on their own judgements than those of others. At the same time, he or she will develop a stronger and more comfortable sense of self-identity, and reference to role models should become less important.

'I spend a lot time thinking about the game beforehand; usually "what if" . . .'

As we mentioned earlier, for many competitors, too much 'focus' before a game can be just as dangerous as too little focus. If this problem seems familiar, you should reflect on what has worked best for you in the past and use this to bring together medium and short-term pre-competition schedules that are effective. This may well involve keeping busy with other things if thinking about the game doesn't help. What is more, when thinking about the forthcoming game, it is important to follow one of the golden rules of imagery as outlined in Chapter 6 – always use imagery in a constructive way by visualising positive targets and actions. Time spent in mental practice should be deliberate and planned, using whatever techniques are appropriate for your sport and for you. After all, why hurt yourself? What is the point? Just lying and thinking about the game is often a recipe for disaster, and filling time more productively can often overcome this problem.

'I can't get to sleep before a game'

A common problem that is often made worse because before competition we try to get a good night's sleep, go to bed earlier than usual, and so disturb our normal sleep patterns. The result – we end up lying awake. The first rule is, don't break with routine – before competition go to bed at the usual time. Second, try this simple technique for drifting off, known as 'chaining'. You have to concentrate hard on this technique but with practice it can be very effective. The trick is simply to allow your mind to wander from one thought or image to the next without ever questioning why or reflecting where the chain is going. It can be random; it can be circular, but never question it. Just allow your mind to drift, until you drift into sleep.

'I'm finding it hard to come back from injury'

This is a familiar problem for many athletes, especially when the injury is sudden or perhaps interrupts a run of good form.

The Irish rugby player, Paul O'Connell, returned from the British Lions rugby tour to New Zealand in 2005 knowing that he faced surgery and a period of enforced rest, but also knowing that he had not played to his potential on tour. His solution was simple. He determined that he would return from injury not only as well as when he left but even better. This is a good example of the type of personal-best approach that motivates winners in sport (see also above, 'I can't seem to rise to the occasion'). He then decided to use the time out to reflect on how he could improve as a player, and left no stone unturned in the process. So instead of the injury time being a frustrating, enforced absence from the game, he structured it with a goal in mind – to come back stronger, and he did, emerging as probably the world's greatest forward in 2006/7.

In contact sports, awareness of an injury can inhibit play. To overcome this heightened state of awareness, it can be helpful to concentrate attention on highly

Paul O'Connell (courtesy of Inpho Photography)

structured, short-term performance goals. In this way, one's attention is diverted from the dominant thought, 'how does it feel?' to the more helpful question, 'how did I play?'

'If my first touch goes well, that's a great sign, but if it doesn't, forget it!'

Fortune-telling is bad news for athletes. In our experience, the above statement is a prime example of people who admit being out of control and who believe that luck, chance or fate is controlling their performance. On good days, if things start well, this can inspire confidence, but, unfortunately, on bad days the chances of turning a situation around are slim. This type of player will spend the early minutes of a game testing whether or not things are right, and may try to make amends by 'upping the ante' each time to remedy earlier errors. The lack of perceived control in such circumstances is disconcerting. If this problem applies to you, a good solution is to put yourself centre-stage and to highlight the degree of control that you have over your own performance. In particular, in the early stages of competition it is important to emphasise not the first touch but general work rate and activity. Also, remember that the only people who don't make mistakes are people who never try anything at all.

'If I make a mistake, I can't get it out of my head'

So many of the issues we have already discussed can reveal themselves in a situation where the spontaneous becomes thoughtful, where thought interferes with action, and, in particular, where past mistakes continue to cast a shadow over present performance. Staying in the here-and-now is critical to good performance. Look ahead and you lose sight of what you are doing; look behind and you will find that 'what ifs' cloud your judgement. With practice there are many mental skills that can be learned to draw the line – to consign to history previous mistakes and instead to play it as it comes. A good coach will not choose to burden players with history but will have effective ways of clearing away the detritus to allow freedom of expression.

FAQs about team performance

'They're slow starters'

This statement may characterise teams that are not entirely sure of themselves, and so wait for the game to spark them into action or dictate the play, when they could be far more proactive than reactive. Often teams that wait for a catalyst such as a setback or a bad decision to spur them to action have developed this reactive approach because they have spent too long dwelling on how to counter the opposition instead of how to stamp their mark on the game. In these situations there may be a need to instil a greater sense of identity and hunger based on longer-term goals, and to ensure that the team shares a common sense of purpose. Practical pre-match techniques such as focusing all attention on the first 5 minutes ('big five') can help.

'They're poor finishers'

This can often reflect one of two issues – either the team lacks self-belief and its capacity to win through, or the team has too much self-belief and eases up because it thinks the contest is over. In the first case, it could be that the team is not entirely sure what it is about (does it know what its strengths or 'weapons' are?) and how to win. When the chips are down, there may be a lack of confidence in the winning formula for the team as a whole, and so players may start to adopt their own styles of play. Reinforcing team strategies and game plans can overcome this problem, and using previous occasions where the team won through will help to bolster confidence. However, if the problem is more deep-seated, it may be time to reflect on more radical measures involving the make-up of the team.

At the other extreme, a team that is too confident may expect that the game will eventually drift its way, rather than devising strategies to take control and move the game in its direction. Again, these problems may call for radical solutions involving changes to personnel in order to change the culture of the team, or strategies can be devised to remind the team how to take charge.

'They drift in and out of games'

As with individual players, where a team plays in fits and starts, individually and collectively, it may be useful to break the game down into much smaller units, and to make sure that evaluation looks across all facets of the game, and not just the last few minutes. Also, with 'drifting' teams, it is helpful to set an objective before the game – such as for each player to focus on the here-and-now and make a big effort to win his or her individual battle with opponents – and for the team to win each half.

'They seem to leave it all on the training pitch'

When teams seem to play better in practice than in competition, an obvious question arises. Have players developed the right preparation techniques to control their own stress levels or has this been left to chance? Are training routines artificial or have they been designed to simulate match conditions? (See also Chapter 5 for some suggestions about simulating some common distractions in practice situations.) Are players being asked to consider the big picture too much, or are they given freedom only to think of their own task – such as the player who is their immediate opponent? There should be no reason why training performances cannot be replicated during competition, and a systematic review of obstacles to this objective should be undertaken. There may be broader issues, however, in terms of personal motivations, and time should be spent understanding these problems.

'They just haven't come together as a unit'

If a team seems to lack any obvious sense of identity or cohesion, it may be that sufficient time has not been spent buying into a common goal, or there may be different agenda at work within the team. Before proceeding, it is important to make sure that task cohesion is really the issue, or do they play well together but simply choose not to mix away from their sport? Has money or other rewards got in the way? Do they know who they are? Have they forged an identity? One remedy may be to use a few key buzzwords to remind the team who they are and what they are about (one example is 'BLAH' – *b*uzzing, *l*ight, *a*ngry, *h*onest).

'They always seem to fall at the critical hurdle'

The team that does well in early rounds of competitions but folds when it comes to the crunch game may be carrying too much baggage around with them. For example, are they burdened by the history of the club or carrying the weight of expectation because of previous failures? In these circumstances there is a need to cocoon the team from the wider club and supporters, to define the identity from within the group of players and not by external forces or history.

Another technique is to describe a championship campaign as a series of hurdles to be overcome, each one essentially the same but with unique characteristics. A good team meets the last hurdle just like the first, and has in place pre-match routines that never vary, so when the big games come along it is just another day; the same task, just different venue and opposition. With this in mind, to avoid 'overheating', it is important not to change routines in later rounds of a competition but to consolidate them over time and as a tournament progresses.

'They're a very quiet team'

Quietness can signify two things – either a team that knows what it is about and so has no need to talk, or a team that lacks the self-belief to express itself. Which explanation is more accurate in any given case must be worked through, to find out if there is actually a problem or not. The answer lies in having a level of communication that does not ebb and flow as the tide of a game changes but is used to manage the game and the impression created. For example, if the team becomes quiet when the tide is flowing against them, this is quickly picked up by the opposition as a sign of a lack of confidence.

Beforehand, it may be useful to designate key players with the responsibility to keep the 'noise level' at the right pitch across the pitch. Positions such as goalkeeper are crucial in this regard along with key players in specific areas (e.g. defence, midfield, attack). Also, bench players can be given specific responsibility for keeping the volume high. At the same time you should also consider whether there is a more deep-seated problem of management's making – that they don't talk because they don't have anything to say. In other words, they are merely acting to your instructions. The remedy does not need repeating – learn to let go.

'They never seem to follow the game plan'

This is often indicative of different agenda at work within a team and often charac-terises either young teams (who have never been on message) or mature teams (who have drifted off message). In both situations, it is useful to identify the cliques within the team or among management. Do same players sit together and train together, or do younger and older players not mix? The solution involves gentle social engineering to mix the team up and break alliances; for example by intro-ducing intrateam competition, reorganising changing arrangements, travel arrangements, accommodation, etc.

'They lack flair and only do what they're told'

This may be a consequence of being too 'hands on' – whatever instructions have been given in the past have worked so why bother thinking when you just do what you are told? This can be a hard nut to crack but has to begin with an honest acceptance that a culture of dependency has been fostered and it is now starting to have an adverse effect on performance. For example, they may turn up for games expecting to be motivated by someone else. What walks into the changing room is more important than what walks out, and danger lies in placing too much emphasis on that short time in the changing room prior to games.

'It's a lazy team'

Labelling any team as 'lazy' without sufficient evidence is a big mistake. However, if it becomes apparent that certain team members are not working hard enough, perhaps the label is justified. Laziness can occur in a team that has achieved too much, too soon and is finding it difficult to re-energise, or a team that has set its sights too low, or a team that has become too tight or too cohesive. In each case, the solution must involve ways of shattering the collective comfort zone, piece by piece. Unexpected changes in personnel may often be called for to stem the drift towards mediocrity, but often drastic action is the only cure.

'There are one or two in the squad who just aren't team players'

In any team there will always be those who do not appear to pull in the same direction as everyone else. Dealing with these players can be very difficult and time-consuming, especially when their individual talent is considerable. Eventually, there is no alternative but to sit down with a balance sheet and calculate the pros and cons – what does the player cost in terms of collective action and what does he or she give in personal performance? On the basis of this analysis, hard decisions must be made, but do not be fooled into assuming that yet more attention will be the solution; it often rewards attention-seeking behaviour, and sends the wrong signal to other players. Often, the harder you try, the easier it will be for the player to keep running away.

'How can I get my substitutes to make an impact?'

Increasingly, coaches and managers are becoming interested in practical ways of ensuring that their substitutes are as alert and focused as possible while they wait to be called into action in the match. This is a difficult challenge because it's hard to keep players' minds active when they're sitting on the bench. In general, however, it's helpful to ask players to look for certain patterns of play arising in their position and to encourage them to warm-up regularly by jogging along the sidelines during the game. Also, reminding substitutes about their strengths or 'weapons' can give them an edge when they enter the fray.

There's more!

For those whose thirst for psychological knowledge has yet to be sated, here are just a few texts that may be of interest.

Further reading

Andersen, M. B. (2000). (ed.) *Doing Sport Psychology*. Champaign, IL: Human Kinetics.

Andersen, M. B. (2005). *Sport Psychology in Practice*. Champaign, IL: Human Kinetics.

Beswick, B. (2001). *Focused for Soccer*. Champaign, IL: Human Kinetics.

Bull, S. J. (2000). *Sport Psychology, A Self-Help Guide*. Marlborough: Crowood Press.

Butler, R. J. (1996). *Sports Psychology in Action*. London: Butterworth/Heinemann.

Butler, R. J. (2000). *Sport Psychology in Performance*. London: Butterworth/Heinemann.

Cashmore, E. (2002). *Sport Psychology: The Key Concepts*. London: Routledge.

Cockerill, I. (ed.) (2002). *Solutions in Sport Psychology*. London: Thomson.

Cox, R. H. (2002). *Sport Psychology: Concepts and Applications* (5th ed.). St Louis, MO: McGraw-Hill.

Gardner, F. L. and Moore, Z. E. (2006). *Clinical Sport Psychology*. Champaign, IL: Human Kinetics.

Gill, D. L. (2000). *Psychological Dynamics of Sport and Exercise*. Champaign, IL: Human Kinetics.

Goldberg, A. (1998). *Sports Slump Busting: 10 Steps to Mental Toughness and Peak Performance*. Champaign, IL: Human Kinetics.

Greenlees, I. and Moran, A. P. (2003). *Concentration Skills Training in Sport*. Leicester: British Psychological Society, Sport and Exercise Psychology Section.

Halden-Brown, S. (2003). *Mistakes Worth Making: How to Turn Sports Errors into Athletic Excellence*. Champaign, IL: Human Kinetics.

Horn, T. S. (2002). *Advances in Sport Psychology*. Champaign, IL: Human Kinetics.

Jackson, S. and Csikszentmihalyi, M. (1999). *Flow in Sports: The Key to Optimal Experiences and Performances*. Leeds: Human Kinetics.

Jowett, S. and Lavallee, D. (2006). *Social Psychology in Sport*. Champaign, IL: Human Kinetics.

Lavallee, D., Kremer, J., Moran, A. and Williams, M. (2004). *Sport Psychology: Contemporary Themes*. London: Palgrave Macmillan.

Lavallee, D., Williams, J. and Jones, M. (2007). *Key Studies in Sport and Exercise Psychology*. Maidenhead, Berkshire: Open University Press.

LeUnes, A. and Nation, J. R. (2002). *Sport Psychology: An Introduction* (3rd ed.). Pacific Grove, CA: Brooks/Cole.

Lidor, R. and Henschen, K. (eds) (2002). *The Psychology of Team Sports*. Morgantown, WV: Fitness Information Technology.

Lidor, R., Morris, T., Bardaxoglou, N. and Becker, B. (2001). *The World Sport Psychology Sourcebook*. Morgantown, WV: Fitness Information Technology.

Moran, A. (2004). *Sport and Exercise Psychology: A Critical Introduction*. London: Psychology Press/Routledge.

Morris, T. and Gordon, S. (Eds) (2007). *Sport and Exercise Psychology: An International Perspective*. Morgantown, WV: Fitness Information Technology.

Morris, T. and Summers, J. (2004). *Sport Psychology: Theories, Applications and Issues* (2nd ed.). Chichester: Wiley.

Morris, T., Spittle, M. and Watt, A. P. (2005). *Imagery in Sport*. Champaign, IL: Human Kinetics.

Murphy, S. M. (ed) (1994). *Sport Psychology Interventions*. Champaign, IL: Human Kinetics.

Murphy, S. M. (ed) (2005). *The Sport Psych Handbook*. Champaign, IL: Human Kinetics.

Orlick, T. (2000). *In Pursuit of Excellence: How to Win in Sport and Life Through Mental Training*. Champaign, IL: Leisure Press.

Shaw, D., Gorely, T. and Corban, R. (2005). *Sport and Exercise Psychology*. Abingdon: BIOS Academic Publishers.

Taylor, J. and Wilson, G. S. (2005). *Applying Sport Psychology*. Champaign, IL: Human Kinetics.

Wann, D. L. (1997). *Sport Psychology*. Upper Saddle River, NJ: Prentice-Hall.

Weinberg, R. and Gould, D. (2007). *Foundations of Sport and Exercise Psychology*. Champaign, IL: Human Kinetics.

Williams, J. M. (2001). *Applied Sport Psychology: Personal Growth to Peak Performance*. Maidenhead: McGraw-Hill.

Wood, B. (1998). *Applying Psychology to Sport*. London: Hodder and Stoughton.

Notes

Chapter 1

1 How a swing doctor and a mind reader bolster the home defence (2006, Sept 20). *Guardian*, p. 7.
2 England need group therapy after Beswick fails to provide head start (2007, March 27). *The Times*, p. 76.
3 Golf psychologist banned after scuffle (2005, Nov 18). *The Irish Times*, p. 23 *http://news.bbc.co.uk/solpda/ukfs_sport/hi/newsid_4447000/4447124.stm*; *Irish Times*, Nov 18 2005.
4 Cited in Pelé, Pelé: My story (2006, 13 May). *Guardian*, p. 8.
5 Keeping sensible (2003, Oct 20). *The Irish Times*, p. 7.
6 Lewin, K. (1951). *Field Theory in Social Science*. New York: Harper.
7 Cited in MacRury, D. (1997) *Golfers on Golf*. London: Virgin Books, p. 95.
8 Chen, C. and Stevenson, H. W. (1995). Motivation and mathematics achievement: A comparative study of Asian-American, Caucasian-American, and East Asian high school students. *Child Development*, 66, 1215–1234.
9 Wooden, J. (with S. Jamison) (1997). *Wooden: A Lifetime of Observations and Reflections on and off the Court*. Lincolnwood, IL: Contemporary Books.
10 Cited in Reinharz, P. and Anderson, B. (2000), Bring back sportsmanship. *City Journal*, Spring 2000 (http://www.city-journal.org/html/10_2_bring_back_sportsmanship.html).
11 A potter's tale: Any colour will do (2002, April 20). *Guardian*, pp. 10–11.
12 Cited in LeUnes, A., and Nation, J. (2002). *Sport Psychology* (3rd ed). Pacific Grove, CA: Wadsworth, p. 18.
13 Cited in Global Hawaii – Michelle Wie website (www.global-hawaii.com/golf/michellewie/).
14 Black Knight of the fairways (2005, July 10). *Sunday Independent*, p. 12.

15 Ericsson, K. A., Krampe, R. T. and Tesch-Römer, C. (1993), The role of deliberate practice in the acquisition of expert performance. *Psychological Review*, 100, 363–406.
16 Harris, H. A. (1964) *Greek Athletes and Athletics*. Westport, CA: Greenwood Press.
17 Triplett, N. (1998). The dynamogenic factors in pace-making and competition. *American Journal of Psychology*, 9, 505–523.
18 Green, C. D. (2003). Psychology strikes out: Coleman R. Griffith and the Chicago Cubs. *History of Psychology*, 6, 267–283.
19 Thelwell, R. C. and Maynard, I. W. (2003). The effects of a mental skills package on 'repeatable good performance' in cricketers. *Psychology of Sport and Exercise*, 4, 377–396.
20 Cited in Patmore, A. (1986). *Sportsmen Under Stress*. London: Stanley Paul, p. 231.

Chapter 2

1 http://www.wada-ama.org/en/.
2 Green, C. D. (2003). Psychology strikes out: Coleman R. Griffith and the Chicago Cubs. *History of Psychology*, 6, 267–283.
3 Schnall, M. (2002). *What Doesn't Kill You Makes You Stronger: Turning Bad Breaks into Blessings*. Cambridge, MA: Perseus Publishing,
4 Keane, R. (with Eamon Dunphy, 2002). *Keane – The Autobiography*. London: Michael Joseph, p. 181.
5 Ferguson assumes full control in title campaign (1999, Feb 17). *Guardian*, p. 26.
6 Shaw, D., Gorely, T. and Corban, R. (2005). *Sport and Exercise Psychology*. Abingdon: BIOS Scientific Publishers, p. 62.
7 Ross, L. (1977). The intuitive psychologist and his shortcomings: Distortions in the attribution process. In L. Berkowitz (Ed), *Advances in Experimental Social Psychology*, vol. 10 (pp. 174–221). New York: Academic Press.

Chapter 3

1 Billie Jean King (2007, Sept.) *Weston Star*, p. 22.
2 Maslow, A. H. (1953). *Motivation and Personality*. New York: Harper & Row.
3 Porter, L. W. and Lawler, E. E. (1968). *Managerial Attitudes and Performance*. Homewood, IL: Dorsey Press.
4 Butler, R. J. (1996). *Sport Psychology in Action*. Oxford: Butterworth-Heinemann.
5 Cited in D. Fletcher (2006). British swimming, sports psychology, and Olympic medals: It's all in the mind. *World Swimming Coaches Association Newsletter*, 6, 5.
6 Locke, E. A. (1968). Toward a theory of task motivation and incentives. *Organizational Behaviour and Human Performance*, 3, 157–189.
7 Naber, J. (Ed.) (2005). *Awaken the Olympian Within: Stories from America's Greatest Olympic Motivators*. Irvine, CA: Griffin Publishing Group.

Chapter 4

1 How relaxed Chelsea took complete control (2005, Oct 15). *Guardian* (Sport), p. 3.
2 Relaxed Woods identifies the major pressure points (2001, April 6). *Guardian*, p. 26.
3 It's a kind of religion (2004, Oct 23). *Guardian*, p. 14 (*Weekend Magazine*).

4 Faldo dismisses fear of failure in a heartbeat (2004, July 15). *The Daily Telegraph*, p. 3 (*The Open*, special supplement).

5 Captain steers a steady ship (2002, Sept 26). *The Irish Times*, p. 19.

6 Getting up for the Ashes (1998, Nov 20). *Guardian* (Sport), p. 2.

7 Wilkinson, J. (2006). *My World*. London: Headline Book Publishing, pp. 49–50.

8 Dunn, J. G. H. and Syrotuik, D. G. (2003). An investigation of multidimensional worry dispositions in a high contact sport. *Psychology of Sport and Exercise*, 4, 265–282.

9 Wilkinson, J. (2006). *My World*. London: Headline Book Publishing.

10 O'Sullivan faces censure after walking out on Hendry match (2006, Dec 15). *Guardian* (Sport), p. 1.

11 Jonny just the latest star to suffer paralysis by analysis (2003, Nov 11). *The Daily Telegraph*, p. S4.

12 Christie's final race against time (1996, July 14). *The Sunday Times* (Sport), p. 4.

13 Blame it on the boogie (2003, May 9). *The Daily Telegraph*, p. S3.

14 Seigne's only song: 'Je ne regrette rien' (1997, Oct 5). *The Sunday Times* (Sport), p. 14.

15 Vealey, R. S. and Walter, S. M. (1994). On target with mental skills: An interview with Darrell Pace. *The Sport Psychologist*, 8, 428–441.

16 Interview: Ian Woosnam (2002, July 15). *Guardian* (Sport), p. 22.

17 England must find the cure for the spot-kick 'disease' (2000, May 19). *Guardian*, p. 35.

18 Woosnam, op. cit.

19 Breathe deeply and be happy with second (1996, Sep 27). *The Irish Times*, p. 7.

20 A loss of fate (2007, Feb 18). *Sunday Tribune*, p. 35.

21 Keeping cool with Michael Phelps (May 2 2007), *BBC Sport Academy*. www.news.bbc.co.uk/sportacademy/hi/sa/swimming/features/newsid_3921000/3921525/stm.

Chapter 5

1 Clarke enjoys special K day (1999, Aug 1). *The Sunday Times*, p. 13.

2 Cited in Clarke, D. and Morris, K. (2005). *Golf – The Mind Factor*. London: Hodder & Stoughton, p. 63.

3 Ibid.

4 Cited in Miller, B. (1997). *Gold Minds: The Psychology of Winning in Sport*. Marlborough, Wiltshire: Crowood Press, p. 64.

5 Just running (2004, Nov). *Cork Now*, pp. 5–8.

6 Focused Cech puts records low on his list of priorities (2005, April 30). *The Times*, p. 100.

7 Crowning my career in a major way (2004, June 22). *The Irish Times* (Sport), p. 2.

8 A photo at the finish fails to spoil Woods' day (2002, Sept 23). *The Daily Telegraph*, p. S9.

9 The top 10 sporting distractions (2004, Oct 24). *The Sunday Times* (Sport), p. 2.

10 Oh dear, so near but so far away (2005, July 12). *The Irish Times*, p. 21.

11 The golf pro who missed from 3 ft and lost £230,000 (2006, March 21). *The Times*, p. 5.

12 Brodkin, J. (2001) Pumped up for the mind games (Sept 14). *Guardian* (Sport), p. 34.

13 Cited in English, A. (2006). *Munster: Our Road to Glory*. Dublin: Penguin, p. 9.

14 Interview: Garry Sobers (2002, June 10). *Guardian* (Sport), p. 20.

15 Cool Goosen rides the storm (2004, June 22). *The Daily Telegraph*, p. S10.

16 Fear of failure haunted me right to the last second (2004, May 1). *Guardian* (Sport), p.12.

17 Cited in Moran, A. (1997). *The Pressure Putt: Doing Your Best When It Matters Most in Golf*. Aldergrove: Tutorial Services Ltd.

18 Holmes finds self-belief and double delight (2004, Aug 30). *Guardian*, p. 6.

19 Cited in English, A. (2006). *Munster: Our Road to Glory*. Dublin: Penguin, p. 233.

20 It's all in the hands (2003, Nov 20). *Guardian* (G2), p, 2.

21 Cited in Clarke, D. and Morris, K. (2005). *Golf – The Mind Factor*. London: Hodder & Stoughton, p. 3.

22 It's all in the hands (2003, Nov 20). *Guardian* (G2), p. 2.

23 One 'Tiger' that will never crouch (2001, April 9). *Evening Herald*, p. 61.

24 Coping with a stress factor (2002, Oct 6). *Sunday Independent* (Sport), p. 6.

Chapter 6

1 Not quite time to take gloves off yet: An interview with Ronan O'Gara (2005, Feb 2). *Irish Times* (Sports Supplement), p. 5.

2 Pitt, N. (1998, July 19). Out of the Woods, *The Sunday Times*, p. 5.

3 English, A. (2006). *Munster: Our Road to Glory*. Dublin: Penguin, p. 9.

4 Fear of failure haunted me right to the last second (2004, May 1). *Guardian* (Sport), p. 12.

5 I am ready and able to handle the real thing, Sven (2003, March 22). *The Times* (Sport), p. 36.

6 Nicklaus, J. and Boden, K. (1974). *Golf My Way*. New York: Simon & Schuster, p. 79.

7 Plod and panache a recipe for success at the home of golf (2005, July 11). *The Independent* (Sport), p. 58.

8 Cited in Hodge, K. (2000). *Sports Thoughts*. Auckland: Reed Publishing, p. 28.

9 Murphy, S. (2005). Imagery: Inner theatre becomes reality. In S. Murphy (ed.), *The Sport Psych Handbook* (pp. 127–151). Champaign, IL: Human Kinetics.

10 Kosslyn, S. M., Thompson, W. L. and Alpert, N. M. (1997). Neural systems shared by visual imagery and visual perception: A positron emission tomography study. *Neuro-Image*, 6, 320–334.

11 Kosslyn, S., Ganis, G. and Thompson, W. L. (2001). Neural foundations of imagery. *Nature Reviews. Neuroscience*, 2, 635–642.

12 Morris, T., Spittle, M. and Watt, A. (2005). *Imagery in Sport*. Champaign, IL: Human Kinetics, p. 130.

13 Moran, A. P. and MacIntyre, T. (1998). There's more to an image than meets the eye: A qualitative study of kinaesthetic imagery in elite canoe-slalomists. *Irish Journal of Psychology*, 19, 406–423.

14 Nadal leaves Hewitt with no excuse (2006, June 6). *The Irish Times*, p. 16.

15 Getting up for the Ashes (1998, Nov 20). *Guardian* (Sport), p. 2.

16 Ice-man Faulds keeps cool to shoot gold (2000, Sept 21). *Guardian*, p. 7.

17 Faldo dismisses fear of failure in a heartbeat (2004, July 15). *The Daily Telegraph* (Sport: Open Special Supplement), p. 2.

18 It's all in the hands (2003, Nov 20). *Guardian*, G2, p. 2.

19 James, W. (1890). *Principles of Psychology*. New York: Holt, Rinehart and Winston.

20 Driskell, J. E., Copper, C. M. and Moran, A. (1994). Does mental practice enhance performance? *Journal of Applied Psychology*, 79, 481–492.

21 Moran, A. (2004). *Sport and Exercise Psychology: A Critical Introduction*. London: Routledge/Psychology Press.

Chapter 7

1 Knowles, E. (1999). *The Oxford Dictionary of Quotations*. Oxford: Oxford University Press, p. 575.

2 Knowles, E. (1999). *The Oxford Dictionary of Quotations*. Oxford: Oxford University Press, p. 60.

3 One fine day (2006, Nov 5). *Sunday Tribune*, p. 31.

4 Murray returns to roots with approach for Perlas (2006, April 20). *The Times*, p. 82.

5 O'Sullivan, E. and Smyth, P. J. (2002). The attacking mindset. In B. D. Hale and D. J. Collins (eds), *Rugby Tough* (pp. 155–170). Champaign, IL: Human Kinetics.

6 One fine day (2006, Nov 5). *Sunday Tribune*, p. 31.

7 Carlson, R. (1998). *The Don't Sweat the Small Stuff Workbook*. London: Hodder and Stoughton, p. 7.

8 Beswick, B. (2001). *Focused for Soccer*. Champaign, IL: Human Kinetics, p. 44.

9 Pioline presses self-destruct button. BBC Sport, 28 June 2000 http://mews.bbc.co.uk/1/hi/wimbledon2000.

10 Kirschbaum, E. (2004, Aug 22). Wrong target drama cost US gold. Reuters Olympic Games: Athens 2004, www.iol.co.za.

11 Cragg takes the scalp of Bekele (2005, Jan 31). *The Irish Times* (Sport), p. 6.

12 Cited in The greatest of them all turns 65. International Sports Press Association (AIPS) website, January 2007.

13 Ibid.

14 One fine day (2006, Nov 5). *Sunday Tribune*, p. 31.

15 Mood swings and hot tempers (2002, May 28). *The Irish Times*, p. 22.

16 Relax and watch the birdies (1997, June 8). Stress Manager, supplement to *The Sunday Times*, pp. 8–9.

17 Morgan, W. P., Ellickson, K. A., O'Connor, P. J. and Bradley, P. W. (1992). Elite male distance runners: Personality structure, mood states and performance. *Track and Field Quarterly*, 92, 59–62.

18 Eriksson pleads with fans not to take it out on Rooney (2006, July 3). *Guardian* (Sport), p. 1.

19 O'Sullivan to pay for obscenities (2004, April 26). *The Daily Telegraph*, p. S12.

20 Hodge, K. (2000). *Sports Thoughts*. Auckland: Reed, p. 72.

21 O'Sullivan, E. and Smyth, P. J. (2002). The attacking mindset. In B. D. Hale and D. J. Collins (eds), *Rugby Tough* (pp. 155–170). *Rugby Tough*. Champaign, IL: Human Kinetics.

22 MacRury, D. (1997). *Golfers on Golf*. London: Virgin Books, p. 47.

23 Polished Souey joins NDL ranks (2001, March 12). *Evening Herald*, p. 62.

24 Beswick, B. (2001). *Focused for Soccer*. Champaign, IL: Human Kinetics, p. 44.

25 Esgate, A. and Groome, D. (2005). *An Introduction to Applied Cognitive Psychology*. Hove, East Sussex: Psychology Press.

26 Ibid.

27 Gilbert, B. (1994, with S. Jamison). *Winning Ugly: Mental Warfare in Tennis – Lessons from a Master*. New York: Fireside Books.

28 Woodward, C. (2004). *Winning! The Story of England's Rise to Rugby World Cup Glory*. London: Hodder and Stoughton, p. 259.

29 Grout, J. and Perrin, S. (2004). *Mind Games*. Chichester, West Sussex: Capstone Publishing Ltd.

30 Petersen, C., Semmel, A., Von Baeyer, C. et al. (1982). The Attributional Style Questionnaire. *Cognitive Therapy and Research*, 6, 287–299.

31 Biddle, S. J., Hanrahan, S. J. and Sellars, C. (2001). Attributions: Past, present and future. In R. N. Singer, H. A. Hausenblas and C. M. Janelle (eds.), *Handbook of Sport Psychology* (2nd ed) (pp. 444–471). New York: Wiley.

32 Seligman, M. E. P., Nolen-Hoeksema, S., Thornton, N. and Thornton, K. M. (1990). Explanatory style as a mechanism of disappointing athletic performance. *Psychological Science*, 1, 143–146.

33 Jacob, G. (2007). It's not over . . . (2007, 3 Jan). *The Times* (Sport), p. 66.

34 One fine day (2006, Nov 5). *Sunday Tribune*, p. 31.

Chapter 8

1 See http://news.bbc.co.uk/sport1/hi/other_sports/sailing/4246831.stm

2 Latané, B. (1981). The psychology of social impact. *American Psychologist*, 36, 343–356.

3 Forsyth, D. (2006) *Group Dynamics* (4th ed). San Francisco, CA: Thomson, pp. 7–11.

4 See http://content-uk.cricinfo.com/ci/content/player/9187.html

5 Winning the war before a ball has been kicked (2004, Oct 22). *Guardian*, p. 37.

6 Welcome to Leicester where a punch from the captain is just a sign that you've arrived (2007, May 19). *Guardian*, p. 35.

7 Op. cit.

8 Tuckman, B. (1965). Development sequence in small groups. *Psychological Bulletin*, 63, 384–399.

9 Baron, R. S. (2005). So right it's wrong: groupthink and the ubiquitous nature of polarized group decision making. In M. P. Zanna (ed.) *Advances in Experimental Social Psychology*, vol. 37 (pp. 219–253). San Diego, CA: Elsevier Academic Press.

10 Clough, B. (with J. Sandler) (2003). *Cloughie: Walking on Water*. London: Headline, p. 124.

11 Wilko, a deep thinker trapped by his image (2004, Nov 16). *Sunday Independent* (Sport), p. 5.

12 http://en.wikipedia.org/wiki/Kamp_Staaldraad

13 Forsyth, D. (2006). *Group Dynamics* (4th ed). San Francisco, CA: Thomson, p. 168.

14 Subtle captaincy gave Europe edge (2002, Oct 6). *The Sunday Times* (Sport), p. 22.

15 Courneya, K. S. and Carron, A. V. (1992). Home advantage in sport competitions: a literature review. *Journal of Sport and Exercise Psychology*, 14, 13–27.

16 Jones, M. V., Bray, S. R. and Lavallee, D. (2007). All the worlds a stage: impact of an audience on sport performers. In S. Jowett and D. Lavallee (ed.), *Social Psychology in Sport*. Champaign, IL: Human Kinetics, pp. 91–102.

17 Triplett, N. (1898). The dynamogenic factors in pacemaking and competition. *American Journal of Psychology*, 9, 505–523.

18 Lavallee, D., Kremer, J., Moran, A. and Williams, M. (2004). *Sport Psychology: Contemporary Themes*. London: Palgrave, p. 184.

19 Michaels, J. W., Blommel, J. M., Brocato, R. M. et al. (1982). Social facilitation and inhibition in a natural setting. *Replications in Social Psychology*, 2, 21–24.

20 Lavallee, D., Kremer, J., Moran, A. and William, M. (2004). *Sport Psychology: Contemporary Themes*. London: Palgrave, p. 185.

21 Cited in Hodge, K. (2000). *Sports Thoughts*. Auckland, New Zealand: Reed, p. 79.

22 Clough, B. (with J. Sandler) (2003). *Cloughie: Walking on Water*. London: Headline, p. 232.

Chapter 9

1 http://www.rateitall.com/i-53312-john-wooden.aspx.

2 Wooden, J. (with S. Jamison) (1997). *Wooden: A Lifetime of Observations and Reflections on and off the Court*. Lincolnwood, IL: Contemporary Books.

3 Wooden, J. (with S. Jamison) (2007). *The Essential Wooden: A Lifetime of Lessons on Leaders and Leadership*. New York: McGraw-Hill.

4 The brains and bravado that define O'Neill (2006, Sept 30). *Guardian*, p. 31.

5 Quotation from Ron Yeats, cited in the Bill Shankly Tribute Website (shankly.com).

6 Woodward, C. (2004). *Winning!* London: Hodder and Stoughton.

7 Marcotti, G. Made not born (2001, 7 Oct). *The Sunday Tribune* (Sport), p. 9.

8 Ibid.

9 Clough, B. (with J. Sadler) (2002). *Cloughie: Walking on Water. My Life*. London: Headline Books, p. 266.

10 Ibid., p. 220.

11 Duffy, P. J., Lyons, D. C., Moran, A. P., Warrington, G. D. and MacManus, C. (2006). How we got here: Perceived influences on the development and success of international athletes. *Irish Journal of Psychology*, 27 (3–4), 150–167.

12 Chelladurai, P. (1993). Leadership. In R. N. Singer, M. Murphey and L. K. Tennant (eds), *Handbook of Research in Sport Psychology* (pp. 647–671). New York: Macmillan.

13 Talking the talk (2007, April 15). *The Observer* (Sport), p. 12.

Chapter 10

1 Kipling, R. (1895). 'If.' (First published in the 'Brother Square Toes' chapter of *Rewards and Fairies*, 1910).

2 Wooden, J. (with S. Jamison) (2007). *The Essential Wooden: A Lifetime of Lessons on Leaders and Leadership*. New York: McGraw-Hill, p. 78.

3 Psychologist Mourinho inspires with group therapy (2007, April 1). *The Sunday Times* (Sport), p. 2.

4 Casey in prime condition for best shot at green jacket (2007, April 4). *Guardian*, p. 32.

5 Carron, A. V., Prapavessis, H. and Grove, J. R. (1994). Group effects and self-handicapping. *Journal of Sport and Exercise Psychology*, 16, 246–257.

Index

Note: entries in italics denote illustrations.